DATE DUE

Nixon, Kissinger, and the Shah

Nixon, Kissinger, and the Shah

The United States and Iran in the Cold War

ROHAM ALVANDI

OXFORD
UNIVERSITY PRESS

OXFORD
UNIVERSITY PRESS

Oxford University Press is a department of the University of Oxford.
It furthers the University's objective of excellence in research, scholarship,
and education by publishing worldwide.

Oxford   New York
Auckland   Cape Town   Dar es Salaam   Hong Kong   Karachi
Kuala Lumpur   Madrid   Melbourne   Mexico City   Nairobi
New Delhi   Shanghai   Taipei   Toronto

With offices in
Argentina   Austria   Brazil   Chile   Czech Republic   France   Greece
Guatemala   Hungary   Italy   Japan   Poland   Portugal   Singapore
South Korea   Switzerland   Thailand   Turkey   Ukraine   Vietnam

Oxford is a registered trademark of Oxford University Press
in the UK and certain other countries.

Published in the United States of America by
Oxford University Press
198 Madison Avenue, New York, NY 10016

© Oxford University Press 2014

Chapter 2 has appeared in an earlier form as Roham Alvandi, "Nixon, Kissinger, and the
Shah: The Origins of Iranian Primacy in the Persian Gulf," *Diplomatic History* (2012) 36(2):
337–372. © Society for Historians of American Foreign Relations. By permission of Oxford
University Press.

Library of Congress Cataloging-in-Publication Data

Alvandi, Roham, 1979–
Nixon, Kissinger, and the shah : the United States and Iran in the Cold War / Roham Alvandi.
pages cm
Includes bibliographical references and index.
ISBN 978–0–19–937569–1 (alk. paper)
1. United States—Foreign relations—Iran.   2. Iran—Foreign relations—United States.
3. United States—Foreign relations—1969–1974.   4. Nixon, Richard M. (Richard Milhous),
1913-1994.   5. Kissinger, Henry, 1923– 6. Cold War—Diplomatic history.   I. Title. II. Title:
United States and Iran in the Cold War.
E183.8.I55A598 2014
327.7305509'04—dc23
2013048498

9 8 7 6 5
Printed in the United States of America
on acid-free paper

To my parents and in memory of my grandfather

Contents

Acknowledgments

THIS BOOK IS adapted from my DPhil thesis at the University of Oxford. I doubt that any doctoral student reading this will believe me, but I enjoyed writing it. To have spent those years reading, writing, and discussing Iran's international history was a privilege. Perhaps that is something you can only say with the benefit of hindsight. From the first autumn day in 2005 when I arrived at St. Antony's College, I came into contact with an extraordinary community of scholars who have enriched my life with their teaching and friendship. I am forever indebted to my kind and patient tutor and thesis supervisor, Louise Fawcett, who not only gently guided this work from conception to completion, but also taught me the importance of taking a historical approach to the study of international relations. Her *Iran and the Cold War: The Azerbaijan Crisis of 1946* firmly established Iran's place in Cold War historiography, and it gives me great satisfaction to follow in her footsteps. I owe special thanks to the unfailingly generous and good humored Avi Shlaim, who examined and commented on my thesis and whose ideas about the nature of the Cold War in the Middle East have shaped the arguments of this book. I am deeply grateful to Homa Katouzian, who commented on earlier drafts of this book and shared with me his encyclopedic knowledge of Iranian history, which is only matched by his kindness toward his students. I miss my late friend Wilfrid Knapp, who warmly welcomed me to St. Catherine's College in 2007. Wilfrid generously commented on early drafts of this book, and I hope he would be pleased with the result.

Many of the basic assumptions about the nature of international politics that underlie this study were imparted to me by Devin Hagerty, who taught me how to think and write about foreign policy when I was an undergraduate at the University of Sydney. With Devin's encouragement, I went on to study at his *alma mater*, the Fletcher School of Law and Diplomacy at Tufts University, where I gained an invaluable firsthand understanding of how Americans view Iran and the wider world. Abiodun Williams, another member of the Fletcher mafia, then kindly hired me to work on his staff in the office of UN Secretary-General Kofi Annan. I am indebted to Abi, a true scholar-diplomat, for not only giving me a front-row seat to the world of diplomacy, but also a master class in bureaucratic politics that came in very handy when I was trying to make sense of the mountain of documents produced by officialdom in Washington.

A number of friends and colleagues around the world helped me track down sources for this book. I am indebted to Mahdi Ahouie for his help in Geneva; to Bill Samii and Noa Schonmann for sharing with me their research on Iranian and Israeli covert operations in Iraqi Kurdistan; and to Bill Burr and Malcolm Byrne at the National Security Archive for their invaluable work in tracking down and declassifying many of the US documents cited here. I owe special thanks to Christian Goos and Donna Lehman at the Gerald R. Ford Presidential Library for generously sifting through countless files for me in Ann Arbor and efficiently processing my numerous mandatory review requests. I am grateful to Daryoush Bayandor, Harold Saunders, Brent Scowcroft, Ardeshir Zahedi, and a former US Central Intelligence Agency (CIA) officer (who asked to remain anonymous) for kindly sharing with me their memories of the Nixon-Kissinger-Pahlavi partnership. The research for this book was made possible by the warm hospitality of many friends and family around the world. My thanks to Bahram Asgarian; Aras Berenjforoush; Karen, Mitchell, and Sam Charap; Rudy and Tiffany Costanzo; Marshall, Robin, David, and Trudi Cloyd; Obaida El-Dandarawy and Shaden Khallaf; Farhad Diba; Shirin Hakimzadeh; James and Marcy Plunkett; Anthony Seretakis; Zenon Severis; and Jose Urrutia for kindly welcoming me into their homes during my travels. This book was written with the generous financial support of the Department of Politics and International Relations and St. Catherine's College at the University of Oxford, the George C. Marshall Foundation, the Lyndon Baines Johnson Foundation, the Gerald R. Ford Presidential Foundation, the British Institute of Persian Studies, the Europaeum, the British Library's Eccles Centre for American Studies, and the Royal Historical Society. I was honored to receive the Foundation for Iranian Studies' 2011 Dissertation Prize and the University of Oxford's 2011 Dasturzada Dr. Jal Pavry Memorial Thesis Prize. I thank all these institutions for their kind recognition and generous support of this work.

In the course of writing this book at Oxford and the London School of Economics (LSE), during visits to far flung archives, or at meetings of the

International Society for Iranian Studies and the Society for Historians of American Foreign Relations, I met many talented scholars who gladly offered me advice, feedback, and camaraderie, as well as some cautionary tales, which all contributed to this book. In particular, I want to thank Gholam Reza Afkhami, Ali Ansari, Målfrid Braut-Hegghammer, Claudia Castiglioni, Houchang Chehabi, Anne Deighton, Toby Dodge, Chris Emery, W. Taylor Fain, Greg Gause, Fawaz Gerges, Ali Gheissari, Jim Goode, Jussi Hanhimäki, Sir Alistair Horne, Adam Howard, Artemy Kalinovsky, Barin Kayaoglu, Matteo Legrenzi, Douglas Little, William Roger Louis, Vali Nasr, Behlul Ozkan, Richard Parish, David Patrikarakos, Roland Popp, Jaideep Prabhu, Siavush Randjbar-Daemi, Sir Adam Roberts, Tom Schwartz, Matt Shannon, Kristian Coates Ulrichsen, Fred Wehrey, and Tom Zeiler for their support and encouragement. My thanks are also due to Nigel Ashton, Mathew Betts, Demetra Frini, Arne Westad, and all my colleagues in the Department of International History at the LSE for giving me the opportunity to work alongside some of the world's foremost historians. They took a gamble by hiring me before I had completed my doctorate and generously afforded me the time to finish this book. I am also grateful to Paul Horsler and his colleagues at the LSE Library for helping me track down books and periodicals, and to Mina Moshkeri for creating the maps in this book. Special thanks are due to Susan Ferber, my editor at Oxford University Press, for taking on this book project when so many other would-be authors were clamoring for her attention, as well as the two reviewers, whose helpful comments made this a much stronger book.

My fondest memories of the years I spent working on this book are of my fellow graduate students at Oxford. There was no better end to a long day spent toiling away in the Bodleian or the Manor Road Building than an evening with them in the Late Bar at St. Antony's. In particular, I want to thank Farid Boussaid, Alex Buck, Milos Damnjanovic, Matt Eagleton-Pierce, Jon Gharraie, Jaideep Gupte, Kai Hebel, Nadiya Kravets, Ahmed Mehdi, Florian Nickels-Teske, Naysan Rafati, Tania Saeed, Shohei Sato, Arman Shafieloo, Dorian Singh, Richard Stanley, and Pegah Zohouri Haghian for their friendship all these years. My partner throughout this long and difficult endeavor was Eliza Gheorghe, who supported me with her love and kindness. Although she was hard at work researching her own Cold War autocrat, she always found the time to patiently read and comment on countless drafts of this book. I owe the greatest debt of gratitude to my parents, Hamid Alvandi and Fatemeh Asgarian Tafreshi, for their unconditional love and for always encouraging me to pursue my passion for history and politics. Only they and I know how much they have done for me, not the least of which was patiently teaching me to read and write Persian as a young boy, when we were so far from home. Without the extraordinary sacrifices they made, I would never have had the opportunity to study at Oxford or write this book. I dedicate this book to them and to the memory of my grandfather, Mirza Ramazan Ali Asgarian Tafreshi, whose legacy to me was his love of Iran and its rich history.

Nixon, Kissinger, and the Shah

Introduction

ON JULY 29, 1980, in the sweltering heat of the Egyptian summer, the funeral cortege of Mohammad Reza Pahlavi, the last shah of Iran, slowly wound its way through the streets of Cairo.[1] Thousands of Egyptian soldiers escorted the shah's casket, lying on a horse-drawn gun carriage, draped with the Iranian flag. Behind the casket walked the exiled Iranian royal family, led by the widowed Empress Farah, veiled in black. The world's leaders were not invited to the funeral of the deposed shah, who had fled Iran in 1979 following a popular revolution that had toppled the Pahlavi dynasty and established an Islamic Republic. The kings and queens, presidents, and prime ministers who had enjoyed the shah's hospitality at the lavish 1971 Persepolis celebration were conspicuous by their absence. Only Egyptian president Anwar Sadat, former US president Richard M. Nixon, and the exiled King Constantine of Greece were on hand to witness the burial of Mohammad Reza Shah, and with him, more than two and a half millennia of Persian monarchy.

No senior official had been sent from Washington to represent President Jimmy Carter at the funeral.[2] The Carter administration had tried to distance itself from the reviled Iranian monarch, refusing him permission to settle in the United States. They hoped to salvage some kind of relationship with the Islamic Republic from the ruins of the United States' long-standing friendship with the shah, which every president since Franklin D. Roosevelt had reaffirmed.[3] Carter had begrudgingly allowed the ailing shah to visit the United States in October 1979 for medical treatment, but when American diplomats were taken hostage in Tehran in November, the shah was palmed off to Panama and then Egypt, where he died.[4]

Richard Nixon, like many Republicans, was appalled at the way the Democratic Carter administration had treated the shah, a long-standing friend and ally of the United States. Despite being something of a pariah himself after resigning the presidency in disgrace in 1974, Nixon made a point of flying to Egypt for the funeral. Upon arriving at Cairo airport, he told reporters that Carter's actions had been "shameful" and described the decision to deny the shah asylum as "one of the black pages of America's foreign policy history."[5] Henry Kissinger, who had served Nixon as both national security advisor and secretary of state, had been pressing the White House to admit the shah after he fled Iran in January 1979.[6] Nixon and Kissinger's concern for the shah's fate reflected not only their desire to help an old friend, but also a sense of injustice that they were now being blamed for the shah's downfall and the subsequent Tehran hostage crisis because of their administration's unquestioning support for the shah. A blame game was being waged between Democrats and Republicans over the question of "who lost Iran."[7] While Republicans blamed the shah's downfall on Carter's refusal to sanction a bloody crackdown in Iran, Democrats attacked Nixon and Kissinger for encouraging the shah's megalomania through unrestricted arms sales to Iran.[8]

This political debate has cast its shadow over the literature on US-Iran relations, much of it written in the wake of the Iranian revolution and the Tehran hostage crisis.[9] These historical accounts are largely concerned with identifying and assessing the culpability of various American administrations for the downfall of the shah, which was perhaps the single biggest setback for US policy in the Middle East during the Cold War. Many scholars focus on the Eisenhower administration's pivotal role in the 1953 coup that established a US client state in Iran and forever tainted the shah in Iranian eyes as an instrument of American imperialism.[10] Others are critical of the Kennedy administration for failing to push the shah toward meaningful reform in the early 1960s.[11] As a whole, these works portray the Iranian-American relationship as one of a powerful but short-sighted US patron that was willing to tolerate the abuses and excesses of a weak but restless Iranian client, because of a Cold War logic that saw the stability of Pahlavi Iran and its vast oil reserves as crucial to the US strategy for containing the Soviet Union. While this is a more or less fair assessment of the US-Iran relationship during the Eisenhower and Kennedy presidencies, there is also a consensus that from the mid-1960s onward, during Lyndon B. Johnson's presidency, the dynamics of the relationship began to change.[12] Indeed, during the 1970s, the era of superpower détente, the ongoing Vietnam War, and soaring oil prices, a very different picture of the shah emerges—as that of a commanding international figure who enjoyed tremendous influence in Washington during Nixon's presidency.[13]

This book challenges the popular view of the shah as merely "America's proxy," a position grounded in the US-Iran relationship of the 1950s, by highlighting his role in shaping and implementing American strategies of containment in the 1970s.[14] In the last decade of his reign, the shah forged a partnership with Richard Nixon and Henry Kissinger to contain Soviet influence and to establish Iran's regional primacy in the Persian Gulf. Under the Nixon Doctrine, Iran evolved from a client to a partner of the United States in the Cold War. The Nixon-Kissinger-Pahlavi partnership provides yet another example of how the course of the Cold War was shaped not only by statesmen in Moscow and Washington, but also by their allies in the Third World. The Cold War was a truly global struggle, fought not only along the iron curtain that divided Europe after World War II, but also throughout Africa, Asia, and Latin America, where European colonial empires were quickly receding.[15] Third World actors like Mohammad Reza Shah were not simply bystanders in this global ideological and material struggle, but active agents of history who often abetted and manipulated the superpowers in the pursuit of their own local ambitions and interests.[16]

The gradual declassification of the Nixon and Ford presidential papers, as well as documents produced by Henry Kissinger's State Department and the CIA under Richard Helms, have slowly lifted the veil of secrecy that shrouded much of the dealings between Nixon, Kissinger, and the shah. These new sources underscore the autonomy and leverage the shah enjoyed vis-à-vis Washington.[17] Although Iranian diplomatic records from Mohammad Reza Shah's reign remain generally inaccessible to historians, a number of Persian-language sources that show the view from Tehran of US-Iran relations are available outside Iran. These include the diaries of Asadollah Alam, the shah's closest advisor and minister of the imperial court, which offer a day-by-day account of the politics of the shah's court.[18] In addition to the Alam diaries, two oral history collections, one assembled by the Foundation for Iranian Studies in Bethesda, Maryland, and the other by the Iranian Oral History Project at Harvard University, shed light on the shah's highly secretive decision-making. Finally, I was able to interview a handful of former American and Iranian officials with intimate knowledge of the shah's relationship with Nixon and Kissinger, including

Ardeshir Zahedi, who served as Iran's foreign minister from 1966 to 1973 and as ambassador to the United States from 1973 until 1979.[19]

This book is not intended to be a comprehensive history of the US-Iran bilateral relationship in the 1970s. Rather, it analyzes three key historical episodes that map the rise and fall of the Nixon-Kissinger-Pahlavi partnership. These episodes not only showcase the dynamics of the shah's relationship with Nixon and Kissinger, but are also significant for the Cold War beyond Iran's borders. In doing so, some well-researched aspects of US-Iran relations in this period, like arms sales and oil prices, receive less attention. This book is also not intended as a study of the Cold War's impact on Iran, which already has a number of excellent studies, specifically of how US policies impacted both the Pahlavi state and Iranian society.[20] Instead, it is a study of Iran's impact on how the United States fought the Cold War. The shah was a significant Cold War actor in the 1970s who used his extraordinary influence in the Nixon White House to shape American foreign policy in regional conflicts from the Middle East to South Asia.

Chapter 1 begins with a discussion of the origins of the US-Iran relationship during World War II and the 1946 Azerbaijan crisis. In the early days of the Cold War, Mohammad Reza Shah and his prime ministers succeeded in drawing a reluctant United States into Iran in order to balance the influence of Britain and the Soviet Union. Pahlavi Iran emerged as a US client state after the Anglo-American-sponsored coup that toppled Prime Minister Mohammad Mosaddeq in 1953 and transformed the shah into a dictator. This Cold War patron-client relationship was established by the Eisenhower administration in the 1950s, but continued into the 1960s under the Kennedy and Johnson administrations. The dynamics of the US-Iran relationship in the 1950s and 1960s would sharply differ from the partnership that the shah would forge with Nixon and Kissinger in the 1970s.

Chapter 2 traces the evolution of Iran from a client to a partner of the United States, from the announcement of the British withdrawal from the Persian Gulf in 1968 to the end of Nixon's first term as president in 1972. At the heart of this partnership was the personal friendship between Richard Nixon and Mohammad Reza Pahlavi, forged during Nixon's 1953 visit to Iran as vice president. The shah relentlessly lobbied the Nixon administration to abandon a policy of balancing Iran and Saudi Arabia as the "twin pillars" of the Gulf and to instead embrace Iran's regional primacy. Nixon saw his old friend as a modernizing anti-communist statesman who shared his grand geopolitical view of the Cold War as well as his disdain for liberal intellectuals. Under the Nixon Doctrine, the United States would embrace Iran as the paramount power in the Gulf after the British completed their withdrawal from the region in 1971. Drawing on Iranian sources, this chapter reveals that the shah's decision-making during the 1969 Shatt al-Arab border crisis between Iran and Iraq nearly sparked a war between the two countries. It also details the Nixon administration's illegal funneling of American arms to Pakistan via Iran during the 1971 Indo-Pakistan War.

Chapter 3 examines the zenith of the US-Iran partnership after Nixon and Kissinger's May 1972 visit to Iran. In the first detailed history of the CIA's covert operation in Iraqi Kurdistan from 1972 to 1975, it shows how the Nixon administration worked with Iran and Israel to back the Kurdish insurgency against the Ba'thi regime in Baghdad. The shah took advantage of his influence in the Nixon White House to draw the United States into the conflict in 1972. He then used the Americans to keep the Kurds fighting, in order to paralyze the Iraqi army and thereby neutralize the Iraqi threat to Iran's oil-rich province of Khuzestan and Iranian shipping in the Shatt al-Arab and the Persian Gulf. But as the tide of battle turned against the Kurds and as Iraq signaled its willingness to reach a compromise, the shah defied Kissinger and made a deal with Iraqi strongman Saddam Hussein in March 1975 to abandon the Kurds in exchange for territorial concessions in the Shatt. The partnership with the shah was so vital to the United States that Kissinger had no choice but to accept the shah's decision as a *fait accompli* and suffer subsequent domestic recriminations for having betrayed the Kurds.

Spanning the decline of the US-Iran partnership after Watergate and Nixon's resignation, Chapter 4 focuses on the failure of negotiations between the shah and the Ford administration from 1974 to 1976 on American nuclear exports to Iran. An inability to agree on the terms of nuclear cooperation was symptomatic of an emerging rift in the US-Iran partnership. The shah had hoped that the United States would provide the nuclear technology and material that Iran wanted in order to reach economic and military parity with the great powers following the dramatic increase in oil prices in 1973. However, he did not enjoy an intimate relationship with President Gerald R. Ford, as he had with Nixon. Although Kissinger worked hard to defend the US-Iran partnership from political opponents in the Democratic Congress and critics within the Republican administration, the shah's detractors were no longer sidelined, as they had been under Nixon. Ford ultimately sought to appease these critics by foisting a nuclear agreement on the shah that included safeguards that went beyond Iran's commitments under the 1968 Nuclear Non-Proliferation Treaty. The shah rejected Ford's demands, seeing them as a violation of Iran's sovereignty and a reversion by the United States to treating Iran as a client, rather than a partner of the United States.

Together, these three episodes offer a history of Mohammad Reza Shah's efforts to enlist the United States in his campaign to make Iran a major regional power, and Richard Nixon and Henry Kissinger's willing embrace of that vision as part of their strategy for fighting the Cold War. This partnership between Nixon, Kissinger, and the shah did not imply American domination or exploitation of Iran. Rather, the shah effectively harnessed the Nixon Doctrine to serve Iranian interests. Nor did Iran's rising power threaten the stability of the Persian Gulf. The shah preserved the security of the Gulf at a time when the Nixon administration was unwilling to fill the vacuum created by Britain's withdrawal from the region in 1971. Tehran supported American leadership in the global Cold War, while Washington respected Iranian primacy in the Gulf. The Nixon-Kissinger-Pahlavi partnership represented, therefore, the accommodation of Iran's ambitions and interests within American strategies of containment and remains, to this day, the high-water mark of the United States' relationship with Iran.

1

The United States and Iran in the Cold War

IRAN'S COLD WAR relationship with the United States began during World War II as what historians call "an empire by invitation."[1] That is to say that Mohammad Reza Shah welcomed and encouraged American influence in Iranian affairs in the hope that the rising power of the United States would give his country some respite from the long-standing imperial ambitions of Britain and Russia. Since the nineteenth century, Iran had found itself wedged between the British Empire in India and the Persian Gulf, and Tsarist Russia's encroaching empire in the Caucasus and Central Asia. These two European colonial powers had divided Iran into spheres of influence in the 1907 Anglo-Russian Convention, with Russia taking the north and Britain the south. The 1917 Russian Revolution offered the Iranians a brief lull from Russian expansion, but Moscow soon resumed its interest in northern Iran under its new Bolshevik leaders. Similarly, Britain's control of Iran's oil industry ensured London's continuing interest in southern Iran and the Persian Gulf. Since the arrival of American missionaries in Iran in the 1830s, the United States had remained a disinterested power, refusing to become involved in the country's affairs.[2] However, World War II drew the reluctant Americans into the maelstrom of Iranian politics. Following the German attack on the Soviet Union in June 1941, Britain and the Soviet Union invaded neutral Iran in August in order to secure the Iranian oil fields and the trans-Iranian railway that stretched from the Persian Gulf to the Caspian Sea. After the United States' entry into the war in December, tens of thousands of American troops were deployed in southern Iran under the Persian Gulf Command to manage the Allies' supply corridor through Iran to the Soviet Union.[3]

The Allied invasion threw Iran into chaos. Reza Shah Pahlavi, Iran's modernizing but autocratic ruler, was sent into ignominious exile in South Africa by the Allies. The 21-year-old Crown Prince Mohammad Reza Pahlavi just barely managed to ascend the Peacock Throne in the midst of the political vacuum that had been created by his father's abdication. The young shah and his prime minister, Mohammad Ali Foroughi, secured a Tripartite Treaty with Britain and the Soviet Union in January 1942, which committed both powers to respect Iran's sovereignty and to withdraw their forces from the country within six months of the end of the war. The United States, however, refused to sign the treaty. Despite Franklin D. Roosevelt's support for the ideal of self-determination under the Atlantic Charter, he was reluctant to make any commitment to Iran's independence, which he regarded as a British concern. But as the war progressed and relations between the Allied powers became increasingly strained, Roosevelt slowly came to the view that the United States must steer its own course in Iran.[4] Washington extended Lend Lease assistance to Iran in March 1942, providing the Iranians with desperately needed military aid. The Iranian government meanwhile succeeded in securing the services of a number of private American military and civilian advisors, such as Arthur Millspaugh, who returned to Iran to resume his work as director-general of finances, and Colonel H. Norman Schwarzkopf, who was hired to advise the Iranian Gendarmerie.

The long-awaited American commitment to Iran's independence came at the conclusion of the Tehran Conference between Roosevelt, Soviet premier Josef Stalin, and British prime minister Winston Churchill in December 1943.[5] The three Allied leaders agreed to sign the Declaration of the Three Powers Regarding Iran, in which they recognized Iran's contribution to the war effort and committed themselves to Iran's sovereignty and territorial integrity. Roosevelt and his advisors were increasingly frustrated by Britain's imperialist attitude toward Iran, which was inconsistent with the Atlantic Charter. As the British Empire gradually receded in the Middle East, the United States reluctantly emerged as the new dominant power in the region and gradually took up the task of steering the countries of the region toward its liberal vision of modernity within the context of the emerging Cold War. In Iran, the Americans confronted a culturally rich but economically devastated country where the Pahlavi dynasty was seeking to construct a modern Iranian nation-state on the ruins of the Persian Empire. Roosevelt summed up the changing American attitude in January 1944: "I was rather thrilled with the idea of using Iran as an example of what we could do by an unselfish American policy. We could not take on a more difficult example than Iran."[6] However, American policy was not entirely unselfish, as American oil companies had a major stake in the colossal oil reserves of the Persian Gulf, particularly in Saudi Arabia. Although the British enjoyed a monopoly over Iranian oil, Iran was nonetheless a vital buffer between the Soviet Union and American oil interests in the Arabian Peninsula.[7]

Iran's leaders had few options to deal with the chaos that engulfed the country during World War II. Mohammad Reza Shah and his wartime premiers pursued the traditional Iranian strategy of *movazeneh* (balance), in the hope that the rising power of the United States would check the ambitions of Britain and the Soviet Union and ensure that Iran would survive the war.[8] In addition to engaging the services of American advisors, in February 1943 Iran again offered oil concessions to American companies in the hope of drawing the United States deeper into Iranian affairs. The offer sparked a diplomatic crisis, as Churchill resisted any American encroachment into what he considered Britain's sphere of influence, while Stalin was incensed that the Soviet Union had been excluded from exploiting Iranian oil. A Soviet delegation was dispatched to Tehran in September 1944 to pressure Iranian prime minister Mohammad Sa'ed into granting a Soviet oil concession in northern Iran. Sa'ed sought to defuse the crisis by announcing in October that all discussion of oil concessions would be postponed until after the war. Iran's parliament, or Majlis, went one step further. Under the leadership of Mohammad Mosaddeq, an outspoken and staunchly nationalist deputy, legislation was passed in December that required all future concessions to have the consent of the Majlis.[9] Mosaddeq was opposed to the policy of *movazeneh*, arguing that giving a concession to the Soviets to balance the one given to the British was like "a person with one hand amputated who, in pursuance of balance, would consent to have his other hand being amputated."[10]

Iran and the Origins of the Cold War

Furious at the Iranian rebuff, Stalin sought to pressure Tehran into submission. The Iranians were particularly alarmed that during the Allied conferences in Yalta and Potsdam in 1945, the Soviets gave no indication that they intended to withdraw their troops from Iranian territory once the war ended. Instead, Moscow was actively encouraging ethnic separatist movements among the Azeris and Kurds of Iran's northwestern province of Azerbaijan,[11] which were protected by the Red Army from Iranian government forces. Stalin had placed Mir Jafar Abassovich Baghirov, the first secretary of the Communist Party of Soviet Azerbaijan, in charge of implementing his policies in northern Iran. In April 1945, Baghirov defined the goals of Soviet policy as "the unification of 'southern [Iranian] Azerbaijan with Soviet Azerbaijan, or the formation of an independent southern Azerbaijani People's Republic, or the establishment of independent bourgeois-democratic system or, at least, cultural autonomy in the framework of the Iranian state.' "[12] On July 6, 1945, the Soviet leadership ordered Baghirov to carry out a series of "measures to organize a separatist movement in southern Azerbaijan and other Provinces of Northern Iran." This would lay the groundwork for "a national autonomous Azerbaijan district with broad powers within the Iranian State."[13] One million convertible rubles were placed at Baghirov's disposal to promote pro-Soviet candidates in Iran's Majlis elections, to fund propaganda publications, and to arm partisan groups.[14]

With the surrender of Japan on September 2, 1945, the deadline for the withdrawal of Allied forces from Iran was set for March 2, 1946, as per the terms of the Tripartite Treaty and the Tehran Declaration. However, there was no sign that Stalin had any intention of withdrawing Soviet troops from northern Iran. Instead, in September, the Soviet Union actively backed the creation of two secessionist governments in Iranian Azerbaijan. In Tabriz, the capital of the province, the Azerbaijan Democratic Party (ADP) was founded by a group of pro-Soviet communists from Iran and the Caucasus, led by Ja'far Pishevari, who declared the province's autonomy from Iran. Similarly, in Mahabad in the west of the province, the Kurdish Democratic Party proclaimed the independence of the "Kurdish Republic of Mahabad." The Red Army prevented Iranian military reinforcements from entering the province, and by December the local Iranian gendarmerie and army commanders had surrendered to the rebels.[15]

Stalin's refusal to withdraw the Red Army from Iranian Azerbaijan in 1946 contributed to the emergence of the global Cold War and marked the beginning of Iran's Cold War relationship with the United States. The Azerbaijan crisis was a formative political experience for an entire generation of Iranians, including Mohammad Reza Shah, who would never forget how the Soviets had tried to "nibble away pieces of our territory."[16] As a consequence of the crisis, much of the political and military elite of Pahlavi Iran would harbor a deep mistrust of the Soviet Union, which seemed to be pursuing the same imperial ambitions in Iran as the Romanov tsars. As for the Americans, the crisis crystallized Iran's strategic importance as part of the "Northern Tier" of countries, stretching from Turkey in the west to Pakistan in the east, which separated the Soviet Union from the Persian Gulf and the Indian Ocean.[17] The defense of Iran came to be seen as vital to the success of American strategies of containing communism.

The central figure in the 1946 Azerbaijan crisis was not the young shah, but the patrician 70-year-old Ahmad Qavam, a veteran of Iranian politics who became prime minister in January 1946 for the fourth time. The Soviets had pressured the shah into appointing Qavam as premier because they regarded him as less susceptible to British influence than many of his peers. A firm believer in the *movazeneh* strategy, Qavam tried to secure a deal with Stalin during talks in Moscow in February and March 1946. But with the deadline for the withdrawal of Soviet troops from Iran having passed, Qavam returned to Tehran in March empty-handed. Meanwhile, reports were reaching Washington from the US Consulate in Tabriz that the Red Army was moving deeper into Iranian territory, and the Iranians were desperately appealing to the United States to intervene. It appeared as if Iran might soon join countries like Romania behind the "iron curtain" that Churchill had warned of in his speech at Fulton, Missouri, on March 5. Neither Britain nor the United States objected to a Soviet oil concession in northern Iran per se. The British felt that the USSR had a legitimate interest in northern Iran, and they were perfectly happy to divide the country into spheres of influence, as they had done in 1907. But in the context of Moscow's gains in Central and Eastern Europe, and Soviet ambitions in Greece and Turkey, Harry S. Truman, Roosevelt's successor, put his weight behind Iranian efforts to eject the Soviet Union from northern Iran.[18]

Truman made it clear to Stalin in a telegram delivered on March 6 that the United States could not "remain indifferent" to the continuing presence of Soviet troops in Iran.[19] The Truman administration firmly backed Ambassador Hoseyn Ala, Iran's envoy to the newly created United Nations (UN) in New York, who ratcheted up the pressure on Stalin in March by asking the UN Security Council to intervene in the dispute between Iran and the Soviet Union. Stalin viewed Azeri autonomy in Iran as a means to an end. He resented the fact that the Iranians were trying to exclude the Soviet Union from exploiting Iranian oil, and he tried to use the Azeri and Kurdish separatists and the Red Army to force Tehran into submission.

But Stalin had overplayed his hand, and he now moved to extract the USSR from a full-blown Cold War crisis. On March 24 he issued orders to Baghirov and the commander of the Baku Military District, General Ivan Maslennikov, to organize the withdrawal of Soviet troops from Iran by May 10. The planned Soviet withdrawal was then announced by Moscow Radio and by Ambassador Andrei Gromyko, the Soviet representative at the UN. Meanwhile, the newly appointed Soviet ambassador in Tehran, Ivan Sadchikov, entered into negotiations with Qavam for a face-saving deal that would allow the Soviets to withdraw with their credibility intact.[20]

Qavam leveraged the pressure being exerted on Moscow at the UN to secure an agreement with Sadchikov in Tehran in the early hours of April 5. In a dramatic about-face, the Soviet Union agreed to a complete troop withdrawal within six weeks and acknowledged that the separatist movements in Azerbaijan were an internal Iranian matter. In exchange, Qavam promised the Soviets a 51 percent share in a joint Soviet-Iranian company that would exploit the oil of northern Iran, pending the approval of the Iranian Majlis. As the Red Army completed its withdrawal on May 8, 1946, Pishevari's rebel government was abandoned to its fate. Stalin wrote an extraordinary letter to Pishevari that day, saying that, "You, as I found out, say that we first raised you to the skies and then let you down in the precipice and disgraced you." The Soviet leader explained to Pishevari that his strategy was "to create a threat for the [Iranian] government, to ensure a possibility of concessions on the part of the government." The purpose of the occupation had been to scare Tehran into submission. Now that this goal had been achieved, Stalin explained, there was no reason to maintain troops in Iran. "Such is the law of the revolutionary movement."[21] The ADP government collapsed before the Iranian army even reached Tabriz on December 13, and Pishevari and his comrades fled into exile in the Soviet Union. Two days later, Mahabad also fell to the Iranian army, and its rebel Kurdish leaders were mercilessly hanged. But the Iranian victory was not complete until October 1947, when the 15th Majlis decisively rejected the Qavam-Sadchikov agreement by 102 votes to 2. Qavam had paid a clever game. He had successfully ejected the Soviet Union from Iran, without granting an oil concession to Moscow.

The 1946 Azerbaijan Crisis was not only a diplomatic victory for Iran and the United States over the Soviet Union, but it was also the beginning of Iran's Cold War. The crisis left an indelible mark on the young Mohammad Reza Shah, who concluded that a weak Iran would always invite Soviet aggression and communist subversion. The Soviet threat from abroad and the communist threat from within would come to dominate his strategic thinking for the rest of his reign. To every American president, the shah would argue that the key to preserving Iran's independence in the face of the ceaseless Soviet quest for control of Iranian oil was a strong monarchy, defended by a powerful army, backed by the United States. In the shah's mind, this translated into unqualified American support for his domestic policies and generous US military assistance to build up Iran's armed forces. This was something no American president was willing to give the shah throughout the 1950s and 1960s. From its very inception, Iran's Cold War relationship with the United States was marked by tensions over Iran's military needs and the shah's domestic policies. Under the Truman Doctrine for containing the spread of communism, the United States committed itself to the defense of Greece and Turkey against the threat of Soviet domination by extending considerable economic and military aid to those countries. By comparison, and much to shah's frustration, Iran received a modest amount of development aid under the 1949 Point Four Program, which provided US technical and economic assistance to developing countries, as well as military training and surplus arms with the establishment of the US Military Assistance Advisory Group (MAAG) in Iran in 1950.

As the Cold War heated up with the victory of Mao Zedong and the Communist Party in the Chinese Civil War in October 1949 and the beginning of the Korean War in June 1950, Iran too was plunged into political violence and instability. Radicals on both the Islamist Right and the communist Left carried out assassinations against journalists, intellectuals, and government ministers. An attempt was even made on the life of the shah in February 1949, during a visit to Tehran University's Faculty of Law and Political Science. Despite being shot in the face with a revolver at almost point-blank range, the shah miraculously escaped with only minor injuries. A great deal of mystery surrounded his would-be assassin, who apparently had connections to leaders of the communist Tudeh (Masses) Party of Iran.[22] The shah took the opportunity to first outlaw the Tudeh, forcing the Iranian communists underground, and then to convene a constituent assembly to modify the constitution to give himself the power to dissolve the Majlis. During his first visit to the United States later that year, he pressed the Truman administration for military and financial assistance to build a large conventional army capable of deterring the Soviet Union.[23] In a half-hour meeting with Truman on November 18, the shah spoke of the glories of Persia and its downfall at the hands of invading armies, most recently the Red Army. But from Washington's perspective, the real threat to Iran came from communist subversion, rather than a Soviet invasion. In the first of many such encounters with US presidents, Truman politely declined every one of the shah's requests for more American military and economic aid.[24] When the shah told Secretary of State Dean Acheson of his desire to build a 150,000-man army, Acheson warned him that such a policy would "wreck" the Iranian economy and leave his country so weakened that it "would collapse without even being subjected to military attack."[25]

Mosaddeq and the Iranian Oil Crisis

While Europe rebuilt its postwar economy with generous American assistance, Iran had to look to its income from the British-owned Anglo-Iranian Oil Company (AIOC) to pay for its development plans and military needs. In July 1949 a Supplemental Agreement was negotiated between Iran and the AIOC, revising the terms of the British oil concession in Iran by modestly increasing Iran's share of the profits. British control of Iranian oil quickly became the focus of the rising tide of nationalism in Iran. The unpopular government of Prime Minister Haj Ali Razmara was unable to secure ratification of the agreement in the Majlis. In the hot-house political climate of the day, Razmara was assassinated on March 7, 1951, by the Fada'iyan-e Eslam, a militant Islamist group who branded him a toady of the British.

Soon after Razmara's murder, the Majlis passed legislation nationalizing the AIOC and elected Mohammad Mosaddeq, who had led the campaign against the Supplemental Agreement, as prime minister. Mohammad Reza Shah had little choice but to bow to the tide of public opinion and invite Mosaddeq to form a government on April 29. The elderly Mosaddeq was an aristocrat who had dedicated his life to defending Iran's fledgling parliamentary system under the 1906 Constitution and ending the pervasive influence of foreign powers in Iran.[26] The French- and Swiss-educated lawyer eloquently advocated a policy of *movazeneh-ye manfi* (negative balancing), whereby Iran would not compromise its sovereignty by granting "balancing" concessions to foreign powers.[27] With a reputation for incorruptibility and patriotism, Mosaddeq had blocked a Soviet oil concession in 1944 and had become the leader of a coalition of diverse political groups and individuals known as the National Front, which had united to fight the Supplemental Agreement with the British. After assuming the premiership, he immediately set about implementing the nationalization of the AIOC, sparking a major confrontation between Britain and Iran. The Anglo-Iranian oil crisis would have a dramatic impact on US-Iran relations, as the United States ultimately sided with Britain to topple Mosaddeq and install the shah as a dictator in 1953. Much of the goodwill that the Americans had built up in Iran since the 1830s would evaporate with the 1953 coup, as many Iranians came to see the United States as an imperial power complicit in the oppression and corruption of the shah's regime. The coup was such a traumatic event for the Iranians that the specter of Mosaddeq would loom over US-Iran relations even after the fall of the shah in 1979.

From the outset of the Iranian oil crisis in 1951, it was apparent to Prime Minister Clement Attlee's government in London that Mosaddeq would settle for nothing less than total Iranian control of Iranian oil, which the British stubbornly refused to concede. They feared that the loss of AIOC would have disastrous consequences for Britain's weakened postwar economy and would undermine Britain's authority throughout its empire. The British retaliated against the nationalization of AIOC by imposing economic sanctions on Iran and successfully lobbying for a complete international boycott of Iran's oil exports. Foreign Secretary Herbert Morrison led the charge for military action to seize the AIOC's massive Abadan oil refinery in the Persian Gulf. Attlee, who was more circumspect about such gunboat diplomacy, consulted with Washington in September 1951 about this planned military action and quashed the idea when he ran into stiff opposition from Truman. The British concluded that the only way they could achieve a satisfactory resolution to the oil crisis was to topple Mosaddeq. Robin Zaehner, an eccentric Oxford don and British spy, was sent by Morrison to Tehran to use the British Secret Intelligence Service's (SIS) network of agents to destabilize the National Front and bring down Mosaddeq's government.[28]

The Truman administration was sympathetic to Mosaddeq's brand of liberal nationalism, which it hoped would serve as a bulwark against the spread of communism in Iran.[29] The Americans were also weary of the British policymakers' attitude toward Iran, whom they deemed slow to adapt to the postcolonial era. When Mosaddeq visited the United States in October 1951 to address the UN Security Council, he was warmly received by Truman in Washington. Truman's concern was to keep Iran in the Western camp, not to preserve Britain's stake in Iranian oil. The president warned

Mosaddeq on October 23 that "Russia was sitting like a vulture on the fence, waiting to pounce on the oil. That is why we are so anxious to get these problems resolved."[30] But there were others in Washington, especially in the senior ranks of the CIA, who had lost patience with Mosaddeq and who feared that further instability would invite a communist takeover in Iran. They watched as the pressure mounted on Mosaddeq from the British as well as conservative Iranian royalists, who loathed Mosaddeq's populist politics and feared that the premier would consign the shah to the role of a constitutional monarch. Compounding Mosaddeq's problems was that as his popularity grew, the political divisions, jealousies, and rivalries within the National Front began to tear his coalition apart. Leading members of the National Front's parliamentary faction, such as Seyed Abolqasem Kashani, Mozaffar Baqa'i, and Hossein Makki, would eventually abandon Mosaddeq and join forces with a network of royalists and British agents in the army, the clergy, and the bazaar to topple the prime minister.[31]

Aware of the plots to overthrow him, Mosaddeq arrested a number of the conspirators and broke diplomatic relations with Britain in October 1952. With the British Embassy closed, the SIS handed over its network of agents in Iran to the CIA. Christopher Montague "Monty" Woodhouse, who had been head of the SIS station in Tehran, was sent to Washington in November to secure American support for Mosaddeq's overthrow. "Not wishing to be accused of trying to use the Americans for pulling British chestnuts out of the fire," Woodhouse later recalled, "I decided to emphasize the Communist threat to Iran rather than the need to recover control over the oil industry. I argued that even if a settlement of the oil dispute could be negotiated with Mosaddeq, which was doubtful, he was still incapable of resisting a *coup* by the Tudeh Party, if it were backed by Soviet support. Therefore he must be removed."[32] He received a sympathetic hearing from Frank Wisner and Allen Dulles, both senior figures in the CIA. However, more junior Iran experts in the Agency, as well as Roger Goiran, the CIA station chief in Tehran, were all against "putting U.S. support behind Anglo-French colonialism."[33] Woodhouse encountered a similar negative reaction from the State Department, which continued to push for a negotiated settlement between Britain and Iran. Dulles told Woodhouse that the incoming Republican administration of General Dwight D. Eisenhower, in which he and his brother John Foster Dulles would both serve, would look more favorably on the British proposal.

Much of the detail of the Anglo-American covert operation that toppled Mosaddeq is now well known.[34] Shortly after Eisenhower took office in January 1953, the CIA was given the green light to begin work with the SIS on a plan to topple Mosaddeq. According to the Cold War logic behind the US decision to support the coup, Mosaddeq needed to be removed in order to prevent a communist takeover in Iran. The Americans recognized that Mosaddeq was not a communist and that the Tudeh Party opposed him because of his rejection of a Soviet oil concession in northern Iran. However, in their view, the danger was that Iran's continuing descent into chaos would invite communist subversion.[35]

Mohammad Reza Shah was a reluctant conspirator. The shah wanted to be rid of Mosaddeq, but he feared the premier's popularity and preferred to topple him through ostensibly legal avenues, rather than a military coup. Only after considerable pressure and reassurance from London and Washington did the shah sign the *farmans* (royal decrees) on August 12, 1953, dismissing Mosaddeq and appointing General Fazlollah Zahedi, an ambitious retired army officer and senator, as prime minister. However, Mosaddeq had been tipped off about the conspiracy from a number of sources. Consequently, the first attempt to carry out the coup on August 15 failed as government troops seized key buildings in Tehran and arrested Colonel Nematollah Nasiri, commander of the Imperial Guard, when he tried to deliver the shah's *farman* to Mosaddeq. As the shah fled into exile in Rome, the CIA officer in charge of the operation, Kermit "Kim" Roosevelt, managed to regroup the conspirators for a second coup attempt on August 19, involving the use of paid mobs and pro-shah army and police units. The final showdown was at Mosaddeq's home, where loyal troops fought a pitched battle with Zahedi's forces for many hours, reducing Mosaddeq's house to rubble and leaving hundreds dead. Although Mosaddeq had escaped, he surrendered to Zahedi the following day. The shah returned to Tehran on August 22, bewildered at his dramatic change of fortune. He reportedly told Roosevelt, "I owe my throne to God, my people, my army—and to you!"[36]

The US-Iran Patron-Client Relationship

The Eisenhower administration's support for the overthrow of Mosaddeq marked the beginning of the US-Iran patron-client relationship. US economic and military support not only stabilized Iran after the 1953 coup, but also freed the shah from any significant social constraints on his power, thereby transforming the Pahlavi monarchy into a dictatorship.[37] In exchange, the shah ruthlessly suppressed any communist or nationalist threat to American interests in Iran and kept his country aligned with the United States in the Cold War. Such relationships between a superpower patron and a Third World client were quite common throughout the Cold War. In the Middle East, the United States enjoyed a similar relationship with Jordan, while the Soviet Union's clients included South Yemen.[38] The superpowers often found it difficult to control or influence the behavior of these regional clients.[39] Nonetheless, the vital importance of the economic and military support provided by Moscow or Washington meant that the superpowers were often able to meddle in their clients' internal affairs, so as to preserve their material interests and promote their competing visions of modernity. Like the European imperial powers of the past, the superpowers frequently relied on coercion, rather than persuasion, to fight their battles in the Third World.[40] It was precisely such a patron-client relationship, characterized by constant bargaining of arms and an American willingness to intervene in Iran's domestic affairs, that Nixon inherited from his predecessors.

The CIA's role in the overthrow of Mosaddeq quickly tarred the shah in Iranian eyes as a treacherous client of the United States. In the immediate aftermath of the coup, the US ambassador in Tehran, Loy Henderson, complained to Washington that "[u]nfortunately [the] impression [is] becoming rather widespread that in some way or other this Embassy or at least US Government has contributed with funds and technical assistance to overthrow Mosadeq and establish Zahedi Government." Henderson, who was keenly aware of the damage being done to the shah's legitimacy, warned that "it [is] not in US interest over long run to be given credit for internal political developments in Iran even if those developments might be to Iran's advantage."[41] To stabilize the shah's regime after the Anglo-Iranian oil crisis, the Eisenhower administration poured American aid into Iran. The average amount of annual US economic aid to Iran jumped from $9.7 million under Truman (1949–1953) to $64.5 million under Eisenhower (1954–1961), while military assistance increased from $17.6 million to $60 million.[42] After lengthy negotiations, the new National Iranian Oil Company signed an agreement in August 1954 with an international consortium of oil companies, including five of the major US companies, to produce and market Iranian oil.[43] The profits would be split 50–50 between Iran and the consortium. With the United States gaining a direct stake in Iran's oil, the British monopoly on Iranian oil had been broken. The combination of American patronage and a resumption of oil exports stabilized the Iranian economy.

With the support and encouragement of the Eisenhower administration, Mohammad Reza Shah tightened his grip on the throne. The young shah had played a marginal role in both the Azerbaijan crisis and the Anglo-Iranian oil crisis, when he was overshadowed by formidable prime ministers like Qavam, Mosaddeq, and Zahedi. But in the 1950s he took up the reins of power. Mosaddeq was tried by a military court in the winter of 1953 and was found guilty of treason. He lived under house arrest on his private estate until his death in 1967. This period also marked the beginning of the shah's friendship with Richard Nixon, whose first encounter with the shah was during his December 1953 trip to Iran as Eisenhower's vice president (Figure 1.1). Nixon's notes from those meetings in Tehran indicate that Zahedi did most of the talking.[44] Nixon later recalled, "I found the Shah to be intelligent, dignified, quiet, and not too sure of himself."[45] However, returning to Washington, he reported to the National Security Council (NSC) that "the shah is beginning to have more guts."[46] When the shah met with Eisenhower and Nixon in Washington in December 1954, at the beginning of a long vacation in the United States with his glamorous consort, Queen Soraya, the Americans expressed their "admiration" for the "resolute attitude Iran [is] taking vis-à-vis communists."[47] By April 1955 the shah felt confident enough to dismiss Zahedi, who went into exile in Switzerland. With American support, the shah's security forces brutally suppressed both the communist and nationalist opposition to his dictatorship. A five-man CIA team helped the Iranians create the Sazman-e Ettela'at va Amniyat-e Keshvar (National Security and Intelligence Organization, known by its Persian acronym SAVAK) in 1957. The CIA trained SAVAK in the tradecraft of modern intelligence and counterintelligence, and in time the organization became a notorious instrument of repression and torture.[48]

Despite all this American political, economic, and military support, the deeply insecure shah was never satisfied with the patronage he received from the United States. The lesson he had drawn from the 1946 Azerbaijan crisis and the 1953 coup was that only a strong army, backed by the United States, would protect the Pahlavi monarchy from Soviet aggression and communist subversion.[49] The shah rejected Mosaddeq's neutralist foreign policy and instead made the unpopular decision in 1955 to take Iran into the pro-Western Baghdad Pact, alongside Britain, Iraq, Pakistan, and Turkey.[50]

FIGURE I.I   The shah meets Nixon for the first time in Tehran in December 1953. Courtesy of the Richard M. Nixon Presidential Library.

He had hoped that Iran's membership in the Pact would strengthen the American commitment to Iran's defense.[51] But when the Eisenhower administration refused to join the Pact, because of considerations relating to the Arab-Israeli conflict, Iran was left without the iron-clad security guarantees that neighboring Turkey enjoyed as a member of the North Atlantic

Treaty Organization (NATO).[52] Despite the significant flow of American arms to Iran under the Eisenhower Doctrine, the United States' refusal of membership in the Baghdad Pact was the first of many points of friction between the shah and his American patrons.[53] The shah's unhappiness with the United States intensified after he discovered in February 1958 that Washington had failed to inform him that General Valiollah Qarani, the head of Iranian army intelligence (G-2), had asked for American help to carry out a coup and install a reformist government.[54] The shah's fears were compounded by the bloody military coup that toppled the Hashemite monarchy in neighboring Iraq on July 14. In a bid to reassure the shah, US secretary of state John Foster Dulles ordered his diplomats in Tehran to avoid all contact with "dissident and doubtful characters" and promised a bilateral defense agreement with Iran during discussions at the London ministerial meeting of the Baghdad Pact on July 28.[55]

Dulles's promise of a defense agreement was not enough to satisfy the shah, who felt "ridiculously weak" after the Qarani plot and the Iraqi coup.[56] The shah entered into secret talks with Moscow that winter for a non-aggression pact, which he hoped would diminish the Soviet threat to his regime and reduce his dependence on the United States.[57] Although the Soviet-Iranian talks collapsed under Anglo-American pressure in February 1959, and Iran eventually signed the defense agreement with the United States on March 5, deep concerns remained in both Tehran and Washington about the future of the US-Iran patron-client relationship. On the one hand, the shah resented the Americans' refusal to provide the arms and security guarantees he wanted, at a time when he felt particularly vulnerable. As he told one British official, Washington treated him as "a concubine and not as a wife."[58] On the other hand, the Eisenhower administration worried about the stability of the shah's increasingly unpopular regime. An intelligence assessment issued shortly after the coup in Iraq warned that "the present political situation in Iran is unlikely to last very long" and that "[t]he possibility of a coup to overthrow the monarchy cannot be disregarded."[59] If the shah did not make "some dramatic internal reforms," CIA director Allan Dulles warned, then "his days will be numbered."[60] The Eisenhower administration feared, however, that any attempt to pressure the shah to reform would destabilize his regime or drive him into the arms of the Soviet Union. Secretary of State Christian Herter told the NSC in November 1958 that the shah "was so exceedingly temperamental...that if we really attempted to put the heat on him, he might very well tell us to go to hell and proceed to play ball with the other side."[61] The shah's growing intolerance of any criticism was best exemplified by his treatment of Abolhassan Ebtehaj, the respected head of Iran's Plan and Budget Organization (PBO), who was responsible for carrying out the country's ambitious seven-year development plans. Initially, the shah had supported Ebtehaj and the PBO as a virtual shadow government after the 1953 coup, in order to weaken the power of Zahedi. However, as the shah consolidated all power in his own hands, Ebtehaj fell out of favor because of his opposition to corruption and the diversion of oil revenues from development to military spending. Ebtehaj resigned in February 1959 and was later imprisoned for his public criticism of the shah's policies.[62] The shah reportedly said of Ebtehaj, "I don't understand this man. Iran has been good to him, yet he doesn't like Iranians. He calls us all thieves. He doesn't seem to believe in what we are doing. The worst thing is that he doesn't seem to like his country."[63]

John F. Kennedy's narrow victory over Richard Nixon in the 1960 US presidential election heralded the most difficult days of the shah's relationship with the United States. The new Democratic president was influenced by American social scientists such as Walt Rostow and John Kenneth Galbraith, who saw economic and social modernization, rather than military aid, as the solution to political instability and communist subversion in the Third World.[64] Kennedy had criticized the Republicans for embracing unpopular anti-communist autocrats like the shah, who seemed destined for the dustbin of history.[65] Much to the shah's dismay, Kennedy seemed more interested in engaging with non-aligned countries like Gamal Abdel Nasser's Egypt, which the shah viewed as a Soviet-backed threat to the Persian Gulf, than with staunch US allies in the Third World like Iran.[66] Amidst growing domestic discontent, and in the hope of mollifying the Kennedy administration, the shah appointed the liberal Ali Amini as prime minister in May 1961. Amini was an experienced and independent politician, who was well regarded in Washington following his tour there as ambassador from 1956 to 1958.[67] The Kennedy administration embraced Amini and pressured the shah to allow his prime minister to carry out meaningful reforms, including an anti-corruption drive and a land reform program under the direction of his radical agriculture minister, Hassan Arsanjani.[68]

The shah deeply resented Kennedy's support for Amini, which he regarded as American meddling in Iran's internal affairs. He was finally able to rid himself of his troublesome prime minister in July 1962, when Amini resigned over the shah's refusal to cut Iran's defense spending.

Although the Kennedy administration was displeased with Amini's departure, they felt they had little choice but to continue backing the shah if they wanted to avoid "near political chaos" in Iran. Their only choice, as one of Kennedy's advisors put it, was a policy of "actively pushing, prodding, and cajoling" the shah toward reform.[69] The shah responded by enthusiastically embracing the language of modernization. In 1963 he proclaimed his own bloodless "White Revolution," which he claimed would take the wind out of the sails of his leftist opponents. Its elements included the redistribution of large land holdings to peasants and universal suffrage. But the White Revolution failed to convince the Iranian public that the shah was a "modernizing monarch."[70] As one Iranian senator observed, "His Majesty is trying to become both Xerxes and Fidel Castro; but this is impossible."[71] In fact, the rising tide of anger with the corruption and oppression of the shah's regime erupted into nationwide protests in Iran in June 1963, resulting in the deaths of scores of protesters at the hands of the security forces. But in Washington, Kennedy was convinced of the need to support the shah's modernization efforts. In an extraordinary letter to the shah, Kennedy dismissed the protests as "unfortunate attempts to block your reform programs" and told the shah that "such manifestations will gradually disappear as your people realize the importance of the measures you are taking to establish social justice and equal opportunity for all Iranians."[72] After the brutal suppression of the June 1963 protests, the shah abandoned any pretense of sharing power with the ever diminishing social base of the monarchy. He now ruled Iran personally, which meant that "politics itself began to disappear from the public sphere."[73] Kennedy had hoped to strengthen the shah's regime through reform. Instead, by acquiescing to the shah's crackdown and lauding his White Revolution, Kennedy helped to silence the shah's critics and further entrench his dictatorship.[74]

The US-Iran patron-client relationship was reaffirmed by the Kennedy and Johnson administrations. Kennedy had pushed the shah to reform, albeit with little success, again demonstrating Washington's willingness to intervene in Iran's internal affairs when American interests were threatened. After Kennedy's decision to back the shah's White Revolution in 1963, the focus of the US-Iran relationship would shift away from reform and back to the constant bargaining between Tehran and Washington over transfers of American arms to Iran. During Lyndon B. Johnson's presidency, the shah's leverage with the United States would increase as Iran's rising oil revenues strengthened the autonomy of his regime and reduced his reliance on American patronage.[75] The shah had taken his first modest step toward a more independent posture in the Cold War in September 1962 by normalizing Soviet-Iranian relations. After three turbulent years of negotiations, Iran became the first American ally to pledge to the Soviet Union that no foreign power would be allowed to establish missile bases on its soil.[76] But regardless of the shifting dynamics of the US-Iran relationship, the Johnson administration would show much the same willingness as Eisenhower and Kennedy to meddle in Iran's internal affairs to protect American interests. The prime example was the notorious 1964 US-Iran Status of Forces Agreement (SOFA), which reinforced the shah's image in Iran as a Cold War client of the United States.[77]

The SOFA had first been proposed by the Kennedy administration in March 1962, under intense pressure from the Department of Defense, which was concerned with protecting the growing number of US military personnel in Iran. The United States had asked Iran to extend diplomatic immunity to the civilian and military staff of the US military missions in Iran, as well as their dependents. Under the terms of Article I of the 1961 Vienna Convention on Diplomatic Relations, the Pentagon's personnel in Iran would be classed as "members of the administrative and technical staff" of the US Embassy, giving them immunity from Iranian criminal jurisdiction. Such sweeping immunity, extending to the dependents of the American personnel and covering criminal acts committed outside the course of their duties, went far beyond SOFAs that the United States had negotiated with its NATO allies in Europe. The State Department was aware that "some articulate Iranians" would see such a law as "an infringement on Iranian sovereignty."[78] Not surprisingly, Iran's Foreign Ministry dragged its feet on this controversial agreement as diplomatic notes flew back and forth between Tehran and Washington in 1963.[79] When the immunity law was finally passed by Iran's normally pliant Majlis on October 13, 1964, it did so by a margin of only 74 votes to 61. Then, just 12 days later, the Majlis approved a $200 million loan from private US banks for the purchase of American arms.[80] In an act reminiscent of the capitulations granted by Iran's Qajar rulers to the European powers in the nineteenth century, it seemed as if the shah had sold Iran's sovereignty to the United States in order to indulge his insatiable appetite for more American weapons. The US Embassy concluded that "the Shah's regime has paid an unexpectedly high price in getting this done."[81]

When news of the immunity law reached the Islamic seminary of Qom, the shah's clerical opponents relished the opportunity to attack him for having betrayed Iran to the Americans. Ayatollah Ruhollah Khomeini, who had fomented the protests against the White Revolution the previous summer, told his students, "We must use it [the immunity law] as a weapon to attack the regime so that the whole nation will realize that this Shah is an American agent and this is an American plot." On the morning of October 27, Khomeini delivered a fiery sermon denouncing the shah in language that had not been heard in public since the fall of Mosaddeq:

> They have reduced the Iranian people to a level lower than that of an American dog. If someone runs over a dog, belonging to an American, he will be prosecuted. Even if the Shah himself were to run over a dog belonging to an American, he would be prosecuted. But if an American cook runs over the Shah, the head of state, no one will have the right to interfere with him. Why? Because they wanted a loan and America demanded this in return. The government has sold our independence, reduced us to the level of a colony, and made the Muslim nation of Iran appear more backward than savages in the eyes of the world!

Khomeini warned the shah, "save yourself," and went on to deliver the following message to President Johnson:

> Let the American President know that in the eyes of the Iranian people he is the most repulsive member of the human race today because of the injustice he has imposed on our Muslim nation. Today the Qor'an has become his enemy, the Iranian nation has become his enemy. Let the American government know that its name has been ruined and disgraced in Iran.[82]

In a bid to silence Khomeini, SAVAK arrested the fiery cleric and sent him into exile on November 4. But the immunity law had enraged the shah's opponents and had propelled Khomeini into the national spotlight. Iranian prime minister Hasan Ali Mansur tried to calm tensions by making a speech to the Iranian Senate in which he blatantly lied about the terms of the immunity granted to the Americans in Iran.[83] Three months later he was gunned down in front of the Majlis by an assassin belonging to a shadowy radical Islamist group. This was followed by a second attempt on the life of the shah on April 10, 1965. As the shah arrived for work that morning at the Marble Palace in downtown Tehran, one of his guards, Reza Shamsabadi, opened fire on him with a machine gun. The shah managed to scramble into his office and dive for cover behind his desk, before Shamsabadi was shot by two other guards.[84] The shah nearly paid the ultimate price for his acquiescence to the United States' disregard for Iran's national sovereignty.

Although the United States had provided the shah with significant military and economic aid under Eisenhower, Kennedy, and Johnson, he nonetheless chafed under American patronage. In the context of intense domestic and regional crises in the 1950s and 1960s, the shah harbored deep anxieties about Washington's commitment to the security of his regime, and he resented US efforts to limit Iran's military spending. He felt that the Americans took him for granted and often complained that Washington treated him as a "concubine" rather than a "wife."[85] Moreover, Eisenhower's backing for the 1953 coup, Kennedy's support for Amini in the early 1960s, and Johnson's 1964 SOFA agreement all reinforced popular Iranian perceptions of the shah as a pliant instrument of US policy. The shah told Kim Roosevelt in July 1966 that he was "tired of being treated like a schoolboy" by the United States.[86] He tried to distance himself from Washington by proclaiming his *siyasat-e mostaqell-e melli* (independent national policy), which he hoped would steal the thunder of his pro-Mosaddeq opponents, who advocated a non-aligned foreign policy. This meant that while Iran remained within the Central Treaty Organization (CENTO),[87] the shah also dramatically expanded Iran's economic ties with the USSR in the 1960s, culminating in a high-profile agreement in January 1966 for Soviet financing and construction of a steel mill, a gas pipeline, and a machine tools plant in Iran.[88] A year later, Iran even purchased $100 million of unsophisticated arms from the Soviet Union.[89] Few of the shah's critics were convinced, however, that he was anything other than a loyal US client. Iranian public opinion continued to view the United States as "the chief architect and daily instructor" of the shah's regime, even though, as Iranian historian Homa Katouzian writes, Washington's "real influence had considerably declined since the mid-1960s."[90]

The announcement in January 1968 of the British withdrawal from the Persian Gulf, followed by the election in November of Richard Nixon to the White House, presented the shah with an opportunity to fundamentally transform the US-Iran patron-client relationship. Working closely with President Nixon and his chief foreign policy advisor, Henry Kissinger, the shah would remake Iran as a partner of the United States.

He would no longer rely on American patronage to ensure his regime's survival or pursue his foreign policy ambitions. Nor would the United States continue to interfere in Iran's internal affairs or second-guess the shah's decisions on arms purchases. Grappling with the war in Vietnam, superpower détente, and the opening to China, the United States would rely on Iran to take Britain's place as the defender of the shipping lanes of the oil-rich Persian Gulf from the Soviet Union and its Arab allies. As this took effect, the shah was transformed from the insecure and unsatisfied American client of the 1950s and 1960s into the confident and independent international figure of the 1970s.

2

"Protect Me"

THE NIXON DOCTRINE IN THE PERSIAN GULF

ON THE MORNING of May 31, 1972, the shah received President Richard Nixon and his national security advisor, Henry Kissinger, at Tehran's Saadabad Palace in the foothills of the Alborz Mountains. The three men were in high spirits. Nixon had arrived in Tehran the previous day from his summit meeting in Moscow with General Secretary Leonid Brezhnev, where he had signed a series of arms control agreements with the Soviet Union. This was the era of superpower détente, and Nixon and Kissinger were lauded as its architects. Nixon's popularity was soaring after his momentous trip to Communist China in February. Meanwhile, Henry Kissinger had established a position of unprecedented power in the machinery of American foreign policy, conducting the administration's secret diplomacy in Beijing, Paris, and Moscow, and sidelining the nation's chief diplomat, Secretary of State William Rogers. The shah, too, was at the apogee of his reign. Under his leadership, Iran had enjoyed more than a decade of nearly double-digit GDP growth, commensurate with manifold increases in both oil income and military expenditure.[1] Having normalized relations with his Soviet neighbor in 1962, the shah had turned his attention south to the Persian Gulf, where he sought to establish Iran's regional primacy in the wake of Britain's withdrawal from the region in 1971. Mohammad Reza Shah had seen five American presidents pass through the White House; each in turn had frustrated and disappointed him in his ambition to make Iran a leading regional and international power. But now, under the Nixon Doctrine, the United States would rely on the shah to maintain stability in the Persian Gulf. On that May morning in Tehran, Nixon looked to the shah and uttered the words the Iranian monarch had long waited to hear: "protect me."[2]

Nixon's presidency marked a turning point in the shah's Cold War relationship with the United States. Under this administration, the shah was able to shape the formation and implementation of the Nixon Doctrine in the Persian Gulf region (see Figure 2.1). Although President Johnson and his advisors has seen regional stability as resting on a balance of power between Iran and Saudi Arabia as the "twin pillars" of the Gulf, between 1969 and 1972 the shah convinced Nixon and Kissinger to abandon this policy and tilt in favor of Iran.[3] In the process, Iran was transformed from a client to a partner of the United States in the global struggle to contain the Soviet Union. Examining the formation of this Nixon-Kissinger-Pahlavi partnership, this chapter addresses the question of why Nixon embraced a policy of Iranian primacy in the Gulf, whereas Johnson had rejected it. Declining Anglo-American power in the context of the British withdrawal from the Gulf between 1968 and 1971 and America's quagmire in Vietnam do not provide an adequate explanation.[4] These important constraints confronted both Johnson and Nixon, yet each president adopted quite distinct Gulf policies. Instead, the policy shift reflected a fundamental change in American thinking about Mohammad Reza Pahlavi. Because of his long-standing friendship with the shah, Richard Nixon brought new ideas to the White House about the Pahlavi monarch and his ambitions for Iran, providing fertile ground for the shah's relentless efforts to forge a partnership with the United States by securing Washington's backing for Iran's regional primacy in the Gulf. By lifting virtually all restrictions on US arms sales to Iran, Nixon allowed the shah to assume the regional leadership role that he had always sought for his country.

The Shah and Pax Britannica

The idea that the security of the Persian Gulf rests on a balance of power between Iran and Saudi Arabia originated in London. For more than a century, Her Majesty's Government ruled the Gulf as a British lake on the periphery of India, protecting significant political and economic interests along the southern shore, where Arab rulers governed a series of British-protected states.[5] Britain's balance of power policy in the Gulf consisted of preventing either of the two largest littoral powers, Iran and Saudi Arabia, from dominating their smaller and weaker Arab neighbors, while also deterring any other great power from entering the Gulf. However, by the 1960s it was becoming politically infeasible for

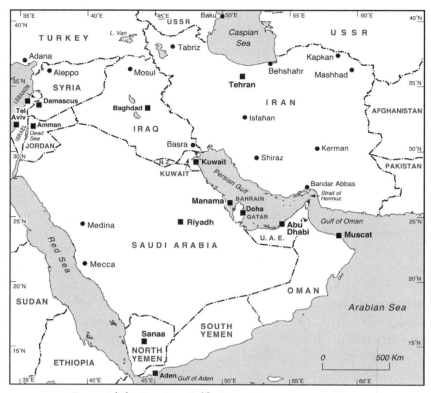

FIGURE 2.1   Iran and the Persian Gulf, circa 1972.

Britain to maintain what was left of its empire in the Middle East.[6] On January 16, 1968, the Labor Government, led by Prime Minister Harold Wilson, announced that Britain would withdraw all its military forces from the Gulf by 1971 as part of a larger withdrawal "East of Suez." The decision was motivated, in part, by the Cabinet's desire to cut defense spending and achieve fiscal austerity in the face of a severe economic crisis, while avoiding painful cuts in social spending. In order to avoid a power vacuum following the British withdrawal, which could result in regional instability and Soviet encroachment, a new regional order would need to emerge to protect British interests.[7]

The solution developed by the mandarins of the British Foreign Office was to strengthen the British-protected states by persuading them to join together in a single Arab federation, and to encourage Saudi Arabia to play a more active role in the Persian Gulf, thereby providing an Arab counterweight to the shah's ambitions for Iranian regional primacy. In 1967 the

Foreign Office had prepared a report on Britain's long-term policy in the Gulf, the conclusions of which were approved by the Cabinet's Defense and Overseas Policy Committee on June 7, 1968. According to this report, Britain would "encourage an indigenous balance of power which does not require our military presence." This balance of power would depend, above all, on Saudi Arabia and Iran, as "they are also the two best placed to bring force to bear in the area, the Saudis by virtue of their commanding geographical position and the Iranians through their growing naval supremacy in the Gulf. If they were at loggerheads with each other, local stability would be unlikely to survive our departure. Conversely if they were to act in concert, or at least with mutual understanding, they could do much to ensure a peaceful transition to whatever new system follows our withdrawal."[8] *Pax Britannica* had been maintained in the Gulf by a preponderance of British naval power. After the British military withdrawal, equilibrium between Iran and Saudi Arabia would prevent either power from dominating the Gulf, thereby protecting the independence of the proposed Arab federation without a substantial British military presence. But such a balance of power would not emerge automatically. Rather, it would have to be constructed and maintained.

From Britain's perspective, the shah's ambitions for Iranian primacy in the Persian Gulf posed a threat to the successful construction and operation of a regional balance of power, particularly as the shah continued to press Iranian territorial claims against the British-protected states of Bahrain, Sharjah, and Ras al Khaimah. At the time of the shah's March 1965 visit to London, British Foreign Secretary Michael Stewart advised Wilson to "disabuse the Shah of the idea that, if and when we ever leave the Persian Gulf, Iran can take our place: given the Arab character of the southern shores of the Persian Gulf, and the pretensions of Saudi Arabia and Iraq (to say nothing of the United Arab Republic) this hope is quite illusory."[9] Given their long-standing political and economic relationships with the Arab rulers of the Gulf, British policy was to contain Iran's ambitions and to reassure their Arab clients. Sir Stewart Crawford, the British resident in the Gulf, advised Foreign Secretary George Brown that Britain should avoid any appearance of endorsing Iran's ambitions, thereby giving the impression that "we shall disregard the interests of the [Arab] Gulf States and sell them down the river."[10] In March 1968, Sir Denis Wright, Britain's ambassador to Iran, warned his colleagues in the Foreign Office that "[t]he Shah remains suspicious of our intentions and of our alleged favouritism of the Arabs against Iran."[11] A few days later Wright traveled to

London to participate in a discussion of Gulf policy convened by Goronwy Roberts, a junior minister in the Foreign Office. When Wright asked his colleagues "whether the balance of British interests in Iran had been considered against those in the Arab world," he was assured that "on an arithmetical calculation the balance was overwhelmingly in favour of the Arabs."[12]

Mohammad Reza Shah shared the ubiquitous Iranian mistrust of perfidious Albion, stemming from more than a century of British imperialism in Iran. He was convinced that London was conspiring with the Arabs against Iran in anticipation of Britain's withdrawal from the Persian Gulf.[13] Although the shah's Anglophobia was acute, given that the British had exiled his father in 1941, his suspicion that British interests favored the Arabs over Iran was not unfounded. In June 1968, Sir Denis Allen, under secretary at the Foreign Office, advised Wright that any attempt to accommodate the shah's ambitions would not only disrupt the stability of the Gulf and "earn us major ill-will from the Arabs," but would in any event fail to "earn us any permanent dividends from the Shah."[14] Although the British privately recognized that Iran would be the single most powerful littoral power following their departure, they feared that the shah's ambitions would spark Arab-Iranian hostility, threatening Britain's economic interests on the Arab shore of the Gulf and generating instability that could be exploited by the Soviet Union.

British disdain for Pahlavi Iran as a revisionist power and support for Saudi Arabia as a status-quo power is apparent in a report written in December 1968 by William Morris, Britain's ambassador to Saudi Arabia, following a visit by the shah to the court of King Faisal. Whereas Morris describes Faisal as "a true conservative, by nature cautious and pessimistic," he calls the shah "our Middle East de Gaulle," "restless, bold, innovative, radical." He denigrates the shah as "the son of the illiterate Persian sergeant, self-consciously masquerading as heir to the 3,000 years old Achaemenid monarchy," in contrast with Faisal, a man who "dislikes pomp, ceremony and luxury, and in a quiet rather snobbish way is certain and therefore undemonstrative about his lineage."[15] The shah would have welcomed the comparison to French President Charles de Gaulle. In his memoirs he wrote that when de Gaulle "spoke of France, he seemed to echo the ambitions which I nurtured for my own country: he wanted an independent France. His quiet eloquence inspired faith in his country's future.... This great patriot was an example to me."[16] But Morris did not intend the comparison as a compliment. He saw the shah as a megalomaniac with ambitions above his station, echoing the Foreign Office's anxiety that Iranian primacy would threaten Britain's long-term interests in the Gulf. These pejorative depictions of the shah, as well as the concept of a balance of power between Iran and Saudi Arabia, were the legacy that the departing British bequeathed to the United States in the Gulf.

Continuity: Johnson's Balancing Policy

In the year between the announcement of the British withdrawal from the Persian Gulf in January 1968 and the inauguration of the Nixon administration in January 1969, Johnson had little time to formulate America's Gulf policy. The Gulf had been a British sphere of influence, and the United States had considered it Britain's responsibility to contain Soviet influence there. Johnson had agreed to subsidize Britain's global military presence, while concentrating his own attention on Vietnam.[17] Although Britain had informed the United States in April 1967 that it would be withdrawing its forces "East of Suez," the announcement in January 1968 that the Gulf would be included in this withdrawal disappointed the Americans, and their reaction was markedly bitter. When British Foreign Secretary George Brown traveled to Washington on January 11, 1968, to deliver the bad news, he reported to London that he had suffered through a "bloody unpleasant" meeting with US Secretary of State Dean Rusk, who was furious at what he saw as Britain's shirking of its global responsibilities at a time when the United States was bogged down in Vietnam. Rusk resented what he called the "acrid aroma of the fait accompli" and contemptuously demanded, "for God's sake, be Britain."[18] That same day Johnson wrote to Wilson, expressing his "deep dismay" at the "British withdrawal from world affairs," which would leave the United States "to man the ramparts all alone."[19] Nonetheless, within a week of these exchanges the US Department of State began what would be a year-long process of formulating a Gulf policy, in close consultation with the Foreign Office.[20]

The Persian Gulf was rather low on Johnson's list of priorities in 1968, as he grappled with the Tet Offensive that was launched by the North Vietnamese in January, followed by his announcement in March that he would not seek re-election.[21] Gulf policy was largely left to the State Department and rarely reached the Oval Office. The Johnson administration quickly dismissed any idea of taking over Britain's role and instead opted for a policy of relying on the littoral states to maintain stability in the Gulf. In a careless statement made during an interview with the Voice of America on January 19, US under secretary of state Eugene Rostow said:

> In the Persian Gulf you have some very strong, and quite active and stable countries, which are interested in taking responsibility for regional security—Iran, Turkey, Pakistan, Saudi Arabia would certainly be a nucleus, and Kuwait—would certainly be a nucleus, around which such security arrangements could hopefully be built, and we can hope that in the long run the policy of Iraq would orient itself in a cooperative direction so that it could join in such efforts.[22]

The statement was careless for two reasons. First, it tarred any regional security arrangement with the imprimatur of the United States, making it more difficult for the Arab rulers of the Gulf to support such an arrangement, lest they be accused by Arab nationalists of collusion with American imperialism. Furthermore, the clumsy reference to Turkey and Pakistan—neither of which border the Gulf—angered both of these governments, as they had not been consulted, and also violated the principle that only the riparian powers would be responsible for Gulf security. In short, Rostow's words had the potential to upset Britain's plans for a regional balance of power arrangement following their withdrawal.[23] The British Embassy in Washington assured the Foreign Office that Rostow's comments were made "off the cuff" and without clearance from Rusk. Soon after, the State Department informed all American diplomatic posts in the region that Washington has "no plan, general or specific, as to future [of the Gulf]."[24]

Following the embarrassment of the Rostow episode, the Johnson administration sought to closely coordinate its Persian Gulf policy with London. Wilson's February 1968 trip to Washington smoothed over any residual hard feelings from the withdrawal announcement; in March, American officials traveled to London for the first of a series of Anglo-American talks on the Gulf. What emerged from these consultations was a division of labor between Britain and the United States, whereby London would manage the negotiations to resolve the outstanding territorial disputes in the Gulf and construct a regional balance of power to replace British hegemony, while Washington would continue to pressure the shah to cooperate with Britain and Saudi Arabia in this endeavor. Theodore Eliot, the country director for Iran at the State Department, assured the British that Washington "could take a hand [with the shah] since the United States military relationship was vital to the Iranians."[25] Johnson had written to the shah in February, after a Saudi-Iranian spat over Bahrain, to remind him that regional stability would require the shah to exercise "patience, understanding and a high degree of statesmanship" in his relations with the Saudis.[26] In his stern reply to the president's patronizing letter, the shah said that in dealing with the Saudis, he had gone "as far as anyone can go, but our efforts so far have, unfortunately, been answered by precisely the opposite reaction to that expected."[27] Nonetheless, the US ambassador to Iran, Armin Meyer, was convinced that Johnson's intervention had exercised a "restraining effect" on the shah.[28] Similarly, the president's national security advisor, Walt Rostow, felt that Johnson had "injected a sobering perspective at a heated moment."[29]

Throughout 1968 the State Department deferred to the Foreign Office to such an extent on Persian Gulf matters that American and British Gulf policy became virtually indistinguishable. In talks held in London in May, Lucius Battle, US assistant secretary of state for Near Eastern and South Asian affairs, assured Goronwy Roberts that the United States "recognized the special British role in the Region and would be heavily influenced by the British view of what it might prove possible to negotiate."[30] In September, Battle reiterated to Sir Denis Allen that the United States was "in complete agreement" with Britain's Gulf policy. He readily admitted that Washington "had no solution to offer, nor indeed any particular suggestions" for managing the various territorial disputes in the Gulf and that "the U.S. and everyone else concerned would look to the British" to manage Gulf problems.[31] Theodore Eliot later recalled that "British interests in Iran were very similar to ours, and their record of experience was much longer" and that in this period "there was a real question as to whether we'd be choosing sides between the Saudis and Iranians, obviously none of us wanted to choose sides."[32] Rather than make a choice, the United States had opted for Britain's balancing policy in the Gulf, which sought to temper the shah's ambitions for Iranian primacy and encourage Saudi-Iranian cooperation.

The United States' wholesale adoption of Britain's balancing policy quickly led to tensions with the shah, who feared that his American allies were toeing a pro-Arab British line. The NSC staff warned of the "basic conflict... between the Iranian assumption that Iran has the mission of controlling the Gulf, and the Saudi assumption that Saudi Arabia is responsible for everything on the Arabian Peninsula." Although the Americans wanted "to stay out of the middle" of this rivalry, the shah worried that Johnson had conspired with the British against Iran.[33] Hushang Ansary, the Iranian ambassador to the United States, had conveyed these concerns to Eugene Rostow in February, and a few weeks later, during a visit to Washington by Iranian foreign minister Ardeshir Zahedi, Dean Rusk informed his Iranian counterpart that he was aware of Tehran's suspicions and assured him that they were unfounded.[34] All Washington wanted, Rusk argued, was to promote Irano-Saudi cooperation as a "prerequisite to peace in [the] Gulf" in the interests of "preventing [the] expansion [of] Soviet influence in area."[35] Despite his protests, however, Rusk shared Britain's concern about the shah's ambitions. In language reminiscent of that used by the British, he would later recall that the shah "was influenced by the dreams of the Persian Empire, he had a very lofty view of what Persia had been and perhaps could be again someday. The sense of glory in the Shah was at least equal to that of President de Gaulle's views about the glory of France."[36]

The shah had tried repeatedly to convince Johnson to tilt toward Iran in the Persian Gulf, using the Soviet threat as his argument for a policy of Iranian primacy. Conscious of the American public's aversion to overseas commitments in the context of Vietnam, the shah had written to Johnson in August 1966, arguing that "[a] strong Iran can...avert the spreading of conflicts in the region, guarantee the smooth and orderly flow of oil to the west and, what is of vital importance and worthy of serious consideration, forestall the repetition of current tragic and costly involvements."[37] The shah firmly believed that radical Arab states like Egypt and Iraq, supported by Moscow, endangered both stability in the Gulf and Iranian national security. He was particularly alarmed by Egypt's military intervention in North Yemen as well as the Soviet- and Chinese-backed rebellion against the sultan of Oman in Dhofar.[38] He feared that Moscow would use radical Arab forces to subvert the conservative Arab monarchies of the Gulf, from which they could disrupt Iran's oil exports through the Strait of Hormuz and press Arab territorial claims against the Iranian province of Khuzestan, where much of Iran's oil reserves are located.[39]

These arguments failed to convince Johnson and his advisors. A succession of American presidents had sought to temper Iranian military spending, fearing that its burgeoning defense expenditure would divert precious resources from economic development, thereby fulfilling the shah's military ambitions at the cost of Iran's domestic stability. Although the dynamics of the US-Iran patron-client relationship were shifting in the shah's favor in the 1960s, he was unable to convince the Johnson

FIGURE 2.2   The shah spars with Johnson in the Oval Office on June 12, 1968.
Courtesy of the Lyndon B. Johnson Presidential Library.

administration to tilt toward Iran in the Persian Gulf. In February 1968
the NSC's interagency review group concluded that the United States
should continue to pursue a balance of power in the Gulf by "avoiding an
undue military build-up by the Gulf littoral states."[40] Despite the shah's
constant requests for ever larger quantities of American arms, in June 1968
Johnson would agree only to continue providing Iran with $100 million in
annual military sales credits, as the United States had done since 1966
(Figure 2.2).[41] In the waning months of Johnson's presidency, Washington
continued "to discourage large military expenditures that would adversely
affect Iran's economic development" and still held that "Iran's armaments
should not be so augmented as to frighten other riparian states and thus
endanger prospects for Arab-Iranian cooperation."[42] Any change in policy
would depend on the next occupant of the White House.

Nixon and the Third World

By the first summer of his presidency, Richard Nixon had already decided
on the contours of the grand strategy that would come to bear his name.
During a tour of East Asia, the presidential party stopped on the island
of Guam. Speaking on background to reporters, and much to Henry

Kissinger's surprise, on July 25, 1969, Nixon outlined his views on a post-Vietnam foreign policy for the United States. He declared that while America would always keep its treaty commitments to its allies, it "must avoid the kind of policy that will make countries in Asia so dependent upon us that we are dragged into conflicts such as the one we have in Vietnam." When it comes to defending its Cold War allies in Asia, "except for the threat of a major power involving nuclear weapons...the United States is going to encourage and has a right to expect that this problem will be handled by, and responsibility for it taken by, the Asian nations themselves."[43] Nixon's statement was intended to signal to America's nervous allies in Southeast Asia that the United States would not abandon them following a withdrawal from Vietnam, while also assuring a profoundly angry American public that they would never again find themselves fighting someone else's civil war. This "Nixon Doctrine" was quickly extended to the rest of the Third World, where the United States would provide material assistance to regional allies like Brazil, Chile, Indonesia, Iran, and Zaire to manage local conflicts and contain Soviet influence without direct American military intervention.[44]

If the Nixon administration was going to rebuild public support for American leadership in the Cold War at a time when the Soviet Union had achieved military parity with the United States, then, as historian Odd Arne Westad argues, Nixon would have to recast America's global role as "an overseer, not an intervener."[45] Third World conflicts were a costly distraction from Nixon's agenda of seeking détente with the Soviet Union and building Washington's leverage over Moscow through the opening to China. Therefore, the Nixon Doctrine and superpower détente were inextricably linked, as the former would redirect American attention and resources to the latter.[46] Nixon and Kissinger were interested in the politics of the Third World only to the extent that it affected relations among the great powers.[47] Nixon famously instructed Kissinger early in his first term not to waste his time on the Third World, "as what happens in those parts of the world is not, in the final analysis, going to have any significant effect on the success of our foreign policy in the foreseeable future."[48] The Middle East was of interest to Nixon and Kissinger mainly because the Arab-Israeli conflict impinged on superpower relations and Persian Gulf oil fueled the economies of America's allies in Asia and Europe. Kissinger readily admitted that in 1969 he had no understanding of Gulf politics: "I did not know how Saudi-Iranian relations worked, my priority was to get the Soviets out of the Middle East."[49] The Nixon Doctrine was a way of limiting and simplifying American intervention in the Third World, and the Gulf was no exception. Preoccupied with superpower détente, engagement with China, and the war in Vietnam, Nixon and Kissinger reduced the complexities of regional politics to a simple question of whether Iran was capable of keeping the peace in the Gulf after the British withdrawal.

Throughout the period of 1969 to 1972, the shah aggressively lobbied Nixon to convince him that Iran could indeed fill the vacuum left by the British in the Persian Gulf. He employed the language of the Nixon Doctrine to argue that the United States should provide Iran with the necessary arms to maintain the security and stability of the Gulf without direct American military intervention. Relations with Iran were higher on the Nixon administration's agenda than formulating a broad Gulf policy, thanks in large measure to the warm personal relationship between Richard Nixon and Mohammad Reza Pahlavi. In his memoirs, Nixon recalled his first impression of the shah during his December 1953 trip to Tehran, after the Eisenhower administration had backed the coup against Mosaddeq: "I sensed an inner strength in him, and I felt that in the years ahead he would become a strong leader."[50] Both men were staunchly anti-communist, and both thought of themselves as practitioners of *realpolitik*. They shared a disdain for American liberal intellectuals who lionized Kennedy and despised Nixon.[51] The shah was even rumored to have made secret financial contributions to Nixon's 1960 presidential election campaign. After Nixon's narrow defeat to Kennedy, the shah maintained a friendship with the former vice president during his years in the political wilderness.[52]

The two old friends had met in Tehran in April 1967 during Nixon's tour of Asia, which was intended to burnish Nixon's already impressive foreign policy credentials ahead of his second bid for the presidency in 1968.[53] The shah had ignored his ministers' entreaties not to meet with Nixon. They feared that their boss would be seen to be backing Nixon's presidential ambitions, as he had reportedly done in 1960, thereby angering the incumbent Democrats.[54] Nixon faced a very different shah in 1967 from the weak figure he had first encountered in 1953. The shah had crushed the protests against his White Revolution in 1963, and he had exiled, imprisoned, or co-opted his Marxist, nationalist, and Islamist opponents.[55] He had replaced his old guard of aging ministers—ambitious aristocratic statesmen who had steered the young shah through the crises of the 1940s and 1950s—with younger Western-educated technocrats who posed no threat to the shah's power.[56] Moreover, by accepting the title of *aryamehr* (light of the Aryans) in 1965 and holding a lavish coronation ceremony in 1967, nearly 26 years after he had assumed the throne, the shah was nurturing a cult of personality that portrayed him as a modern-day Cyrus the Great, taking Iran toward what he called the *tamaddon-e bozorg* (great civilization).[57]

The shah's increasingly imperious rule at home was matched by his determination to restore Iran to what he considered his country's rightful place among the ranks of the great powers. He had been "transformed," according to the CIA, "from a timorous, titular monarch into a self-confident potentate, determined to assert his and Iran's prerogatives against all comers."[58] The shah was not only the *bozorg-e arteshtaran* (supreme commander of the armed forces), but also effectively his own foreign minister. Although he received daily reports from the Foreign Ministry, SAVAK, and other agencies on international developments, he rarely sought the advice of his ministers and frequently presented them with a *fait accompli* on major diplomatic decisions.[59] The shah's tight control over foreign policy meant that he always preferred to receive foreign dignitaries without any other Iranian official present, thereby keeping his own courtiers in the dark about the content of these meetings.[60] His 1967 meeting with Nixon was no exception; the only records of their discussion are Nixon's handwritten notes.

Over lunch at Niavaran Palace on April 22, 1967, Nixon and the shah lamented the loss of American confidence in the age of Vietnam.[61] After surveying the Cold War in Africa, the Middle East, and South Asia, the shah told Nixon that it was "better for [the] U.S. to have Iran able to defend [it]self than to have ... another Vietnam." Nixon recorded that the shah's views echoed the "RN Doctrine." Planting the seed of what would become Nixon's Persian Gulf policy, the shah boasted that by 1971 "Iran will be able to help [the] Saudis if required," though at the time, Nixon thought this claim to be "over optimistic." The shah complained to Nixon that the liberal "Harvard boys" in the Johnson administration, holdovers from the Kennedy presidency, enjoyed far too much influence over US foreign policy. Addressing accusations of corruption and autocracy in his regime, the shah portrayed himself to Nixon as a reformer who "attacks problems—not classes." Unlike the socialists, he was "not imprisoned by any 'ism.'" Nixon found the shah to be "decisive, confident, strong, kind, thoughtful."[62] As president, he would never forget the respect and courtesy the shah had shown him while he was out of office. Returning to the United States, he hailed Iran's "strong monarchy" as a "dramatic economic success." He readily conceded that Iran was not "a representative democracy by Western standards," but he argued that "American style democracy is not necessarily the best form of government for people in Asia, Africa and Latin American with entirely different backgrounds."[63] Writing from exile many years later, the shah recalled that during that 1967 conversation, "we found that we agreed over several very simple geo-political principles."[64]

In the first year of Nixon's presidency, the shah's relentless lobbying quickly overtook the administration's slow and cumbersome consideration of Persian Gulf policy. When the shah visited Washington in April 1969 for President Eisenhower's funeral (Figure 2.3), Nixon's staff warned him that the shah would press the president to abandon balancing in the Gulf and to acknowledge Iran as the paramount power of the region.[65] The US intelligence community had concluded in a January assessment that "with the impending British withdrawal from the Persian Gulf, Iran is vigorously asserting its own claim to a leading position there, thus running afoul of the aspirations of Saudi Arabia." Nixon and Kissinger would confront an Iranian ruler who was certain that "he is master in his own house," confidently "seeking for Iran the position in regional affairs that

FIGURE 2.3 With the shah in attendance, Nixon delivers a eulogy for Eisenhower at the Capitol rotunda on March 30, 1969. Courtesy of the Richard M. Nixon Presidential Library.

he deems to be rightfully his."[66] At his first meeting with Kissinger on the evening of April 1, the shah reiterated the same warnings about the Soviet-backed radical Arab threat to the Gulf that he had expressed to Johnson.[67] The shah was particularly worried about Iraq, where a coup in July 1968 had returned to power the Iraqi branch of the radical Arab Socialist Ba'th (Renaissance) Party, which looked to Moscow for military and economic support to consolidate its grip on power in Baghdad and to defend the "Arabism" of the Gulf against the shah's ambitions for Iranian regional primacy.[68] For the Americans, the shah painted Iran's regional conflict with Iraq in Cold War colors. As he explained to Secretary of Defense Melvyn Laird, "the Soviet Union wanted to penetrate the Persian Gulf area" and he worried that the "reckless" Iraqis were falling under the sway of a "Red regime." The Soviets would never attack Iran directly, the shah said, as this would elicit an American response and spark a global war. Rather, "the more probable and more logical threat was that of a local and limited war." If the United States wanted to avoid being drawn into such a regional conflict, the shah argued, then Washington would have to provide Iran with the necessary arms to build a strong military, capable of deterring any "foolish aggressor" in the region like Ba'thi Iraq.[69] Court Minister Alam, who accompanied his boss to Washington (Figure 2.4), recorded in his diary that the shah

> asked the Americans to consider the advantages they receive from their friendship with us. He stressed that Iran is not an American stooge but that we nevertheless prefer to remain independent of Soviet influence. Iran is a friend of the West sufficiently powerful to maintain her own sovereignty, able to defend her own interests and by implication capable of defending the interests of her western friends.[70]

Crisis in the Shatt

Despite this relentless pressure from the shah, the shift in US Persian Gulf policy was a slow, evolutionary process. Echoes of Johnson's balancing policy were apparent in the American response to the border crisis between Iran and Iraq over the Shatt al-Arab waterway in the spring of 1969, which threatened to escalate into war. The two countries had long disagreed on where their common border lay: the Iraqis asserted sovereignty over the entire Shatt, as stipulated by the 1937 Tehran Treaty, while the Iranians claimed sovereignty up to the *thalweg,* or deepest channel, of the waterway based on common international practice.[71] Tensions had been simmering for some time when the Iraqis sparked, in April 1969, what was the third crisis over the Shatt in a decade. Iraq asserted its sovereignty over the entire waterway by demanding that vessels sailing in the Shatt should neither raise the Iranian flag nor carry Iranian naval personnel. On April 15, Iraq's deputy foreign minister warned the Iranian ambassador in Baghdad that if Iran did not comply, Iraq would use force to block access to Iranian ports. Iran's response was to abrogate the 1937 Treaty and to warn the Iraqis that any interference with Iranian shipping would mean war.[72]

The shah's uncompromising reaction to the Iraqi threat was entirely consistent with the bold claims he had made in Washington just two weeks earlier, as well as the US intelligence assessment from January. However, the shah's advisors worried that if Iran were seen as the aggressor in a war with Iraq, they would then lose the support of the United States and find themselves fighting the Soviet-backed Iraqis all alone. Alam was visiting his family estate in Birjand in eastern Iran when he received a frantic telephone call on April 17 from General Nematollah Nasiri, the chief of SAVAK, urging him to return to Tehran immediately. It seemed that the shah was planning to order an Iranian merchant ship to sail down the Shatt flying the Iranian flag, escorted by the Iranian air force and navy, as a test case to demonstrate Iranian sovereignty. Fearing that hostilities might break out, Nasiri begged Alam to use his influence with the shah to avert a war. Alam concurred, worrying that if Iran were seen as the aggressor, "American public opinion will easily turn against us." He immediately cabled his concerns to the shah, who was then on a state visit to Tunisia.[73]

Ambassador Meyer was aware of the rising military tensions between Iran and Iraq, thanks to reports he was receiving from the US Consulate in Khorramshahr near the border.[74] According to General Fereydun Djam, the acting chief of the Supreme Commander's Staff, the Iranian military had activated contingency plans for a war with Iraq, although there had been considerable confusion and delay in mobilizing the armed forces because of the shah's absence.[75] On the afternoon of April 17, Meyer was attending a reception at the US Officers' Club in Tehran, where he spoke with Djam's deputy, General Mohammad Fazeli, who confirmed that Iran intended to assert its sovereignty in the Shatt with a test-case ship. Meyer, without instructions from Washington,

FIGURE 2.4   As Alam looks on, Nixon bids the shah farewell at the White House on April 1, 1969. Courtesy of the Richard M. Nixon Presidential Library.

expressed to Fazeli "the fervent hope that there would be no shooting." The ambassador later reported to the State Department that he had "mentioned current Congressional sensitivities re things military and I feared repercussions with Iran."[76] Fazeli interpreted Meyer's concerns as a warning that in the event of a war with Iraq, the United States would cut off military supplies to Iran. Shocked by Meyer's comments, he set off for the Supreme Commander's Headquarters, where he was due to attend a meeting that evening with Iran's top military brass, Prime Minister Amir Abbas Hoveyda, and the permanent secretary of the Foreign Ministry, Amir Khosrow Afshar, to discuss the crisis. Fazeli conveyed Meyer's comments to Hoveyda, who then instructed Afshar to report them to the shah in Tunisia.[77]

One can imagine the shah's fury in Tunis upon reading the messages from Alam and Afshar advising restraint in the Shatt, lest Iran's actions anger the United States. He was in no mood to back down, cabling back to Alam that "you are not in the picture on this issue. They [the Iraqis] have caused such offense that these actions are necessary."[78] On instructions from the shah, Afshar summoned Meyer to his home on the morning of April 18, where he conveyed the shah's displeasure with the ambassador's comments to Fazeli and asked Meyer "whether [the] Shah in assuring Iran's legitimate self-defense should seek supplies from quarters where no conditions [are] attached." Meyer responded by refuting Fazeli's account and assuring Afshar that he had spoken without any instructions from Washington. Meyer told Afshar: "I had merely voiced to Fazeli certain concerns as [a] true friend of [the] Shah and Iran." He reported to Washington that he "emphasized that [the] decision as to what to do or not to do in [the] Shatt is strictly for Iran to make." Meyer's sole concern was that Iran's image in the United States not be "tarnished," especially as Congressional authorization would be required for the arms sales that the shah wanted.[79] The State Department approved the steps that Meyer had taken and shared his concern that "military action in the Shatt might tarnish Iran's excellent image in the US" and "hoped that restraint would be shown by both sides."[80]

American officials in Tehran were determined to avoid any entanglement in Iran's confrontation with Iraq, and the Iranians seemed reluctant to push the issue up the chain of command to the White House. General Mohammad Khatam, commander of the Imperial Iranian Air Force (IIAF) and brother-in-law to the shah, had been ordered by the shah to report on the ability of Iran's American-supplied F-4 Phantom jets to support military operations against Iraq. Khatam asked the US Military Assistance Advisory Group (MAAG) in Tehran if they would be willing to transfer the US Air Force (USAF) technicians who maintained Iran's Phantoms to air bases in southern Iran, to support IIAF operations against Iraq. When the request was rejected by General Roy Casbeer, who headed the USAF section of MAAG, Khatam agreed to Meyer's suggestion that the decision not be appealed to Washington, where it would certainly be denied and would only damage Iran's relations with the United States. Meyer was convinced that Khatam and other Iranian officials, knowing that Washington would resist being drawn into the crisis, were using the threat of a rupture in relations with the United States to try to constrain the shah and thus prevent a war with Iraq.[81]

Despite calls for restraint from both the US ambassador and his closest civilian and military advisors, the shah sent Afshar before the Iranian Senate on April 19 to abrogate the 1937 Treaty and warn that Iran would retaliate against any Iraqi attack.[82] In the face of overwhelming Iranian military power, the Iraqis backed down. On April 20, Iraqi defense minister Hardan al-Takriti informed the SAVAK station chief in Baghdad that Iraq had no appetite for a war with Iran.[83] The Iraqis privately relayed a message that they would not challenge the test-case Iranian ship.[84] Waiting until the shah had returned to Tehran, Iran ended the crisis by sailing the freighter *Abu Sina* down the Shatt, flying the Iranian flag with an air and naval escort. As expected, the *Abu Sina* met no resistance from the Iraqis, and the crisis ended in victory for Iran.[85] The Shatt crisis left little doubt about the shah's resolve to assert Iran's power in the Persian Gulf against any regional rival. There were some in the American bureaucracy who were clearly unhappy with the shah's actions. The State Department's Bureau of Intelligence and Research (INR), which had acquired a reputation as a critic of the shah, went so far as to characterize Iran's actions as "belligerence."[86] But the shah's willingness to risk upsetting Washington in pursuit of regional primacy demonstrated Iran's growing autonomy from the United States. Furthermore, Iran's triumph over Iraq in a regional crisis, without any direct American military intervention, was a harbinger of the role that Iran could play under the Nixon Doctrine.

Change: Nixon and Iranian Primacy

The ongoing British withdrawal from the Persian Gulf had clearly tilted the regional balance of power in Iran's favor, requiring a response from the United States. Consequently, in July 1969, Kissinger ordered an interagency review of US Gulf policy in National Security Study Memorandum (NSSM) 66.[87] In Tehran, the shah used the language of the Nixon Doctrine to press the United States to back Iranian primacy. He warned the new US ambassador, Douglas MacArthur II, that the Soviets were pouring arms into Iraq and were encouraging the Ba'th to bring the Iraqi Communist Party (ICP) into a unity government, which would lead to "Soviet domination of Iraq." As the British withdrawal from the Gulf approached, Iran needed a massive infusion of American arms to "deter Iraq, with its increased military capabilities, from making [a] miscalculation and engaging in aggressive steps in [the] Gulf against Iran which could escalate into hostilities." The shah was due to make a state visit to Washington in October (Figure 2.5), where he would press President Nixon directly "to permit Iran to shoulder its responsibilities in this part of the world without having to be dependent on US or other great power intervention."[88]

Both the State Department and Kissinger advised the president to avoid any premature commitment to the shah's entreaties and to continue, for now, with the balancing policy of the Johnson administration.[89] Kissinger advised Nixon to tell the shah that "[t]he President of the US cannot make policy as easily as the imperial ruler of Iran."[90] Every effort was made to ensure that the shah would enjoy his visit, even if the Americans were not yet ready to respond to his calls for a special relationship. As he would not be accompanied by his wife, Empress Farah, the State Department suggested inviting Miss America to join the shah at the state dinner in the White House.[91] The president's personal secretary, Rose Mary Woods, advised against canceling the usual post-dinner entertainment on account of the empress's absence, as the shah, "a man of great interests—great sex appeal," was "much more the 'swinger' type than most visiting dignitaries."[92] Despite these arrangements, the shah must have left Washington a disappointed man. In his private discussions with Nixon, he failed to secure an agreement for increased Iranian oil exports to the United States, the revenue from which he pledged to use to buy more American weapons.[93] He warned the Americans against continuing with the balancing policy of the past, arguing that although King Faisal was a wise leader, Saudi domestic instability and the absence of a strong successor meant that in the long run the United States could not rely on Saudi Arabia to protect the Gulf from Soviet-backed Iraq. Rather, Washington should help Iran "stand by itself if necessary" as the protector of the waterway.[94]

Between 1970 and 1972, Iran and the Persian Gulf became largely synonymous in the minds of Nixon and Kissinger. Nixon wrote to the shah in February 1970 to tell him that he shared the shah's view that Iran should play an important role in the Nixon Doctrine: "As you know, your thoughts and mine coincide at many points on this subject, and a number of the positions I expressed during my Asian trip last summer—as you have

FIGURE 2.5 Nixon and Kissinger greet the shah in the Oval Office on October 23, 1969. Courtesy of the Richard M. Nixon Presidential Library.

noted—would apply to the problems in your region as well."[95] Nixon was clearly intrigued by the idea that Iran, as the paramount power of the Gulf, could contain Soviet influence in that vital theater of the Cold War. In the spring of 1970, during a meeting with the CENTO foreign ministers in Washington, the president asked Joseph Sisco, assistant secretary of state for Near Eastern and South Asian affairs, to prepare a study on whether Iran could indeed play such a role.[96] The first real test of this changing American attitude toward the shah came in April, when Ambassador MacArthur recommended that the United States extend the annual commitment on foreign military sales (FMS) credits that Johnson had made to the shah in June 1968 for an additional three or four years. MacArthur was responding to the shah's repeated demands that Iran's military needed larger quantities of American weapons to prepare for the role they would play after the British withdrawal from the Gulf.[97]

MacArthur's recommendation set off a bureaucratic battle in Washington over arms sales to Iran, with major implications for the ongoing review of Persian Gulf policy. The principal opposition came from the Pentagon, particularly G. Warren Nutter, a University of Chicago–trained economist who served as assistant secretary of defense for international security affairs. The Pentagon objected that Iran did not have the absorptive capacity for integrating the large volume of sophisticated weapons—including four additional squadrons of F-4 Phantoms—in the short span of time that the shah envisaged, and that a decision to increase arms sales to Iran would prejudice the ongoing review of Gulf policy.[98] Others in the administration were eager to avoid angering the shah, whom they saw as a stable and reliable ally in an important region. Jack Miklos, who had replaced Elliot as country director for Iran at the State Department, was a "long-time friend" of Harold Saunders, the principal aide on Kissinger's NSC staff dealing with Iran. Miklos thought that acquiescing to the shah's request was "a very wise, sound approach" and, with support from Saunders at the NSC, was able overcome the Pentagon's objections.[99] The prevailing view, which Under Secretary of State Elliot Richardson expressed to General Earle Wheeler, the chairman of the Joint Chiefs of Staff, was that despite Nutter's concerns, "we have no real option but to bank on Iran."[100] CIA director Richard Helms advised the White House that "it is in our own interest to support this concept of a special relationship with Iran" and reminded his colleagues of the vital intelligence the United States had gathered on the Soviet missile activity from its secret "TACKSMAN" electronic listening posts in Behshahr and Kapkan in northeastern Iran.[101] By April 1970, a consensus had emerged in the administration that Iran—and Iran alone—could be relied upon to contain Soviet influence in the Gulf. After all, the shah asked MacArthur, "who else in the area can supply a credible military deterrent in the Gulf? Pakistan, Saudi Arabia, the small weak Gulf States? Of course not."[102]

Kissinger cautiously weighed in on the side of the shah and, with the president's approval, authorized Under Secretary Richardson to inform the shah in Tehran in April 1970 that the United States would be willing to extend the 1968 FMS commitment.[103] Richardson told the shah that "we fully appreciate [the] unique contribution Iran can make to [the] defense of free world interest in [the] Gulf."[104] The special relationship that the shah had failed to secure in his two trips to Washington in 1969 was now, just a year later, taking shape. Just as the Pentagon had feared, the administration's increasing tilt toward Iran prejudiced the ongoing Persian Gulf policy review. This is hardly surprising, given that Miklos and Saunders, who had supported the shah on FMS credits, were the principal authors of the report that the NSC Interdepartmental Group for the Near East and South Asia (NSC/IG) submitted to Kissinger in June 1970. On the face of it, the report considered five main options for US policy in the

Gulf: (1) assuming the role in the Gulf abandoned by Britain; (2) backing either Iran or Saudi Arabia as a "chosen instrument"; (3) promoting Saudi-Iranian cooperation; (4) establishing bilateral relations and a major US presence in the Lower Gulf; or (5) sponsoring a regional security pact. However, given the American public's complete aversion to any expansion of America's global commitments in the context of Vietnam, the only real choice confronting Nixon was whether to continue with Johnson's balancing policy (Option 3) or to back Iran (Option 2).[105]

Kissinger's staff saw Iranian primacy in the Persian Gulf as a sound choice, given that Iran was "the most powerful and most stable state in the area" and that "there are strong elements of this in what we are already doing." However, they feared that openly backing the shah would "alienate the Saudis." Therefore, they argued, "[t]he logical strategy lies in marrying what is already in fact extensive support for Iran as the unquestioned power in the area with the logic of cooperation between a strong Iran and a weak Saudi Arabia."[106] While the substance of this new Gulf policy would be Iranian primacy, its rhetoric would pay lip service to Saudi-Iranian cooperation so as to avoid offending Arab sensibilities.[107] Miklos later recalled that the idea of Saudi Arabia as a "pillar" of US policy in the Gulf was considered "ludicrous."[108] On June 5, 1970, Kissinger convened a meeting of the NSC's Review Group to discuss the NSC/IG report. In a 20-minute meeting, the Review Group approved the report and agreed that it was ready for the president's consideration.[109] There were signs by the summer of 1970 that Nixon was seriously contemplating whether "the Shah's ideas for Iran ... playing a greater role in the Persian Gulf" were feasible. Despite Joseph Sisco's advice that Iran should be encouraged to gain the "active cooperation" of the Saudis in the Gulf, the administration was inching ever closer to a policy of Iranian primacy.[110]

A One-Pillar Policy

The NSC/IG report did not reach the president's desk until October 1970. In the intervening four months, the White House's attention was focused elsewhere in the Middle East as the War of Attrition between Israel and Egypt raged until August, and then in September a crisis broke out in Jordan, where America's client, King Hussein, was almost overthrown by Palestinian guerrillas and an invading Syrian army.[111] By comparison, the shah looked secure on his throne and Iran seemed to be the cornerstone of a largely stable Persian Gulf. The shah had embarked on a diplomatic charm offensive in the Arab world, peacefully relinquishing Iran's claim to Bahrain in May and restoring diplomatic relations with Egypt in August after a 10-year rupture.[112] It was in this context that Kissinger presented the NSC/IG report to President Nixon, who approved a general US strategy in the Gulf that would "promote Saudi-Iranian cooperation as the mainstay of a stable regional system"; "recognize that Iran is in fact the preponderant power in the Gulf"; and "do what we can to develop a working relationship with the new political entities in the lower Gulf." This strategy rested, according to Kissinger, on the assumption that "[i]f a radical regime were to take over in Saudi Arabia, the U.S. would have little choice but to move closer to Iran—and there is no reason now not to go on preparing Iran for that contingency."[113]

With the benefit of hindsight, it seems counterintuitive that Nixon and Kissinger would see the shah as a safe bet and the Saudis as a long-term liability. While Mohammad Reza Shah would be deposed and exiled in 1979, the Saudi monarchy would survive the assassination of King Faisal in 1975 and would successfully manage the succession to Kings Khalid, Fahd, and Abdullah. But in the autumn of 1970 many American observers imagined that a strong Iran might one day have to come to the aid of a weak Saudi Arabia. At the Islamic summit conference in Rabat in September 1969, the shah had assured Faisal that although a security pact between their two countries was not feasible, he would provide the Saudis with whatever support they asked for in a crisis.[114] As MacArthur observed from Tehran, there was a growing consensus among the Arab rulers of the Persian Gulf that after the British withdrawal, Iran would be the only "moderate neighbor with both the will and the capacity to come to their aid."[115] Just a few months after the Rabat conference, when South Yemeni forces attacked Saudi Arabia, Faisal turned to Iran for help and the shah quickly airlifted anti-aircraft guns and anti-tank recoilless rifles to Saudi Arabia to repel the Yemenis.[116] The shah also assured Faisal that the Iranian air force would provide Saudi Arabia with air cover in the event of a future Yemeni attack.[117] Indeed, in July 1973, Kissinger and the shah would begin secret discussions on a contingency plan for Iran to secure Saudi Arabia's oil fields and restore the Al Saud to their throne if the Saudi monarchy were ever threatened, as other Arab monarchies in Egypt, Iraq, Jordan, Libya, Morocco, and Yemen had been.[118] The vulnerable Saudis were never regarded by the Americans as a "pillar" of Nixon's Persian Gulf policy in the same sense as Iran. From Washington's perspective, it was a role that the Saudis were both unwilling and unable to play. Harold Saunders later recalled that Iran was, in fact, the sole pillar of Nixon's Gulf policy, "with the Saudi pillar being a nominal pillar there for obvious necessary regional political reasons."[119]

The United States had important economic interests in oil-rich Saudi Arabia.[120] By 1969, their bilateral economic relationship contributed $500 million annually to America's balance of payments, and moreover, Saudi Arabia's ability to provide a steady flow of cheap oil to Western Europe and Japan was a vital American interest.[121] However, the Saudis were unwilling to play a regional role that would leave them open to accusations from Arab nationalists of complicity in American or Iranian imperialism. Both British and American diplomats in Saudi Arabia were aware that Saudi reticence was tilting the balance of power in the Persian Gulf in Iran's favor.[122] In Anglo-American discussions in Washington in March 1969, Geoffrey Arthur, assistant under secretary at the Foreign Office, complained to his American counterparts that the Saudis had been "passive in their relations with the Gulf" and asked the Americans for their views on "Saudi inattention to Gulf matters." William Brewer, the State Department's country director for the Arabian Peninsula, responded "that the Saudi attitude could be explained by a combination of slothfulness, statesmanship and preoccupation with other matters," a reference to Saudi fears of growing Israeli power in the aftermath of the Six-Day War of June 1967.[123] Saudi reticence was no match for the shah's vigorous diplomacy. The following year, the British Residency in the Gulf concluded that the Saudis "have chalked up the same nil score as in previous years" in their rivalry with Iran.[124]

King Faisal's commitment to the Arab struggle against Israel severely limited Saudi Arabia's ability to play any leadership role under the Nixon Doctrine. While the shah saw the Nixon Doctrine as an opportunity for Iran to become a major Cold War actor, Faisal saw it as a dangerous development that would only draw the United States and Israel closer together.[125] For Saudi Arabia, the immediate threat to regional stability came from Israel, not the Soviet Union. Faisal was a firm believer in the anti-Semitic "Protocols of Zion," which he had published and distributed, and never tired of telling his American interlocutors that the Zionists and the Communists were conspiring together to drive a wedge between the United States and the Arab world.[126] He warned Nixon in an Oval Office meeting in May 1971 that "Communism is the child, the offspring of Zionism. Zionism is in collusion with Communism for the destruction of the world," and went on to argue that the anti–Vietnam War demonstrations in the United States were in fact part of a Zionist-Communist global conspiracy.[127] This hostility toward Israel, whether rhetorical or indeed "deeply felt," as Kissinger thought it to be, stood in contrast to the shah's quiet military, intelligence, and trade relationship with Israel that dated back to the 1950s.[128] According to General Mansur Qadar, who served as Iran's ambassador to Jordan and Lebanon throughout this period, Iran's close relations with Israel made the shah deeply unpopular in the Arab world.[129] Consequently, the Saudis could not afford to be seen as having too cozy a relationship with Pahlavi Iran. Foreign Minister Zahedi confided to MacArthur in May 1971, after a brief stopover in Tehran by the Saudi king, that "while Faisal and the Saudis make all the right noises in private about [the] desirability and need for close Saudi-Iranian cooperation and coordination in [the] Gulf area, they don't even want to hint about this in public."[130] Nixon's view was that whereas America's alliance with Israel "makes us unpalatable to everybody in the Arab world," the shah is "awfully good on that subject."[131] If there were two states that constituted the "twin pillars" of the Nixon Doctrine in the Middle East, they were Iran and Israel, not Saudi Arabia.[132]

In the evolution of Nixon's Persian Gulf policy between 1969 and 1972, domestic instability and succession problems in Saudi Arabia cast doubt on the Kingdom's ability to act as a viable regional partner for the United States. The shah was seen by the United States as a modernizing monarch, having inaugurated his "White Revolution" of social and economic reforms in the early 1960s.[133] Iran's progress was trumpeted by the US Information Agency as a "model" for the entire region.[134] This stood in stark contrast with the deeply conservative King Faisal, whose leadership was characterized in an April 1970 US intelligence assessment as "more appropriate to the problems of the past than to those of the present and future. He is deeply religious in the context of the rigid Muslim orthodoxy which still characterizes many Saudis, and in large measure he is attuned to the desires of the traditional elements of the society."[135] At the 1969 Rabat conference, the shah had lectured Faisal on the need for social and economic reform in Saudi Arabia, if the monarchy was to weather the political storms ahead.[136] The shah never missed an opportunity to remind his American interlocutors that the Saudis were "very backward" and showed "no inclination to reform."[137] This reluctance to modernize, the shah argued, made them deeply vulnerable to the subversive threat posed by the Soviet-backed radical Arabs.[138]

Although Faisal had managed to wrestle the crown from King Saud in 1964 after a long internal power struggle, American assessments of the stability of the monarchy were cautious. In the summer of 1969 the Saudis uncovered a coup plot that involved air force officers who hoped to overthrow the monarchy and establish a Nasserist regime. The discovery of the coup plot was followed by a brutal and widespread crackdown on anyone suspected of disloyalty. A crisis atmosphere pervaded the kingdom, particularly after the overthrow of the Libyan monarchy in September 1969.[139] By November, the NSC/IG had concluded that although there was little likelihood of unrest in Saudi Arabia in the short term, "in the longer run we cannot assume the continuation of the political and social order upon which US-Saudi cooperation was built."[140] Faisal's health was in doubt, as he made numerous trips to Geneva throughout 1970 for treatment and surgery, and the perennial problem of royal succession loomed.[141] In April 1970 the US intelligence community concluded that in the event of Faisal's death, "a smooth transfer cannot be assured" and that Faisal's designated successor, the reluctant Prince Khaled, would likely only serve as a "figurehead King."[142]

Meeting in Tehran in April 1970, the chiefs of America's diplomatic missions in the region sat down to discuss future US policy in the Persian Gulf. Surveying the two shores, they concluded that "what is impressive is the contrast between the Iranian image of strength and planning and the fact that the Arabs are divided, uncertain, suspicious and fearful.... The lopsided situation has its own seeds of instability. The US problem lies not on the Iranian side—where a firm relationship can be built upon—but on the Arab side."[143] The ghost of Johnson's policy of balancing Iran and Saudi Arabia was now well and truly laid to rest. As Kissinger's deputy, General Alexander Haig, would later recall, the shah "represented the political center in his own country and also in a region in search of a political center of balance."[144] A new policy of Iranian primacy would eventually entail lifting virtually all restrictions on American conventional arms sales to Iran, thereby giving the Iranian armed forces the ability to deter any aggression by a regional rival, independently of the United States. As the shah had explained to Secretary of State William Rogers, Iran "must have an 'over-kill' capability so that should anyone be tempted to attack Iran they would think twice or even three times."[145] Despite the Pentagon's continuing objection that an Iranian deterrence capability would spark a regional arms race, Nixon signed National Security Decision Memorandum (NSDM) 92 on November 7, 1970, ordering a policy of promoting

Saudi-Iranian cooperation while "recognizing the preponderance of Iranian power" in the Gulf.[146] NSDM 92 marked a turning point in the evolution of US Gulf policy from balancing to Iranian primacy and the beginning of the shah's Cold War partnership with Nixon and Kissinger.

Red Star over Baghdad

In accounting for America's policy shift in the Persian Gulf, Kissinger has challenged the view that Nixon's personal relationship with the shah played any role in policymaking: "America's friendship with Iran reflected not individual proclivities but geopolitical realities. Iran's intrinsic importance transcended the personalities of both countries' leaders."[147] Kissinger explains that he and Nixon backed a policy of Iranian primacy in order to contain the radical Soviet-backed Ba'th regime in Iraq. In the chaos that engulfed Baghdad after the Ba'thi coup in July 1968, Iraq's new rulers vacillated between extreme violence and political co-option in their efforts to eliminate all domestic opposition, while looking to Iraq's long-standing relationship with the Soviet Union for military and economic assistance. They signed an agreement with Moscow in July 1969 for exploitation of the North Rumeila oil field, followed by a series of military and economic assistance agreements culminating in a 15-year Treaty of Friendship and Cooperation signed in April 1972. Washington was taking note of Iraq's burgeoning ties with the Soviet Union, as well as the nationalization in June of the Iraq Petroleum Company, which had been owned by a consortium of Western firms, including Mobil and Standard Oil of New Jersey.[148] According to Kissinger, "Iraq was thereby transforming itself into a geopolitical challenge and was on the way to becoming the principal Soviet ally in the area."[149] He and Nixon wanted to ensure that "[t]he vacuum left by British withdrawal, now menaced by Soviet intrusion and radical momentum, would be filled by a local power friendly to us."[150] The logical choice was Iran, given its power and ambitions.

Kissinger's account leaves out, however, the crucial role that the shah played in shaping the White House's views about Iraq and the Persian Gulf. With his superficial understanding of the Gulf region, and his total preoccupation with the Cold War balance of power, Kissinger blithely accepted the shah's assessment of Ba'thi Iraq as a Soviet-backed threat to the Gulf. The shah skillfully employed the logic of the Cold War and the language of the Nixon Doctrine to argue that the Soviets were "gaining domination of the area though a pincer movement, one arm of which started in the UAR and came up the Arabian Peninsula through Yemen. The other arm extended down from Iraq aimed toward Kuwait and Saudi Arabia."[151] In reality, the Ba'thi regime was too busy consolidating its weak position at home to pose much of a subversive threat abroad. By the summer of 1968, the State Department's assessment was that the Ba'th would not last long in power, despite their extensive use of violence.[152] They had to contend not only with their opponents in Baghdad, but also with a Kurdish insurgency in northern Iraq, as well as the threat of another war with Israel.[153] The shah had demonstrated Iran's military superiority over Iraq in the Shatt crisis of April 1969. Iraq, weakened by the purges and instability of a military coup, had far more to fear from Iran, than vice versa. The Ba'th could do little more than broadcast anti-shah propaganda on Radio Baghdad, for example accusing him in July 1969 of being homosexual.[154] Following a particularly vitriolic Iraqi broadcast, Alam recorded in his diary on August 9 that "if our friends and allies let us" Iran would "sort them out."[155] Covertly, Iran tried to overthrow the Ba'th regime, sponsoring two unsuccessful coup attempts in Baghdad in the summer of 1969 and in January 1970.[156] As for the Soviet Union, Moscow took great pains to assure the shah that Soviet support for Iraq posed no threat to Iran.[157] Soviet-Iranian relations had been normalized in 1962, and the trade and investment relationship between the two countries had developed significantly since then.[158] The Soviet Union was playing a "balancing act" between Iran and Iraq, hoping to nudge the shah toward a non-aligned position while cultivating Ba'thi Iraq as its local client.[159]

The advice that Nixon and Kissinger were receiving was that there were tensions in Soviet-Iraqi relations and that Soviet aid to Iraq posed little threat to either Iran or the Persian Gulf.[160] In the briefing papers prepared for Nixon's trip to Tehran in May 1972, written just one month after the signing of the Iraqi-Soviet Treaty of Friendship, the State Department argued that Soviet influence in Iraq might actually constrain and moderate Iraqi behavior, given Moscow's support for a peaceful settlement of the Arab-Israeli conflict and its normalization of relations with Iran.[161] The NSC staff advised Nixon that Ba'thi Iraq was "regarded as about the most unreliable and least realistic of Mid-East states, even in the view of other Arabs. This has meant not only Iraq's isolation within the Arab world but also ambivalent and unsteady relations with the outside world and great powers, including the Soviet Union."[162] Nor did America's British allies see Iraq as a real danger to Gulf stability. For example, Sir William Luce,

Britain's special envoy for the Gulf, told the State Department in January 1971 that "Iraq has relatively little scope for doing mischief in the Persian Gulf states. The people of the area dislike the Iraqis, and Iraq is probably too fearful of Iran's reaction to risk any adventures in the Gulf."[163] Nonetheless, during their May 1972 visit to Tehran, Nixon and Kissinger readily agreed to the shah's request for covert US support to foment the Kurdish insurgency in northern Iraq, in order to paralyze the Soviet-backed Ba'th regime in Baghdad and prevent Soviet domination of Iraq.[164]

Why were Nixon and Kissinger convinced that Ba'thi Iraq represented a Soviet menace to the Persian Gulf, despite all the contradictory advice they were receiving from their own officials and their British allies? The answer lies in the nature of the relationship between Nixon, Kissinger, and the shah. Absorbed with Vietnam, the Soviet Union, China, and a re-election campaign, Nixon and Kissinger had little time to devote to the complexities of Iraqi or Gulf politics. Instead, they deferred to the shah's judgment on local issues as their regional partner under the Nixon Doctrine. This tilt toward Iran in NSDM 92 of November 1970 cannot simply be explained as Washington's response to growing Soviet influence in Iraq. A clear-eyed American assessment, based on the sound advice that Nixon and Kissinger were receiving from their own officials and their British allies, would have recognized that the biggest threat to Gulf security came from a potential regional conflict between Iran and Iraq, not the Soviet Union. But Nixon and Kissinger were looking at the Gulf through the shah's eyes. Kissinger later wrote that some of the shah's "analysis was, of course, self-serving in the sense of providing a rationale for existing policy. But self-interest is no inhibition against accuracy."[165]

Rethinking the Shah

An account of the origins of Nixon's Persian Gulf policy that simply examines the constraints on American decision-making tells only half the story. America's war in Vietnam and the British withdrawal from the Persian Gulf both limited Washington's options in the Gulf. But when confronted with these factors, Johnson and Nixon adopted distinct Gulf policies. To understand why Johnson chose to continue with a British policy of balancing Iran and Saudi Arabia, while Nixon opted for Iranian primacy, demands consideration of the shah's estimation in the two administrations. The view of Mohammad Reza Shah as a megalomaniac whose ambitions would destabilize the Gulf and invite Soviet subversion and the fear that his insatiable appetite for arms was diverting resources away from Iran's economic development were noticeably absent in Nixon and Kissinger's thinking.

An Oval Office conversation in April 1971 between Nixon, Haig, and MacArthur, reveals the clear differences between Nixon's views on the shah, based on their long-standing friendship, and those of Johnson's advisors or the British. Gone is any notion of the shah as a dangerous megalomaniac. The question was no longer how to contain the shah's ambitions, but instead whether the shah was up to the task of fulfilling them. Nixon declares that he is "stronger than horseradish" for the shah but asks his advisors if the shah can "fill that—the role out there, you know, in the whole darn Gulf area." He wants to know if the shah has "got the stuff" or is he "thinking too big"? Nixon tells his advisors, "If he could do it, it'd be wonderful because he's our friend." "I like him, I like him, and I like the country. And some of those other bastards out there I don't like." In Nixon's view, Iran is America's "one friend there" and "by God if we can go with them, and we can have them strong, and they're in the center of it, and a friend of the United States, I couldn't agree more—it's something."[166]

Although Kissinger did not meet the shah until 1969, his views on the Iranian monarch were entirely in accord with those of Nixon. In his memoirs he vigorously refutes the idea that the shah was a megalomaniac whose extravagant weapons purchases needed to be curtailed: "Iran's economic growth was not slowed nor was its political cohesion affected by its defense spending." Far from being a dangerous upstart, Kissinger thought of the shah as a statesman who "[i]n his grasp of the international trends and currents ... was among the most impressive leaders that I met. He had a sure grasp of the importance of both the global and the regional balance of power."[167] Both men were Cold Warriors who firmly believed that containing the Soviet Union "required the tolerance of brutality as a bulwark against worse suffering."[168] The pro-Western Pahlavi monarchy was a perfect fit in such a strategy of containment. The shah was conscious of the importance of this new American thinking, and as the documentary record suggests, he consistently used the language of the Nixon Doctrine to advocate a policy of Iranian primacy in the Persian Gulf. Harold Saunders recalled that in the meetings he attended between Kissinger and the shah, "it was clear that the shah relished speaking to this world-renowned strategist about grand strategy."[169] The shah later wrote that Kissinger's "geo-political ideas coincided perfectly with mine."[170] When the shah argued for Iranian primacy, Foreign Minister Zahedi recalled, Kissinger "understood what we were saying."[171] Iran's role in the Cold War came to be seen by Kissinger as a text-book example of the Nixon Doctrine:

> Under the Shah's leadership, the land bridge between Asia and Europe, so often the hinge of world history, was pro-American and pro-West beyond any challenge. Alone among the countries of the region—Israel aside—Iran made friendship with the United States the starting point of its foreign policy. That it was based on a cold-eyed assessment that a threat to Iran would most likely come from the Soviet Union, in combination with radical Arab states, is only another way of saying that the Shah's views of the realities of the world paralleled our own. Iran's influence was always on our side.... The Shah absorbed the energies of radical Arab neighbors to prevent them from threatening the moderate regimes in Saudi Arabia, Jordan, and the Persian Gulf.[172]

Implementing the Nixon Doctrine

In the year that followed the adoption of NSDM 92 in November 1970, the shah took a number of steps that confirmed Washington's assessment of the preponderance of Iranian power in the Persian Gulf. First, in the land-mark Tehran Agreement of February 14, 1971, between the international oil companies and the oil-producing countries of the Gulf, the shah cajoled the companies into increasing the producers' share of oil profits and raising the price of oil.[173] Then on November 30, 1971, just a day before Britain's defense treaty obligations to the Arab rulers of the Lower Gulf expired, the shah deployed Iranian troops on the Gulf islands of Abu Musa and the Tunbs, which were claimed by both Iran and the British-protected states of Sharjah and Ras al-Khaimah.[174] London could protect neither British Petroleum nor its Arab clients in the Gulf from the shah. Both actions demonstrated that Iran, with the full support of the United States, had taken Britain's place as the principal power in the region.

With the passing of the mantle of regional primacy, the shah would play an increasingly active role in the Nixon Doctrine, beginning with the 1971 South Asian crisis. The crisis was sparked when the martial law regime of General Agha Mohammad Yahya Khan, who had come to power in Pakistan in a military coup in March 1969, held national and provincial elections in both East and West Pakistan in December 1970 in order to transfer power to civilian hands. In elections for the federal National Assembly, the Awami League, led by Sheikh Mujib al-Rahman and representing the Bengalis of East Pakistan, achieved an absolute majority, defeating the Pakistan People's Party (PPP), which held seats only in West Pakistan. Negotiations between the Awami League and the PPP on forming a government failed, and when the Pakistani army attempted to impose a military solution in late March, a civil war erupted. The Awami League declared East Pakistan's secession as the independent state of Bangladesh, while the Pakistani army pursued a brutal crackdown on the Bengali separatists, creating a massive flow of refugees into India. The civil war became an Indo-Pakistan war on November 21, 1971, when the Indian military intervened on the side of Bangladesh, leading to the surrender of Pakistan on December 16.[175]

Throughout the crisis, Nixon wanted to help Pakistan, which was not only aligned with the United States but was also acting as an intermediary between Washington and Communist China, with which Nixon and Kissinger were secretly cultivating a détente. Furthermore, Pakistan was pitted against India, which had signed a treaty of friendship with the Soviet Union in August 1971. However, American public opinion had turned against Pakistan because of the massacres of Bengali civilians. American military transfers to Pakistan were consequently suspended by the State Department in April and economic aid was halted in July. Nixon and Kissinger initially limited their efforts to preventing the United States from aiding India, over the strong objections of a State Department that had been left in the dark about the opening to China.[176] It was in this context that the shah played a secret role in providing American arms from Iran's own inventories to Pakistan.

Pakistan was Iran's CENTO ally, and the shah had already intervened once in 1965 to help the Pakistanis against India. With the outbreak of the 1971 crisis, the shah worried that if Pakistan were not given assistance Yahya Khan would increasingly turn to Beijing, extending Communist influence along Iran's borders. Foreign Minister Zahedi described such an eventuality as a "disaster for Iran."[177] Moreover, the shah's greatest fear was that an Indian victory in East Pakistan might also lead to the collapse of West Pakistan. This was a nightmare scenario for Iran, given the Baluchi separatist movement along the Iranian-Pakistani border regions.[178] The shah had quietly taken a number of steps throughout 1971 to defuse tensions and encourage a negotiated solution. In April he had advised the Pakistani ambassador in Tehran that it was futile to try to use force to control 75 million people in East Pakistan.[179] After the Pakistanis arrested Mujib and threatened to put him on trial, the shah acted on an American request in August to press Yahya Khan not to make a "martyr" of Mujib by trying and executing him.[180] As the situation in East Pakistan deteriorated, Yahya Khan made a sudden 24-hour trip to Tehran on September 14 and 15 to ask for the shah's assurance that Iran would provide military aid to Pakistan if war broke out with India. According to American intelligence sources, the shah's response was "reserved." He agreed only to "provide some limited military material" and his good offices for resolving the crisis, but refused to join Pakistan in any war with India.[181]

In October, the shah played host to a multitude of foreign leaders at a lavish celebration for the 2,500-year anniversary of the founding of the Persian Empire at the ancient Achaemenid capital of Persepolis. The event was ridiculed by the shah's opponents as an extravagance, designed to impress foreigners and indulge the shah's delusions of grandeur, rather than celebrate Iran's national heritage.[182] While his guests enjoyed roast peacock flown in from Maxim's of Paris and 25,000 bottles of fine French wine, served in specially commissioned Baccarat crystal, the shah was busy mediating the South Asian crisis by arranging a meeting with Indian President V. V. Giri, Soviet leader Nikolai Podgorny, and Yahya Khan, all of whom were in attendance. Despite the shah's efforts, however, nothing emerged from the Persepolis meeting other than a quiet Soviet warning to Iran not to provide military assistance to Pakistan.[183] After his mediation efforts had come to naught, and with India's military intervention in late November, the shah began working with the Nixon administration to secretly support Pakistan. Following an urgent appeal for help from Yahya Khan on December 4, 1971, Nixon decided to covertly provide assistance to Pakistan via Iran. This way, the president told Kissinger, "[i]f it is leaking we can have it denied. Have it done one step away."[184] The need for secrecy stemmed from the problem that such third-party transfers of US arms were illegal, "unless the United States itself would transfer the defense article under consideration to that country."[185] Kissinger's staff advised him that "[t]he President could, of course, give his consent to third-party transfers if he were also willing to establish, as a matter of policy, our willingness to supply the same items directly."[186] But given the popular mood against Pakistan among the public and in Congress, Nixon was unwilling to pay the political price of lifting the embargo, so he looked to the shah for help.

An unnamed American official, most likely the CIA station chief in Tehran, met with the shah on December 5 and secured his agreement to Nixon's request.[187] The next day, Nixon confirmed the arrangement with Kissinger, who warned the president that these secret arms transfers were "not legal ... strictly speaking" and that the White House should make sure "the Democrats don't know about it and we keep our mouths shut."[188] Four days later in New York, Kissinger assured the Chinese ambassador to the United Nations, Huang Ha, that the United States would supply military assistance to Pakistan through third parties, including Iran. He reported to the Chinese that the White House had assured the shah that if Iran's "security requires shipment of American arms to Pakistan, we are obliged to protest, but we will understand. We will not protest with great intensity. And we will make up to them in next year's budget whatever difficulties they have."[189] This was the Nixon Doctrine in action: Iran was intervening in the Third World where the United States could not.

"Protect Me"

The US policy of Iranian regional primacy under the Nixon Doctrine, formulated in NSDM 92 and tested in South Asia, was ratified during Nixon's May 1972 trip to Tehran (Figure 2.6), the first visit by a sitting American president to Iran in nearly 13 years.[190] Iran was the president's first port of call after the historic Moscow summit between Nixon and Brezhnev, which in itself was an indication of Nixon's esteem for Mohammad Reza Shah. Nixon, Kissinger, and the shah held two private meetings during the president's visit to Tehran, with no other officials present.[191] In the first meeting, on the afternoon of May 30, Nixon thanked the shah for the role Iran had played in supporting Pakistan. He briefed the shah on his discussions with Brezhnev and asked if America's allies had anything to fear from US-Soviet détente, implying that détente did not mean a weakening of America's commitment to Iran. The shah replied, "Not if you have the right allies.... If they are self-reliant they will welcome it. If they have the principle of fighting until the last American they will not welcome it." Clearly alluding to the Nixon Doctrine, the shah emphasized that "Iran, like Israel, must be able to stand alone."[192] The following morning, the shah finally received the American acknowledgment that all of Nixon's predecessors had denied him. In his minutes of the May 31

FIGURE 2.6 Crowds cheer Nixon and the shah as the presidential motorcade makes its way through the streets of Tehran on May 30, 1972, at the beginning of Nixon's historic visit to Iran. Courtesy of the Richard M. Nixon Presidential Library.

meeting, Kissinger recorded that Nixon "asked the shah to understand the purpose of American policy. 'Protect me,' he said. 'Don't look at détente as something that weakens you but as a way for the United States to gain influence.' The Nixon Doctrine was a way for the US to build a new long-term policy on [the] support of allies."[193] Nixon's choice of words was extraordinary. The president of the United States had traveled to the court of the shah of Iran to ask Mohammad Reza Pahlavi to protect him. In addition to a commitment to support Iran's secret war in Iraqi Kurdistan, Nixon also assured the shah that his administration would authorize the sale of advanced F-14 and F-15 fighter jets to Iran, as well as laser-guided bombs.[194] The shah rightly boasted to Alam that Nixon "gave me everything I asked for."[195]

The Tehran summit was, as Harold Saunders later recalled, the "capstone event" in the shift in US Persian Gulf policy to Iranian primacy. Nixon had made commitments to the shah in Tehran that were, in Saunders's words, "a ratification of a posture that had long since crystallized."[196] But after returning to Washington from Tehran, Kissinger found that Nixon's Gulf policy was encountering resistance in the

American bureaucracy, particularly in the Pentagon, where many officials objected to giving the shah a blank check on conventional arms
sales to Iran. Kissinger was compelled to write to both Secretary of
Defense Melvin Laird and Secretary of State William Rogers in July
to remind them that "decisions on the acquisition of military equipment should be left primarily to the government of Iran."[197] At the time
of the 1972 Tehran meeting, Iran's military expenditure was already
three times that of Iraq and nearly twice that of Saudi Arabia.[198] During
Nixon's presidency, annual US military sales to Iran would grow more
than sevenfold, from $94.9 million in 1969 to $682.8 million in 1974.
They would go on to reach a peak of more than $2.55 billion in 1977.[199]
This burgeoning military spending would give Iran a position of largely
uncontested power in the Gulf. The Iranian military were deployed in
the Dhofar region of Oman from 1972 until 1979, playing a pivotal role
in defeating the communist-backed insurgency against Sultan Qaboos
bin Said, which threatened to spread to the other conservative monarchies of the Arabian Peninsula.[200] Far from being an "Anglo-American
lake," for a decade the Gulf was a region where Iranian power was profoundly felt.[201]

3

Iran's Secret War with Iraq

THE CIA AND THE SHAH-FORSAKEN KURDS

THE NIXON-KISSINGER-PAHLAVI PARTNERSHIP reached its zenith after Nixon and Kissinger's 1972 visit to Iran. The shah's regime was no longer seen as a Cold War liability by the United States, vulnerable to communist subversion, but as an emerging middle power in the global Cold War, able to contribute to American strategies of containment. US-Iran relations took on a "new texture," according to the US Embassy in Tehran, characterized by a "sense of greater equality by Iran in its cooperative dealing with [the] US." The United States had "mastered [the] tendency in recent years to second-guess [the] Shah about his policies while Iran in turn has recovered from its client status attitude."[1] Mohammad Reza Shah was now working with his American partners to defend Iran's pro-Western neighbors against their Soviet-backed enemies. Both overtly and covertly, Iran was aiding Pakistan against India, Jordan against the Palestinians, Saudi Arabia against South Yemen, and the sultan of Oman against the Dhofari rebels. The shah's ambitions seemed limitless, as he began discussions with such distant countries as Australia, Mauritius, and South Africa on plans to project Iran's naval power into the Indian Ocean.[2] This dramatic change in the shah's relationship with the United States took place against a backdrop of Iran's burgeoning oil wealth, which soared as the shah led the oil-producing countries in their quest to wrestle control of oil prices from the American and European oil companies. In 1969, the year Nixon came into office, Iran's annual oil revenues had reached roughly $900 million. By 1972, when Nixon visited Tehran, this figure had nearly tripled, reaching $2.4 billion.[3] This wealth encouraged an Iranian spending spree that would have devastating consequences for the Iranian economy in the late 1970s, but it also allowed the shah to plow money into Iran's armed forces, which became one of the most formidable anywhere in the world. Iran's annual military expenditure increased more than eightfold from nearly $557 million in 1969 to more than $1 billion in 1972, with an increasing share of this money going toward purchasing the latest military hardware from the United States.[4]

At home, the shah had never enjoyed such unfettered power. Iran's oil wealth not only accelerated his ambitious development plans, but also lifted the few remaining constraints and inhibitions on his arbitrary rule. There was little concern within the Nixon administration that the shah faced any serious domestic threat to his rule. The older generation of communist and nationalist opponents of the shah had been largely neutralized. Ayatollah Khomeini, who had fomented the June 1963 protests against the White Revolution, was in exile in Iraq, and the conservative clergy had been cowed or co-opted. The only threat seemed to come from a new generation of militant Iranian students who had been inspired by Mao's China and Third World revolutionary movements in Algeria, Cuba, Palestine, and Vietnam, to take up an armed struggle against the shah and his American partners.[5] Militant groups such as the Islamist Sazman-e Mojahedin-e Khalq-e Iran (Organization of the Iranian People's Holy Warriors) and the Marxist Sazman-e Cherik'ha-ye Fada'i-ye Khalq (Organization of the Iranian People's Sacrificing Guerrillas) carried out sporadic violent attacks in Iran throughout the 1970s. SAVAK dealt ruthlessly with these armed groups, who attempted to abduct Ambassador MacArthur in December 1970 and murdered a US Army colonel in June 1973.[6] A January 1973 assessment by the US Embassy in Tehran concluded that the shah was "standing astride the Iranian political scene like a colossus, with all the reins of power in his hands and admitting of no rival.... His total success has enhanced his prestige and underlined his multifaceted position as stern ruler, national guide and mentor, remote but omniscient father-figure and, to some, reactionary oppressor and destroyer of individual liberties."[7] Few, if any, American observers would have predicted that the shah's regime would collapse by the end of the decade.

Iran's wealth and military power presented the shah with an opportunity to redress a number of Iran's historical grievances with its neighbors. These included settling Iran's numerous territorial disputes in the Persian Gulf, where the shah relinquished Iran's claim to Bahrain in 1970 and seized the islands of Abu Musa and the Tunbs in 1971. The most contentious dispute was with neighboring Iraq, over their common border along the Shatt al-Arab waterway (Figure 3.1). The shah was determined to rid himself of the Tehran Treaty that his father, Reza Shah, had agreed to in 1937 under pressure from the British, which established Iraqi sovereignty over the entire waterway.[8]

FIGURE 3.1   The Iran-Iraq border, circa 1972.

The shah's principal leverage over the Iraqis was the support that Iran, and to a lesser extent Israel, provided to the Kurdish insurgency in northern Iraq. Between 1972 and 1975, the United States covertly backed this Iranian operation in Iraqi Kurdistan as part of the American commitment to Iranian primacy under the Nixon Doctrine. Nixon, Kissinger, and the shah worked together to paralyze the Iraqi army in a guerrilla war in Kurdistan. Their goal was to prevent Soviet-backed Iraq from posing a threat to Iran or the Persian Gulf. Tied down by the war with the Kurds, the Iraqis could neither challenge Iran in the Shatt nor project their influence into the Gulf.

The shah's pivotal role in the origins, conduct, and termination of covert US support for the Iraqi Kurds illustrates the complex dynamics of the Nixon-Kissinger-Pahlavi partnership. The Nixon administration agreed to support the Iraqi Kurds in 1972 at the shah's behest, despite a long-standing US policy of non-intervention in Kurdistan. As the pressure on the Kurds mounted from Baghdad and Moscow in 1973, Nixon and Kissinger granted the shah's request for additional support for the Kurds, despite the rising cost of the operation and diminishing prospects of success. Kissinger kept the operation going in the shadow of the Watergate crisis, which paralyzed Nixon and ultimately led to the president's resignation in 1974. Then, when the shah deemed it expedient to abandon the Kurds in 1975 in order to make a deal with Iraq over the Shatt, the Ford administration, and Kissinger in particular, had little choice but to acquiesce to the shah's decision and to accept the embarrassment and domestic recriminations that followed.

The Origins of Iranian Support for the Iraqi Kurds

The Kurdish tribes that live along the mountainous border between Iran and Iraq have been pawns in the perennial conflict between Iran and its western neighbors since the wars of the Safavid shahs and Ottoman sultans in the sixteenth century. The emergence of the modern state system in the Middle East after World War I left the Kurds without a state of their own. The Kurds of Iran and Iraq found themselves fighting for autonomy from both the Hashemite kings in Baghdad and the Pahlavi shahs in Tehran. Mulla Mustafa Barzani, a tribal leader from Iraqi Kurdistan, rose to prominence in the 1940s when he led a number of revolts against the Hashemites and their British patrons.[9] Driven out of Iraq, in 1945 he crossed the border into Iran, where he fought to defend the short-lived Kurdish "Republic of Mahabad," which was supported by the Soviet Union during its wartime occupation of northwestern Iran. But the Mahabad republic collapsed in December 1946 as the Red Army withdrew from Iran. Barzani fled into exile in the Soviet Union, while the erstwhile president of Mahabad, Qazi Mohammad, was left to face the advancing Iranian army and ultimately the shah's gallows.[10] Mohammad Reza Shah would be eternally suspicious of Barzani because of his support for Iran's secessionist Kurds and his ties to the Soviet Union, where he lived in exile for more than a decade under the surname "Mamedov" and studied at the Higher Party School.[11]

Barzani was elected chairman of the Kurdish Democratic Party (KDP) in 1946 while still in exile, but he returned to Iraq in 1958 after Brigadier Abd al-Karim Qasim overthrew the pro-Western Hashemite monarchy in a bloody military coup. For the next two decades Barzani would work both with and against a succession of radical regimes in Baghdad in the hope of gaining autonomy for the Kurds of Iraq. As Iraq abandoned its alliance with Britain and Iran in the Baghdad Pact, seeking instead closer ties with the Soviet Union, the shah began to see Barzani as a potential ally against an emerging Iraqi threat. Worried about the growing communist influence among the Kurds of both Iran and Iraq, SAVAK established contact with Barzani in 1958 as a source of political and military intelligence on both Qasim's regime and the Iranian Kurds. Under the direction of General Hassan Pakravan, then in charge of SAVAK's foreign intelligence operations, Colonel Mujtaba Pashai, chief of Middle East operations, and Major Isa Pejman, the head of the Kurdish desk, SAVAK orchestrated a propaganda campaign to counter subversive Kurdish-language broadcasts from the Soviet Union and to encourage the Kurds' loyalty to Iran. This hearts-and-minds campaign was premised on the view that the Kurds were, in the shah's words, "the purest Persians, pure Aryans, from their tradition, their language and their history."[12] SAVAK's activities included Kurdish-language radio broadcasts from Mashhad and Kermanshah, sponsoring international conferences among the Kurdish émigré communities in Europe, and publishing a Kurdish-language newspaper. Iran also began providing Barzani with modest amounts of material assistance, including a small amount of arms and ammunition, as well as allowing a KDP radio station to operate from Iranian territory.[13]

However, Iran's support for Barzani did not begin in earnest until the early 1960s, when the pan-Arabist regime of Iraqi president Abdul Salam

Arif began pressing Iraq's claims of sovereignty over both the Shatt al-Arab and Iran's oil-rich province of Khuzestan, with its large Arabic-speaking population.[14] Barzani and his army of Pesh Merga ("those who face death") guerrillas had launched a full-scale Kurdish rebellion against Iraq's central government in 1961. By providing money and arms for this Kurdish insurgency, the shah hoped to inhibit the pan-Arab ambitions of the regime in Baghdad, to paralyze the Iraqi army and prevent it from meddling in Khuzestan and the Persian Gulf, and to provide a valuable bargaining chip in any future negotiations with Iraq over the Shatt. The significance of Iran's assistance to the Kurds was evident in Iraq's decision to launch a major military offensive in May 1966 to sever the mountain supply routes from the Iranian border to Rawanduz in Iraqi Kurdistan, where Barzani's headquarters were located. The Iraqi offensive involved a commitment of 40,000 troops, supported by 100 combat aircraft. However, the Iraqis soon found themselves trapped at Mount Handrin at the eastern entrance to the Rawanduz Gorge, where they were routed by Barzani's Pesh Merga on May 11 and 12, resulting in thousands of Iraqi casualties and the loss of large quantities of abandoned arms and ammunition. According to the British military historian Edgar O'Ballance, "The Mount Handrin ambush severely shook Iraqi military morale and confidence, and prematurely brought the ... Offensive to an abrupt and humiliating end."[15] The Iraqi military would not launch another offensive in Kurdistan until January 1969.

Despite this military success, the shah's support for the Iraqi Kurds was never wholehearted, and Barzani and the shah were not natural allies. The danger always existed that the Kurdish insurgency in Iraq would spill over into Iranian Kurdistan. What if Barzani was in fact a Soviet agent, working with Moscow to create a Kurdish state on Iran's doorstep, as they had tried to do in Mahabad in 1946? Barzani was aware of the shah's suspicions of his ties to Moscow, so he regularly handed over to SAVAK Iranian Communists, including Kurds, who had sought refuge in his territory, in an effort to reassure the shah about his intentions.[16] Barzani also realized that the shah did not share his goal of autonomy or independence for the Iraqi Kurds. Rather, Iran's interests lay in a stalemate between Baghdad and the Kurds, which would paralyze the Iraqi army on Iran's western border and give the shah some leverage over Iraq in the Shatt. Whenever the Iraqis came close to resolving their differences with Barzani, or to defeating him on the battlefield, the shah would escalate Iran's support for the Kurds. Conversely, whenever the Kurds came close to achieving autonomy, the shah would urge restraint. Consequently, Barzani was interested in diversifying his sources of external support, looking in particular to Israel and the United States as potential allies against Iraq.

Israel also had cause to worry about the radical direction that Iraq had taken after 1958. The covert support that Israel gave to Barzani was part of a broader strategy to balance against the rising tide of Arab nationalism following the disastrous 1956 Suez War. Prime Minister David Ben-Gurion sought to consolidate Israel's regional position by seeking an informal "peripheral pact" with other non-Arab states encircling the Arab world: Ethiopia, Iran, and Turkey. These pro-Western non-Arab allies would provide Israel with a counterweight to its Soviet-backed Arab enemies like Iraq.[17] The shah had extended de facto recognition to Israel in 1950, and by 1958 was secretly working with the Israelis to construct the Eilat-Eshkalon oil pipeline from the Gulf of Aqaba to the Mediterranean Sea, allowing Iran to export oil to Europe via Israel while bypassing the Egyptian-controlled Suez Canal.[18] A formal trilateral intelligence relationship between Iran, Israel, and Turkey was established in 1958 with the name "Trident," which involved intelligence sharing and semi-annual meetings of the three countries' intelligence chiefs. Mossad, Israel's foreign intelligence service, assisted SAVAK with intelligence operations in Iraqi Kurdistan, Lebanon, and Yemen, and provided the shah with intelligence on any threats to Iran emanating from the Arab world.[19]

At the same time that the peripheral pact was taking shape, Barzani reached out to the Israelis for help against their common foe in Baghdad. He sent an envoy, Kamuran Ali Bedir Khan, to meet with Israeli foreign minister Golda Meir in Zurich in 1959 to ask her for Israel's political and diplomatic support against Qasim. After Barzani launched his rebellion against Baghdad in 1961, the Israelis were eager to support the Kurds as a way of weakening Iraq. By keeping the Iraqi army pinned down in a guerrilla war in Kurdistan, the Israelis hoped to prevent Iraq from entering the Arab-Israeli conflict on the Jordanian or Syrian fronts. However, Israel faced considerable logistical difficulties in supplying the Kurds, given that it does not share a land border with Iraq. The only possible conduit for Israeli assistance to the Iraqi Kurds was Iran, but SAVAK was initially quite hesitant to allow Mossad to establish a presence in Kurdistan.[20] While the Israelis saw support for the Iraqi Kurds as a logical part of the periphery strategy, their interests in Kurdistan were not the same as those of Iran or Turkey. Worried about their own Kurdish secessionists, neither Iran nor Turkey wanted to see an independent Kurdish entity emerge in

Iraq. Aware of these concerns, Ben-Gurion warned Mossad to support Barzani "without stepping on Iranian and Turkish toes."[21] These obstacles were eventually overcome, and Israel's support for Barzani began in the mid-1960s in tandem with Iran's decision to escalate its support for the Iraqi Kurds.

Bedir Khan returned to Israel in 1963, where he met again with Golda Meir, Ben-Gurion, Mossad chief Meir Amit, and General Tzvi Tzur, the chief of staff of the Israel Defense Forces (IDF). He asked the Israelis for money, a powerful radio transmitter, and anti-tank and anti-aircraft weapons. Ben-Gurion authorized Mossad to discreetly help the Kurds, in coordination with SAVAK, and a Mossad envoy met with Barzani in Iraq in May 1963 to discuss the arrangement. The following month, Amit himself traveled to Paris to discuss the operation with his Iranian counterpart, Pakravan, who had been promoted to chief of SAVAK. Addressing Iran's anxieties about the threat of Kurdish nationalism, Amit and Pakravan agreed that the purpose of any assistance to the Kurds was to keep "the coals [of rebellion] burning, without letting them burst into flames."[22] Knowledge of the Kurdish operation would be kept strictly secret within their two governments and would be withheld from other allies. If the operation was exposed, both governments would deny any knowledge. By the winter of 1963, the first Israeli shipment of weapons and ammunition had reached Barzani via Iran, and in May 1965 Pejman, the SAVAK liaison with Barzani, escorted General Tzur and two senior Israeli military intelligence officers to Barzani's headquarters for two days of talks on military cooperation.[23]

After Tzur's meeting with Barzani, Israeli assistance expanded to include a permanent IDF and Mossad presence at Barzani's headquarters. The Israelis established a four-man radio relay team there, so that they could have direct communications with Israel, and provided the Kurds with a full field hospital, medical training, military instructors, and a regular supply of arms, ammunition, and funds. While Iran provided the bulk of the material assistance for the Kurds, the Israelis supplemented this with a $50,000 monthly stipend. They also established a three-month officers' training course for the Kurds, while Mossad and SAVAK worked together to train a Kurdish intelligence organization called Parastin, with the goal of collecting military intelligence on the Iraqi army.[24] The most crucial Israeli role in the Kurdish operation was providing the Kurds with Soviet weapons that they had captured from the Arabs. While American-made weapons in the hands of the Kurds would suggest Iranian or Israeli involvement, the presence of Soviet-made weapons on the battle-fields of Kurdistan would not raise any eyebrows. Soviet arms were ubiquitous throughout the Third World and would allow the Kurds' foreign sponsors to plausibly deny any involvement in Iraq's civil war.

The Reluctant Americans

Despite Washington's concerns about Iraq's burgeoning relationship with the Soviet Union after 1958, successive American administrations steadfastly refused to be drawn into the conflict in Kurdistan. The Americans were suspicious of Barzani's ties to Moscow and feared that a civil war in Iraq would not only generate instability that the Iraqi Communists could exploit, but also make Baghdad more dependent on military assistance from the Soviet Union.[25] The United States consistently rejected Barzani's appeals for military and financial assistance, despite promises that he would purge any Communists from his ranks and "burn all bridges to Russia" if American aid was forthcoming.[26] After Qasim's overthrow in a coup by the Ba'th Party in February 1963, the United States sought to improve relations with Iraq as part of the Kennedy administration's broader strategy of placating Arab nationalism in the Middle East as a bulwark against Soviet influence.[27] The Americans warned the shah to "keep [his] hands off" Iraq, and in August they secretly provided arms for the Iraqi army, which were most likely used in the ongoing fighting with the Kurds.[28] Washington regarded the Kurds' dispute with the central government as "strictly an internal matter" and consistently encouraged Barzani and the KDP to reach an "equitable settlement" with Baghdad.[29] As Iran and Israel escalated their support for the Kurds in the mid-1960s, the Johnson administration kept Barzani at arm's length. While the shah urged the Kurds to resume their fighting against the Iraqi army, after Barzani had agreed to a cease-fire in 1964, American diplomats in Baghdad congratulated the Kurds for having "wisely resisted Persian blandishments" and encouraged them to "remain calm and try [to] work out [a] solution with GOI [Government of Iraq]."[30] By April 1965 the cease-fire had broken down and Iran and Israel were escalating their support for the Kurds. But the United States continued to turn down Kurdish requests for arms and money, despite Barzani's promises that an independent Kurdistan would be "another state of the union" where American firms would enjoy privileged access to Kirkuk's oil fields.[31]

Contrary to the claims that Iranian support for the Iraqi Kurds in the 1960s amounted to "indirect US intervention" in Iraq, the United States consistently opposed Iran's strategy of using the Kurds to paralyze Iraq.[32] Whereas the shah wanted to keep the Iraqi army bogged down in Kurdistan, in order to prevent Iraq from posing a direct military threat in the Shatt or an indirect threat of subversion in Khuzestan or the Persian Gulf, the United States wanted to end the Kurdish war so that Baghdad would be less dependent on Soviet military aid.[33] Robert Strong, the US ambassador to Iraq, advised Washington in October 1965 that "continued Iranian/Israeli intervention is a threat to the United States position in Iraq but, unfortunately, neither country is likely to be heedful of United States interests in the matter."[34] While the Americans could do little about the flow of Iranian aid to the Kurds, they continued to rebuff repeated Kurdish attempts to draw them into the war in Kurdistan in the late 1960s.[35] Strong's analysis was correct; the shah was not about to heed American warnings to keep his hands off Iraq. Not only did the shah defy the Americans on Iraq, he would eventually draw them into the Kurdish war against Baghdad alongside Iran.

After six failed offensives against the Kurds since 1961, Iraq's leaders begrudgingly came to the conclusion in 1970 that there were only two ways to end the debilitating war in Kurdistan. One option was to give the shah the territorial concessions he wanted in the Shatt, in exchange for an end to Iranian support for Barzani. The problem with this solution was that the fragile legitimacy of Iraq's Ba'thi regime, which had returned to power in a military coup in 1968, rested on its claim to being champions of Arab nationalism. Therefore, the Ba'th could hardly afford to be seen to surrender Arab territory to the Persian shah.[36] The second, more palatable, option was to pursue Iraqi national unity through a negotiated settlement with Barzani, who could not have been happy that Iran and Israel were using the Kurds to tie down the Iraqi army.[37] Negotiations between the KDP and the central government began in December 1969. After face-to-face talks in February 1970 between Barzani and Saddam Hussein, then vice chairman of Iraq's Revolutionary Command Council, an agreement was finally announced by the Iraqi government on March 11. The new accord guaranteed the cultural and linguistic rights of the Kurds, gave them full autonomy in Kurdish-majority areas, and also assured them a share of power in Baghdad. As a result of the accord, the Kurdish language was taught for the first time in schools throughout Iraqi Kurdistan, Kurds were appointed to the cabinet in Baghdad and to provincial posts throughout

Kurdistan, and government funds began to flow into the impoverished Kurdish region. Barzani was given a generous monthly stipend, and his soldiers were put on the government payroll as "border guards." By mutual agreement, a census would be conducted the following spring to determine which Kurdish-majority areas of Iraq would fall within the autonomous Kurdish province that was to be established by 1974. In effect, therefore, the March 1970 accord amounted to a four-year truce in the war between the Kurds and the Iraqi army.

The shah was furious that Barzani had signed the accord. If implemented, it would mean an end to the stalemate in Iraqi Kurdistan, in which Iran had so heavily invested. Iranian prime minister Amir Abbas Hoveyda informed the US ambassador in Tehran, Douglas MacArthur II, that the shah wanted the "top level" of the US government to know that the accord was a "very grave development greatly increasing [the] threat to [the] Gulf area and [the] Arabian Peninsula." The agreement would allow Iraq to redeploy troops and resources from Kurdistan to the Persian Gulf "for subversion and other mischief against [the] small Gulf states." This was all part of Moscow's master plan, the shah argued, for creating an independent Kurdish state that would border with the Soviet Union and "thus enable [the] Soviets to overcome [the] present Turkey-Iran barrier to their direct penetration of [the] Middle East." The accord was all the more reason, the shah argued, for the United States to back Iranian primacy in the Gulf as a bulwark against Soviet encroachment in the region after the British withdrawal.[38] The State Department, however, was unconvinced and instructed Ambassador MacArthur to convey to the shah their view that the agreement would not last very long. They doubted that the Iraqis would redirect their forces away from Kurdistan, as they were hardly likely to trust Barzani to abide by the agreement, and they were also skeptical that the Soviets wanted a "Kurdish corridor" into the Gulf.[39] The initiative for the March Accord had come from Baghdad, not Moscow, though the Soviet Union had encouraged and warmly welcomed the development. Soviet president Nikolai Podgorny and Premier Alexei Kosygin congratulated Iraq on the agreement in an official telegram on March 17, and Soviet Arabists like Yevgeni Primakov and Alexei Vassiliev lauded the accord in the pages of *Pravda* as a blow against both the "reactionary forces" within Iraq and the "agents of Israel and of the imperialist powers."[40] A border conflict between Iran and Iraq was now taking on a distinctive Cold War shade, because of the economic and military support that Iraq received from the Soviet Union and the partnership between Iran and the United

States under the Nixon Doctrine. Despite the State Department's skepticism, the shah saw an opportunity to push the United States to abandon its long-standing hands-off policy toward the Iraqi Kurds and to become directly involved in the Kurdish conflict on Iran's side.

The State Department was correct in its assessment that the accord would not last. There was precious little trust between the Ba'th and Barzani. But as the Kurdish leader later explained, he could hardly tell his own people that he had refused the Iraqi offer of self-rule after so many years of war and suffering. Instead, Barzani accepted the offer while also maintaining his ties with Iran and Israel.[41] Shortly after the accord was reached, SAVAK asked for consultations with the Kurds on their agreement with Baghdad. Barzani's son, Idriss, led a delegation to Tehran from March 4 to 7, where he met with the chief of SAVAK, General Nematollah Nasiri, as well as Israeli intelligence officers. In a coordinated effort, the Iranian and Israeli officials told the Kurds that they were ready to supply them with anti-aircraft guns, artillery pieces, and even captured Soviet tanks, if they would continue their rebellion against Baghdad. In the month of February 1970 alone, Iranian and Israeli financial assistance to the Kurds amounted to more than $3.3 million.[42] Barzani's ambivalence about the accord was matched by that of the Ba'th, who dragged their feet on the appointment of a Kurdish vice president in the central government, resisted Kurdish demands that oil-rich Kirkuk be included in the autonomous Kurdish area, and continued an "Arabization" policy of resettling Arabs and Kurds in order to create demographic facts on the ground ahead of the planned census. Barzani found himself confronting the very difficult choice of siding with either Iran or Iraq, neither of which favored any meaningful Kurdish autonomy. He realized that the autonomy that the Ba'th were offering was a trap. If his Pesh Merga stood down and allowed the Iraqi army to take up positions along the border with Iran, his supply routes would be cut off. And if the Kurds were denied control of the revenues from Kirkuk's oil, they would be left at the mercy of the central government in Baghdad. As the US Embassy in Beirut concluded, Barzani was not prepared to settle for "the mere trappings of an autonomy" where the Ba'th would "retain all the essentials of real political power in their own hands."[43] By the summer of 1970, the CIA was already receiving intelligence that the Kurds were "anticipating a showdown with the Iraqi government" and had begun "strengthening their forces and lining up potential allies."[44] Barzani was willing to continue fighting for meaningful autonomy, but first he needed a guarantee that the shah would not sell him out when the prospect of an autonomous Kurdistan materialized. For this guarantee, he looked to Iran's Cold War partner, the United States.

Drawing the United States into the Kurdish Conflict

It would not be easy for the shah and Barzani to draw the United States into the war in Kurdistan. For more than two decades the Americans had steadfastly refused to become embroiled in Iraq's civil war, and in the early years of Nixon's presidency they were still unconvinced that Iraq's growing military and economic ties with the Soviet Union necessitated a revision of that long-standing policy. Soviet-backed Iraq did not look very menacing, and it appeared to the State Department that the Iraqis had "turned inward" and were "isolated even from mainstream of Arab world."[45] The Americans saw "little likelihood that Iraq will be able to expand its influence very much in [the] Arab world."[46] Despite repeated efforts in 1971, the Kurds were unable to convince the Nixon administration to help them resume their war against Baghdad. Zayd Uthman, a Barzani envoy, contacted the US Embassy in Beirut in July. He complained that the Kurds were tired of Iran's "heavy-handed" attitude and asked for direct high-level talks with Washington, but this request was rebuffed.[47] After Barzani narrowly escaped an assassination attempt in September, which was almost certainly the work of the Iraqi security services, the Kurds redoubled their diplomatic efforts to secure American backing.[48] Another Kurdish envoy, Habib Mohammad Karim, approached the US Embassy in Beirut in November and reiterated Barzani's request for high-level talks, which was again rejected.[49]

Having signed the March 1970 accord with Barzani, Iraq's Ba'thi rulers were close to achieving their goal of neutralizing all domestic threats to their power. In November 1971 they promulgated a National Action Charter (NAC), a manifesto of sorts that spelled out the Ba'th's determination to maintain their grip on power while also expressing ideological affinity with other "progressive" leftist groups like the Iraqi Communist Party (ICP). The Ba'th invited the ICP to reach an accommodation with them, as the Kurds had, by agreeing to the principles in the Charter and joining the government. Since taking power in 1968, the Ba'th had alternated between brutally suppressing the Iraqi Communists and trying to co-opt them into the government.[50] The Soviet Union was putting pressure on the Ba'th to bring the ICP and the Kurds into a national unity government in the hope of ending Iraq's chronic domestic instability. Moscow had a clear interest in a strong unified Iraq, which could act as the Soviet Union's local client in the Persian Gulf and balance the rising power of Iran, the regional partner of the United States.[51] Saddam Hussein visited Moscow in February 1972, where he met with Brezhnev and signed a number of agreements on military supply and economic cooperation, particularly in the area of oil production.[52] Soviet officials made it clear to Hussein that their continuing support for Iraq was conditional on bringing the ICP into the government.[53] But the Ba'th never had any intention of sharing power with the Communists. Instead, by making conciliatory gestures toward the ICP, they hoped to secure Soviet support against Iran, while luring the Iraqi Communists into the open where they could be more easily eliminated.[54] As for the ICP, they saw an opportunity to revive their party in Iraq, and so they accepted the Ba'th's offer to join the government following a visit by Kosygin to Iraq in April 1972.[55] Two Communists were appointed to the cabinet in May, and the attacks by the Iraqi security services on the ICP abated. The Communists were allowed to operate openly in Iraq for a number of years and the ICP formally joined the Ba'th in a National Patriotic Front in July 1973. But the Communists were not given any real political power by the Ba'th; at best, they were tolerated. When Iraq's oil revenue skyrocketed in 1973–1974, reducing Iraq's need for Soviet assistance, the Ba'th's violent suppression of the ICP slowly resumed.[56]

The Kurds' military strength in northern Iraq meant that they were able to resist the combined Ba'thi and Soviet pressure to join the NAC and submit to Ba'thi rule in a national front, but it was not clear how long they would be able to hold out. Given the Ba'th's determination to end the conflict in Kurdistan once and for all, Barzani would soon have to choose between capitulating to Baghdad or resuming the fight for meaningful autonomy. Shortly after Hussein's visit to Moscow in February 1972, a Soviet delegation visited Barzani's headquarters in Kurdistan, led by V. P. Rumanytsev of the Central Committee of the Communist Party of the Soviet Union. Rumanytsev pressured Barzani to join a national front with the Ba'th, in exchange for guarantees of Soviet support. When Barzani replied that he could not trust the Ba'th, particularly after the attempt on his life the previous year, Rumanytsev offered to station a permanent Soviet liaison at his headquarters to monitor Iraqi compliance with any agreement. The Soviet envoy advised Barzani to reduce his dependence on Iran, warning him implicitly that he should not trust the shah. Barzani agreed to consider the Soviet proposal, in order to buy himself more time to secure American support for a renewed campaign against Baghdad.[57] Meanwhile, the shah was desperate to prevent the Kurds from submitting to Ba'thi and Soviet pressure. He could sense Iran's leverage over Iraq slipping away, and he knew that only an American commitment to the Kurds could keep Barzani from giving in. Through SAVAK and the CIA, the shah put his weight behind the Kurdish appeals for the United States to join Iran in supporting Barzani. In late November 1971, shortly after the NAC was announced, SAVAK had advised the CIA that Barzani "represented the only available figure around whom effective anti-BPI [Ba'th Party of Iraq] activity could be organized."[58] On March 6, 1972, shortly after Rumanytsev's visit to Barzani, SAVAK again warned the CIA that Soviet efforts to establish a national unity government in Baghdad "presage further Soviet inroads into Iraq with consequent difficulties for Iran and for the Persian Gulf."[59] A week later, SAVAK relayed a warning from Barzani to the Americans "that if the present trend continued, Iraq would assume a status similar to that of the East European satellites."[60] This Iranian intervention was crucial to bringing the Kurdish conflict to the direct attention of the White House.

Soviet influence in Iraq was undeniably an important consideration in American thinking about the Kurds. But the growing Soviet role in Iraq, in and of itself, was not enough to draw the United States into Kurdistan. An obscure local conflict in the faraway mountains of northern Iraq was hardly a top priority for the superpower. Harold Saunders, the principal aide on Kissinger's NSC staff dealing with the Middle East, later recalled, "I doubt that Nixon and Kissinger would have had it at the top of their personal agendas."[61] Kurdish developments were monitored by mid-level officials in the State Department, few of whom considered Soviet influence in Iraq much of a threat to Iran or the Persian Gulf. But SAVAK's warnings to the CIA bypassed the State Department and propelled the Kurdish issue up the chain of command to the personal attention of Kissinger, because of the high priority that Nixon gave to relations with Iran. The shah's request for American assistance for the Kurds could not be ignored, as similar requests from various Kurdish envoys had been. The Iranian backchannel messages prompted a discussion within the Nixon administration of whether the United States should abandon its long-standing policy of non-intervention in Kurdistan. Without the shah's intervention, it seems unlikely that any such debate would have taken place.

The advice that Nixon and Kissinger were receiving from the State Department, the CIA, and the NSC staff in the early months of 1972 consistently contradicted the shah's claims that Soviet influence in Iraq posed a threat to Iran or the Persian Gulf. The State Department's view was that the various military and economic agreements that Moscow had signed with Iraq were "designed to placate Baghdad, not to pose [a] threat to [the] Shah."[62] The US Embassy in Beirut was convinced that the Ba'th's purges of the Iraqi army had been so extensive that, according to one of their sources, Iraq "could not fight its way out of a wet paper bag."[63] Both the CIA and the State Department advised the White House to stick with the long-standing non-intervention policy in Kurdistan. Harold Saunders told Kissinger on March 27 that "for one thing, any assistance that may be needed by Barzani is fully within the capability of Iran or Israel to provide. There is nothing absolutely needed from us except that they want to involve us. Another factor is that the odds are against the Kurds succeeding. Also, our involving ourselves for the first time at this point could be regarded by the Soviets as a move directed against them." With Nixon's historic summit meeting with Brezhnev only months away, Kissinger recognized that he could not risk upsetting Moscow by encouraging the Kurds to resume fighting in Iraq. Therefore he concurred with the advice he was receiving and instructed his staff to turn down Barzani's request "in [the] least abrasive way possible."[64] As he explained in his memoirs, "we did not want to provoke a further influx of Soviet arms and influence [into Iraq]."[65]

Barzani and SAVAK were now coordinating a plan to overthrow the Ba'thi regime with a coalition of Iraqi opposition forces operating from Kurdish territory in northern Iraq. In March 1972, Kurdish envoys were dispatched to Amman, London, and Washington to ask the Jordanian, British, and US governments to back the plan and to recruit the exiled former Iraqi premier, Colonel Abd al-Razzaq al-Nayif, for the operation. A former chief of Iraqi military intelligence, Colonel Nayif had helped the Ba'th seize power in 1968 and was briefly prime minister before being ousted and sent into exile. Just weeks earlier, on February 18, Iraqi agents had tried to assassinate him at his home in London.[66] Meanwhile, the Iranians had asked Idriss Barzani to send a list of all the Kurds' military and financial needs for the operation, which the Kurds had done. But, as CIA director Richard Helms reported, Barzani still "did not trust the Iranians to implement their promises." The Iraqi opposition, both Arabs and Kurds, made it very clear to the Americans that "while accepting their [Iran's] military and other material assistance, they would not welcome direct control or intervention by Iran in Iraqi internal affairs."[67] This was one reason why Barzani sought to involve King Hussein of Jordan in his plans. Given the king's close friendship with the shah, Jordan could act as a mediator between Iran and the Kurds. Furthermore, the Kurds suggested that Jordan could serve as an alternative to Iran as a conduit for American aid to the Kurds.[68]

The appeal for American aid was reiterated in April 1972 by another Kurdish envoy, Zayd Uthman, who warned the Americans that if the United States did not intervene, Barzani would have no choice but to join the national front with the Ba'th. But the State Department continued to resist the idea of US intervention in Kurdistan. They warned that even if Barzani were able to overthrow the Ba'th, the new Iraqi regime would be very weak and heavily dependent on the Soviet Union. Furthermore, empowering the Iraqi Kurds would surely inflame Kurdish nationalism in Iran and Turkey, and any American involvement in a coup in an Arab country would further harm US relations with the Arab world.[69] Shortly after Uthman's visit to Washington, Iraq and the Soviet Union signed a 15-year Treaty of Friendship and Cooperation on April 9. But even this did not cause the State Department to change its position on the Kurds. They saw the treaty as a watered-down version of the agreements that the Soviet Union had signed with Egypt and India. It was the product of an Iraqi initiative, orchestrated by Saddam Hussein, who wanted Soviet backing to consolidate his own position at home.[70] Nor, in fact, did the treaty cause the White House to reconsider its attitude toward Barzani, as Kissinger claims in his memoirs.[71] In fact, when Kissinger had rejected the Kurdish appeals for help in March, he was well aware that "a Soviet treaty with Iraq similar to that one with Egypt is in the offing."[72] The decisive factor in the ultimate American decision to back Barzani was not Soviet influence in Iraq, but the pressure that the shah was bringing to bear on the White House. As the shah explained to Israeli prime minister Golda Meir, during her secret trip to Tehran on May 18, he was optimistic that he could convince the Americans to help Iran and Israel to support the Iraqi Kurds and he intended to raise the issue with Nixon and Kissinger during their visit to Iran later that month.[73] The president and his national security advisor went into their meetings with the shah in Tehran on May 30 and 31 having rejected the Kurdish appeals for help. In fact, the Kurds had tried to arrange a meeting with Kissinger in Tehran, but had again been rebuffed.[74] However, the Americans emerged from their talks with the shah convinced of the need to support Barzani.

While Nixon and Kissinger were in Tehran, the State Department's INR issued an insightful analysis of the Kurdish situation, outlining the difficult choices that lay ahead for the United States. At the age of 69, INR concluded, Barzani saw "the goals that his people fought for and almost attained slipping away unless he can force some substantial political gains in what may be his last campaign." Barzani knew that the unity government that Baghdad and Moscow were pressuring him to join would mean the end of any meaningful autonomy for the Kurds in Iraq. His only other choice was to fight a "long-drawn-out insurgency," which at best might lead to the overthrow of the Ba'th, but even then the new regime would still have to reach some sort of accommodation with the Soviet Union, given Moscow's entrenched position in Iraq. At worst, Barzani would be defeated, leaving "[a] complaisant pro-Ba'th or even pro-Soviet clique in control of Iraqi Kurdistan [that] could of course bring pressure on Iran and even create a nuisance in eastern Turkey."[75] For the United States, backing the Kurds in order to contain Soviet influence in Iraq was a lose-lose proposition. But for Iran, it was imperative to bring the United States into the conflict in order to prevent Barzani from capitulating to Baghdad. If Barzani were to succumb to the combined Iraqi-Soviet pressure, join the national front, and stand down his Pesh Merga, then the Ba'th would be free to dedicate more of their military resources to challenging Iran in the Shatt al-Arab and projecting Iraqi influence into Khuzestan and the Persian Gulf.

In his meetings with Nixon and Kissinger in Tehran, the shah portrayed the Kurdish conflict to the Americans as a Cold War struggle to block Soviet penetration into the Persian Gulf, rather than a long-standing conflict between Iran and Iraq over regional supremacy. On the afternoon of May 30, the shah expressed to Nixon and Kissinger his fear that Moscow was working in Iraq to "establish a coalition of the Kurds, the Baathists, and the Communists." If they succeeded, "the Kurdish problem instead of being a thorn in the side [of the Ba'th] could become an asset to the Communists." When Kissinger asked "what could be done," the shah replied, "Iran can help with the Kurds."[76] Just as Iran had worked with the United States to secretly assist Pakistan against Soviet-backed India, now the shah asked the Americans to help him finance and arm the Kurds so that they could continue to resist Soviet-backed Iraq. The next morning, the shah complained to Nixon and Kissinger that the immediate danger to Iran came "mostly from Baghdad, or at least Baghdad would take credit for it."[77] Alam recorded in his diary on June 1 that Kissinger had agreed that "the Russians have advanced quite far in Iraq, and we must stop them."[78] In his memoirs, Kissinger writes that he and Nixon were swayed by the shah's argument that "without American support, the existing Kurdish uprising against the Baghdad government would collapse." Kissinger parrots the shah's argument that if Kurdistan fell to the Iraqi army, it would become "a base for subversion of Kurdish areas in all the neighboring countries. In time, this subversion, backed by the rapidly growing Iraqi armed forces, had the potential to become a powerful weapon against the Gulf States, Iran, and even Turkey." He writes that Nixon confronted a "Hobson's choice" in Iraq: while US intervention might eventually lead to an escalation of Soviet assistance to Iraq, non-intervention would certainly result in the collapse of the Iraqi Kurds and the domination of Kurdistan by the Ba'th and their Soviet patrons. As Kissinger explained, "In a choice between the certain and the conjectural danger, the far-off risk tends to appear more attractive."[79] Therefore, Nixon agreed in Tehran to work with the shah to support the Iraqi Kurds.[80]

The shah quickly acted on Nixon's assurance of support. Just one week later he sent a backchannel message to Kissinger via the CIA asking him to receive Idriss Barzani and Mahmoud Uthman, the KDP's de facto foreign minister, who would present the joint Iranian-Kurdish plan to overthrow the Ba'th. The shah was asking Kissinger to agree to the highest-level contacts the Kurds had ever had with the US government. Harold Saunders reiterated to Kissinger the same advice he had given his boss in March: avoid becoming embroiled in Kurdistan. He warned Kissinger that the best that could be achieved would be a stalemate, and "[i]f the battle turned against the Kurds, we would have neither the assets nor the interest to provide decisive support." Rather than becoming directly involved, Saunders advised that the United States should leave it to regional actors like Iran to support the Kurds, in line with the Nixon Doctrine. Furthermore, Saunders was worried that US intervention would be seen by Moscow as a "direct counter-Soviet move." But he acknowledged that Kissinger's decision to receive the Barzani envoys depended "on how committed you feel to the Shah on this particular point." As Saunders recognized, the decision to receive the Kurds was as much about the White House's relationship with the shah as it was about containing the Soviet Union in Iraq. Saunders offered to meet with the two Kurdish envoys in Kissinger's place, so as to avoid giving Barzani the impression of a commitment by the White House to his cause. But Nixon's decision to support the Kurds had already been made in Tehran, without any consultation with the NSC staff, the State Department, or the CIA. Kissinger scribbled on Saunders's memo, "I thought we arranged," which suggests that plans had already been made for the visit without Saunders's knowledge.[81]

Kissinger's decision to receive the Kurdish envoys at senior levels of the US government was a reversal of the United States' long-standing policy toward the Kurds and marked the beginning of covert US involvement in Iraq's civil war, at the behest of the shah. Both the State Department and the NSC staff had warned against becoming embroiled in the Iranian-backed Kurdish rebellion. But Nixon and Kissinger ignored the advice of their own officials and heeded the shah's counsel to back Barzani. Although repeated Kurdish appeals for help had been rejected by the Nixon administration, including by Kissinger himself in March 1972, the shah's intervention had changed the White House's calculations. During their meetings in Tehran in May 1972, the shah had successfully convinced Nixon and Kissinger that if Barzani capitulated and joined a national front with the Ba'th and the ICP, then Kurdistan would fall to the Iraqi army, from where the Ba'th would project Soviet influence into Iran and the Persian Gulf. Nixon and Kissinger knew precious little about the war in Kurdistan. As Kissinger later recalled, "we did not know much about the Kurds—we thought they were some kind of hill tribe."[82] Instead, they relied on the advice and judgment of their regional partner in the Gulf. If the shah said that a Kurdish collapse would increase the Soviet threat to Iran and the Gulf, then Nixon and Kissinger listened, regardless of what their own advisors were telling them. They were persuaded that the war in Kurdistan was not only a regional conflict between Iran and Iraq, but also a battle in the global Cold War. Saunders recalled that his boss wanted to show the Iraqis that "they would pay a certain price for being an ally of the Soviet Union."[83] Without the shah's intervention, Nixon and Kissinger would most likely have continued to ignore the Kurds' appeals for help, much as they had done during their first three years in office. But thanks to the shah's vigorous backchannel diplomacy, the United States agreed to join Iran in supporting the Iraqi Kurds.

CIA Covert Action in Iraqi Kurdistan

Having agreed to a high-level meeting with the Kurds in Washington, Kissinger took Saunders's advice not to personally receive the Kurdish envoys, perhaps to avoid directly implicating himself or the president in this *sub rosa* affair. The State Department was also kept completely in the dark about this change in Kurdish policy. Instead, it was decided that CIA director Richard Helms and Colonel Richard Kennedy, a senior member of the NSC staff, would receive the Kurdish emissaries.[84] The CIA warned the White House that the Kurds' goal would be to secure both American "moral" support to balance Soviet support for the Ba'th, and also American material support for a major military operation to defeat the Iraqi army and overthrow the Ba'th. They estimated that Barzani would need as much as $24 million annually just to pay the salaries of the 50,000-man army he hoped to recruit.[85] Again Saunders advised caution, emphasizing that "[t]he major view in town is that we should stay out of direct support for the Kurds." The US role was unlikely to remain secret, Saunders warned, and would damage America's relations with Moscow and its position in the Arab world if it were revealed. Furthermore, the Iranians and the Israelis were already committed to supporting Barzani, so US support was not essential.[86] But all these arguments fell on deaf ears. Before the two Kurdish emissaries had even arrived in Washington, Nixon asked his friend and political ally John Connally, who had just stepped down as treasury secretary, to stop off in Tehran during a world tour and personally inform the shah that the US was committed to helping Barzani.[87] The purpose of the Idriss-Uthman visit to Washington would be to discuss how, not whether, the US could aid the Iraqi Kurds.[88]

Thanks to the shah's lobbying, the Kurds' long awaited high-level meeting with the Americans took place in Washington on June 30, 1972. Idriss Barzani and Mahmoud Uthman explained to Helms and Kennedy that without more assistance they could only resist the combined Iraqi-Soviet pressure to join the national front for another six months. The Kurds asked for US recognition of the "Kurdish objective of autonomy," and sufficient financial, military, and intelligence assistance to create a Kurdish "offensive military force" that could launch a major attack on the Iraqi army and overthrow the Ba'th regime. They also argued, rather naively, that an American commitment to the Kurdish cause would reassure Iran and Turkey that they had nothing to fear from a Kurdish victory. Helms told the Kurds that "he and Colonel Kennedy have been authorized by Dr. Kissinger to express the sympathy of the United States Government for the Kurdish movement under Mulla Barzani." He assured the Kurdish envoys that the very fact that this meeting was taking place was a break with previous policy and "was proof of our position and readiness to consider their requests for assistance." He asked the Kurds for a comprehensive briefing on the material assistance they needed so that the United States could "provide assistance as quickly as possible." But there were two strict caveats to US support. First, Helms told the Kurds that the only reason they were being received in Washington was, as Uthman later recalled, "because the Shah wanted the American government to help us."[89] Therefore, the Kurds should not entertain any idea of circumventing the shah in order to deal directly with the United States. Second, Helms emphasized that the US role must remain hidden and warned the Kurds that "the relationship could indeed be soured by a failure to honor our need for such secrecy." For both of these reasons, all US assistance would be channeled through Iran. The following day, CIA officials held a second meeting with the Kurdish envoys to discuss the Kurds' needs in detail. These meetings marked the beginning of a covert US operation that was undertaken at the behest of Iran as a way for Barzani to overcome his mistrust of the shah.[90]

It took the CIA less than a month to put together a Kurdish operation for the president's approval. In late July 1972, Helms advised the White House that while Barzani was asking for approximately $60 million annually to raise an army and build a Kurdish government infrastructure, the CIA felt that the Kurds should be discouraged from "such an ambitious, highly provocative, and probably impractical scale of activity, which would exceed the limits of covert capability." The Kurds needed only $18 million annually, the CIA argued, to maintain their current strength of 25,000 Pesh Merga soldiers "for guerrilla warfare of an essentially defensive nature." The Iranians would pay $9 million and the United States would contribute $3 million in financial aid and $2 million worth of munitions, while the balance of $4 million would be covered by Britain and Israel.[91] The weapons that the CIA would provide would consist of "non-attributable" foreign manufactured arms and ammunition in American inventories or US ordnance ordinarily in Iranian and Iraqi inventories. The Agency advised against providing the Kurds with American-made anti-aircraft weapons or tanks, the source of which could not be disguised.[92] The limited operation that the CIA was proposing was designed to serve Iranian, not Kurdish, interests. The goal was to keep the Iraqi army pinned down in Kurdistan and to prevent the formation of a national front government in Baghdad, not to achieve autonomy or independence for the Iraqi Kurds.

Although the CIA had initially opposed any American involvement with the Kurds, like Kissinger they now reversed their position. Their assessment was that "[t]here can be no doubt that it is in the interests of ourselves, our allies, and other friendly governments in the area to see the Ba'thi regime in Iraq kept off balance and if possible overthrown, if this can be done without increasing Soviet influence in Iraq or escalating hostilities to a dangerous international level." How can we account for this dramatic change in the CIA's position? The Agency's own explanation was that increasing Soviet support for Iraq now warranted a revision of US policy toward the Kurds: "While Ba'thi aspirations heretofore may have seemed far beyond their capabilities, developments of the past few months suggest that they now should be taken much more seriously." But another explanation was provided by a CIA officer who later told Congressional investigators that after the White House had decided to back the Iraqi Kurds, the "CIA was told to prepare a paper on 'how' the project could be done, not 'whether' the project should be done."[93] The best that the Agency could do was to limit the scale of the operation to the modest goal of preventing Barzani from joining a national unity government and "keeping Kurdish resistance alive." Providing the Kurds with the offensive military capability that Barzani wanted would be "unrealistic." Instead, the CIA argued that "the Kurds do best against the Iraqi army when they remain well within their mountains and engage in aggressive guerrilla tactics, hitting the Iraqis in many places and keeping them off balance." The situation called for a limited war that would allow "plausible denial" of US involvement.[94] Kissinger writes that this plan for a limited war was conveyed by the shah to Barzani, after discussions between the shah and King Hussein of Jordan from July 31 to August 2 at the shah's summer palace in Nowshahr on the Caspian Sea. The two monarchs had discussed the ground rules for the Kurdish operation, and the shah warned Barzani to "avoid dramatic moves that might trigger an all-out Iraqi assault, such as declaring a separate Kurdish state."[95]

Nixon approved the CIA operation on August 1, 1972, and Kissinger dispatched a brief memorandum of no more than a few sentences, which was hand-delivered to the members of the NSC's 40 Committee to ensure secrecy.[96] Chaired by Kissinger, the 40 Committee included CIA director Helms, Under Secretary of State Alexis Johnson, Deputy Secretary of Defense Bill Clements, and Admiral Thomas Moorer, chairman of the Joint Chiefs of Staff, and was charged with approving sensitive US covert operations.[97] But Connally had already communicated the go-ahead for the Kurdish operation to the shah in June, and this bureaucratic exercise with the 40 Committee was, according to Haig, an insurance policy so that "in

the event that something blows ... we could insist that established proce-
dures were followed."[98] Kissinger's decision not to meet with the Kurdish
envoys in late June, Helms's warning to the Kurds about the need for secrecy, and Kissinger's attempts to cover his tracks and avoid a paper trail
all indicate a keen awareness by the White House of the risks they were
running by going along with the shah's plans to back Barzani, against the
advice of their own officials.[99] If it were revealed that the United States was
covertly working with Iran to fuel a civil war in an Arab country allied with
Moscow, it could set back the détente with the Soviet Union that Nixon
and Kissinger had so carefully crafted.[100] Kissinger's desire for secrecy was
understandable, but it also seems likely that he did not want to directly
implicate himself or the president in a covert operation, which, as he was
being warned, might ultimately end in disaster. If so, his political instincts
would prove to be correct.

As the CIA's covert operation in Kurdistan got underway, Nixon's
focus was on his domestic political fortunes. With elections looming in
November, he spent much of the autumn trying to cover up his staff's
role in a break-in at the Democratic National Committee's headquarters in Washington's Watergate complex in June. A Federal Grand Jury
indicted the Watergate burglars in September, but Nixon successfully
obstructed the investigation by paying off the burglars to keep them
quiet.[101] When Nixon was re-elected in a landslide victory against his
Democratic rival, Senator George McGovern, Helms relayed a message
of congratulations from Barzani to Nixon, telling Kissinger that "[t]he
President might enjoy seeing this message from his new friends."[102]
That autumn, the first deliveries of CIA arms and money were reaching the Iraqi Kurds via SAVAK; in October, Kissinger reported to the
president that the operation was proceeding "without a hitch." Monthly
cash payments were reaching the Kurds, and more were in the pipeline.
The first planeload of 10 tons of Soviet-made arms and ammunition,
including 500 AK-47 rifles, 500 submachine guns, and 200,000 rounds
of ammunition, had already been delivered. By the end of October, the
Kurds would have received 222,000 pounds of arms and ammunition
from CIA stocks and a further 142,000 pounds from the other countries
involved. The operation was achieving its objective, Helms reported, of
protecting Iran's western border by strengthening the Kurds' defenses
against the Iraqi army: "Barzani's maintenance of a secure redoubt
will continue to pin down two-thirds of the Iraqi army and deprive the

Bathists of a secure base from which to launch sabotage and assassination teams against Iran."[103]

By the end of the year, the State Department had opened a US Interests Section in Baghdad, after five years during which the United States had no diplomatic presence in Iraq. The head of the new US mission, Arthur Lowrie, was being kept in the dark about the CIA's Kurdish operation, like the rest of his colleagues in the State Department.[104] Writing from Baghdad, "a city of whispered conversations and glances over the shoulder," Lowrie reported that the situation in Kurdistan had settled into an uneasy stalemate with sporadic minor clashes. "Neither side seems to want a renewal of large scale fighting, but neither is there sufficient mutual confidence to bring about the implementation of the agreement."[105] This must have been music to Kissinger's ears. The stalemate in Kurdistan had been maintained, without the kind of dramatic escalation that would lead the Soviets to pour more arms and money into Iraq and upset superpower détente. This is not to say that the Iraqis were unaware that Barzani was receiving aid from a variety of foreign sources. As Lowrie reported, an Iraqi government newspaper declared on December 17 that, "What is now going on is close coordination between Tehran and Amman and some other Arab capitals under overall supervision of imperialistic intelligence services with [the] object of launching [a] fresh onslaught on [the] Arab national liberation movement and on revolutionary Iraq in particular."[106] But without proof, such accusations could be dismissed as the usual vitriolic propaganda that emanated from Baghdad. The shah, too, must have been delighted. He had kept Barzani out of the national front while the Iraqi army remained in Kurdistan, unable to pose a threat to Iran. As the US intelligence community concluded in December, Iran had the upper hand and wanted to maintain the status quo: "Iraqi leaders have a healthy respect for the Shah's military edge and have backed down from military confrontation whenever large-scale action seemed likely. This caution is likely to persist even in the face of provocations by the Shah. We do not think Iran is likely to initiate major military action against Iraq."[107]

Beneath the surface of the initial success of the Kurdish operation lurked a nagging problem that would eventually undermine the entire effort: the goals of Barzani and his foreign sponsors were entirely disparate. Barzani sought, at a minimum, to establish an autonomous Kurdish government in northern Iraq. But Iran, Israel, and the United States had the far more limited objective of maintaining the stalemate between the Kurds and the Iraqi army, thereby keeping the Iraqis tied down in Kurdistan and preventing them from entering the Arab-Israeli conflict or making

mischief in Iran or the Persian Gulf. The cost of maintaining this stalemate steadily rose in 1973, as Iran and the United States offered more aid
to Barzani to counter the intense pressure on the Kurds from the Ba'th
and the Soviet Union to join the national front. At the same time that the
United States was trying to extricate itself from the war in Vietnam, with
the signing of the Paris Peace Accords in January, it found itself being
drawn ever deeper into Kurdistan. The Kurds remained in their mountain strongholds and the Iraqi army controlled the plains of northern Iraq.
While skirmishes between Iraqi and Kurdish troops were a regular occur-
rence, neither the Ba'th nor Barzani were ready in 1973 to renew open warfare. But as US intelligence had concluded, the stalemate in Kurdistan was
"inherently fragile," and after the harsh winter a renewal of fighting was
likely when the snow and ice melted in the spring of 1974.[108] Ultimately,
Barzani's international sponsors would have to confront the unpleasant
truth that the stalemate was unsustainable.

Despite the grave risks involved in pursuing this unsustainable stalemate in Kurdistan, there were no dissenting voices reaching Nixon and
Kissinger regarding support for Barzani. For one thing, knowledge of the
CIA's covert Kurdish operation was a closely guarded secret in Washington.
Only Kissinger and a handful of officials in the NSC and the CIA were aware
of the full extent of the operation. Helms oversaw the operation and acted
as the channel of communication between Washington and Tehran, even
after Nixon fired him as director of central intelligence in November 1972.
Helms had clashed with the White House when he resisted Nixon's efforts
to use the CIA to cover up the Watergate scandal. The president offered
him an ambassadorship as compensation and Helms chose Iran, a country
he had become familiar with during his long career in the CIA.[109] Helms
took up his post in Tehran in March 1973, taking over from Ambassador
Joseph Farland, a loyal Republican who had been abruptly told to resign
after only a year in the job. When the shah heard that Helms was to be
sent to Tehran, he was delighted. In the words of Arthur Callahan, the
CIA station chief in Tehran, the shah saw it as the "ultimate recognition of
his country's importance."[110] The Soviet ambassador to Iran criticized the
Americans for sending the former head of the CIA to Tehran, but Prime
Minister Hoveyda is said to have joked that while the Soviets only send
their tenth-ranking KGB officer, at least the Americans send their number
one spy.[111] While some suspected that Helms's appointment was a com-
fortable exile, his role as the backchannel for communications between the
White House and the shah was vital to keeping the American hand in the

Kurdish operation hidden, especially from the State Department bureaucracy, which neither Nixon nor Kissinger trusted.[112]

Within the CIA, Helms's views were still the last word on Iran and the Kurds. The subsequent director, James Schlesinger, did not question the wisdom of the Kurdish operation he had inherited and deferred to Helms's judgment on matters relating to Iran. He later recalled, "In general, the attitude within the agency was that you had as ambassador there a man who was quite knowledgeable about such matters and his sense of things probably was good enough. I think that there may have been some tendency for the agency to grow a little complacent with a former director as the ambassador."[113] On the ground in Tehran, the Kurdish operation was managed by Callahan and one other CIA officer who acted as the liaison with Barzani. The operation was run in close coordination with General Manuchehr Hashemi, the head of SAVAK's Eighth Directorate (Counter-Intelligence).[114] Both Callahan and Barzani's CIA liaison were experienced Middle East hands. They were worried that the shah would never accept Kurdish autonomy and would inevitably betray Barzani to the Iraqis. When one of them asked General Hashemi, "How is this going to end?," Hashemi's disconcerting reply was that "it's up to His Majesty." These two CIA officers considered the Kurdish operation "the dumbest thing we'd done in our careers" and cabled their concerns to Langley, warning that "this effort is not going to rebound to the benefit of the United States, or the Kurds, or the Iranians." Their concerns, however, were ignored. Planeloads of CIA-supplied weapons continued to arrive at Tehran's Mehrabad airport and then were transported by SAVAK to Iraqi Kurdistan. By the end of March 1973, the Agency had supplied more than 1,000 tons of arms, medicines, and blankets to Barzani's Pesh Merga.[115] The CIA did its best to keep its hand in the Kurdish conflict hidden. For example, Barzani had invited his CIA liaison to travel from Tehran to his headquarters in Iraqi Kurdistan, offering to disguise the CIA officer in the uniform of an Iranian army colonel for the trip. But Langley refused to sanction any such visit. Unlike the Israelis, who maintained permanent military and intelligence liaison officers at Barzani's headquarters, the CIA refused to send any of its officers into Iraqi Kurdistan.[116]

Escalation in the Shadow of Watergate

With Nixon severely weakened by Watergate, the shah began to question the United States' long-term commitment not only to the Kurds, but also to the US-Iran partnership. He worried whether the Nixon Doctrine could endure without Nixon. The US role was the glue that held the disparate actors in the operation together. But how much longer could the shah count on American support for the Kurdish effort? If full-scale fighting between the Kurds and Iraq was renewed, could Iran depend on help from the crippled Nixon administration to balance Soviet support for Iraq, at a time when the United States was pulling its last troops out of Vietnam? On March 29, 1973, Nixon approved Kissinger's recommendation for continuing support for the Kurds at roughly $5 million per year. The Ba'th were a regime, Kissinger argued, "whose instability we should continue to promote."[117] At the same time, the Soviet Union was ratcheting up the pressure on both Iran and Iraq to settle their differences and end the stalemate in Kurdistan. Moscow had cultivated economic ties with both countries and did not want to jeopardize its relations with either if the fighting in Kurdistan flared up. During a visit to Tehran from March 14 to 16, Kosygin told the shah that the Soviet Union was urging Iraq to resolve its differences with Iran peacefully.[118] The shah would later boast to the Americans that he had taken a very hard line with Kosygin, warning him that Iran could "crush Iraq in a few hours."[119] But his actions after Kosygin's visit suggest that he was, in fact, far more circumspect in his approach to Iraq. While we can never know for certain what the shah's calculations were, it appears that he began to hedge his bets.

The shah authorized his foreign minister, Abbas-Ali Khalatbari, to travel to Geneva in April 1973 for the first of a series of meetings with the Iraqis aimed at a diplomatic solution to Iran's dispute with Iraq over the Shatt al-Arab waterway. In May, Khalatbari informed both the American and British ambassadors in Tehran that the Geneva talks, which had been brokered by Turkey, had produced neither an agreement on the Shatt nor a resumption of diplomatic relations between the two countries.[120] The Iraqis remained committed to the 1937 Tehran Treaty on the waterway, which Iran had unilaterally abrogated in 1969. Iraq refused to negotiate a new treaty that would recognize Iran's de facto control over the eastern half of the Shatt.[121] Lowrie reported from Baghdad that Iran's support for the Kurds was "probably [the] principal reason for Iraq's desire for détente."[122] Court Minister Asadollah Alam explained to Helms that the shah had decided to "play it tough for the moment" and was demanding that the Iraqis agree to the *thalweg*, or deepest channel, of the Shatt as the border.[123] The shah told British ambassador Sir Peter Ramsbotham that, in exchange for this territorial concession, the Iraqis would want him to give up his Kurdish "trump card," which he might eventually have to do, given that "Barzani would not last forever and his successors, under Iraqi and Russian pressures, would find it difficult to maintain their position."[124] The elements of a deal—Iraqi concessions in the Shatt in exchange for Iran's abandonment of the Kurds—were now on the table.

As further talks between Iran and Iraq continued in the spring of 1973, the shah prepared to make a state visit to the United States that summer.[125] Meanwhile, the US Senate's Watergate Committee had begun live tele-vised hearings in May, and new revelations of presidential wrongdoing were broadcast on an almost daily basis. While the Iran-Iraq talks were ongoing, it was vital for the shah that Nixon and Kissinger should con-tinue supporting the Kurds so as to maintain the pressure on the Ba'th. The shah feared, however, that Watergate had distracted and weakened the White House. According to the CIA, the shah told King Hussein in July 1973 that "the Watergate affair was unfortunate for everyone since it appeared to have brought the U.S. Government to a standstill. There were many problems between the U.S. and its friends which needed attention, the Shah continued, but these days they do not seem to be receiving it."[126] For the shah, it was far from clear how much longer Nixon and Kissinger would be able to support Iran's secret war in Iraqi Kurdistan.

With Nixon under siege, the Soviets intensified their pressure on Barzani to join the national front government with the Ba'th and the ICP. Two diplomats from the Soviet Embassy in Baghdad visited Barzani at his headquarters from June 2 to 5. They warned the Kurdish leader that Iran and Iraq were negotiating, implying that the shah would soon sell them out in a deal with Baghdad. Barzani had reported the visit to the Iranians and had, rather coyly, asked the shah whether he should join the national unity government in Baghdad. The shah reportedly replied, "Do so if you want to commit suicide!"[127] Despite the shah's warning, however, Barzani received an ICP delegation at his headquarters on June 19, led by First Secretary Aziz Mohammad, for discussions on joining the national front.[128] Just days later, Jim Hoagland of the *Washington Post* published an interview with Barzani in which the Kurdish leader made a public appeal for American support, despite the covert aid he was already receiving from the CIA. He offered to give American energy companies access to the oil of Kirkuk if the United States would help "protect us from the wolves."[129] Then, on July 6, Helms and Callahan met in Tehran with Barzani's son, Masoud, who headed Parastin, as well as Mahmoud Uthman, whom Helms had met in Washington the previous summer. The Kurds said that the Ba'th would attack them with "poison gas" unless they agreed to join the national front government, so they had come to Tehran to ask for heavier weapons to launch an offensive against the Iraqi army. They apologized if Barzani's interview with Hoagland had annoyed the Americans, but explained that their public appeal for US support was intended as a "cover" for the covert aid they were receiving.[130] Just as the shah was playing a double game by negotiating with Baghdad while keeping the Iraqi Kurds fighting, Barzani also was performing a delicate balancing act by keeping open the possibility of joining the national front with the Ba'th and the Communists in order to leverage more arms and money from Iran and the United States.

The complex moving pieces of the Kurdish operation came together during the shah's trip to Washington in July 1973, where he hoped to take the pulse of his American partners and secure their commitment to maintaining the stalemate between Barzani's Pesh Merga and the Iraqi army. Barzani had asked the shah, as the "father and protector" of the Kurds, to "speak on our behalf in the United States" and secure "full American understanding and backing" for a Kurdish offensive against the Iraqi army.[131] The line that the shah would take with Nixon and Kissinger in Washington was that the United States and Iran had to back the Kurds in order to prevent Iraq from becoming a "satellite country of the Soviet Union."[132] But during the shah's meetings with Nixon that summer, the president was clearly distracted by Watergate, and their discussion barely advanced beyond generalities. In their first meeting on the morning of July 24, the shah told Nixon, "You are helpful in Iraq. It is important for psychological reasons that the Kurds know that the great United States is behind them." He assured Nixon that "[w]e are preventing a coalition of the Baaths, the Kurds, and the Communists. We are preventing this." There was little resistance from Nixon, who simply replied, "Your analysis convinces me that it is indispensable that we have a policy of total cooperation.... I see the world and the part Iran plays pretty much as you do."[133] During their meeting the next morning (Figure 3.2), Kissinger noted that Nixon was "totally preoccupied" while the shah was "exuberant." The shah sympathized with his old friend's predicament, telling Nixon that the

FIGURE 3.2   In the midst of Watergate, the shah meets with Nixon and Kissinger in the Oval Office on July 25, 1973. Courtesy of the Richard M. Nixon Presidential Library.

Democrats who were attacking him for Watergate were hypocrites: "When liberals are in power, everything goes. When they are not in power, they become moralistic." Nixon agreed that there was "a clear double standard." As they departed, Nixon told the shah that their meetings were "always a pleasure" as they "thought so much alike."[134]

That evening, the shah hosted Nixon for a dinner in the president's honor at the Iranian Embassy, which very nearly ruined the whole visit. Iranian ambassador Ardeshir Zahedi had imprudently invited Katharine Graham, the socialite publisher of the *Washington Post* newspaper that had doggedly pursued the Watergate investigation.[135] Luckily, Graham had called Kissinger to ask if she should attend the dinner, and Kissinger had advised her not to come. "Zahedi isn't very bright is he?" Kissinger later asked Helms. "I don't know what the President would have done if she had been there. He might have left. That would really have ripped it."[136] This was the last time that Nixon and the shah would meet while either was still in power. The next time they would see each other would be in Cuernavaca, Mexico, in July 1979, when the disgraced former president would visit the exiled shah.

The real business of the shah's visit was not conducted in the Oval Office with the beleaguered president, but in separate meetings with Kissinger and Helms, who had come to Washington to participate in the talks. On July 23, Helms reported to Kissinger that, so far, the CIA had managed to keep the Kurdish operation under wraps. He advised Kissinger to stick with their policy of not arming the Kurds for offensive operations, but perhaps modestly increasingly their monthly payments to the Kurds. Kissinger agreed, saying that "[t]hey ought to have enough money so that they can remain a thorn in the side of the [Iraqi] government."[137] When Helms and Kissinger met with the shah the following day, the Iranian monarch pressed the Americans to give more aid to Barzani. Kissinger responded, "If you think more needs to be done, we will seriously consider it." The shah reiterated that he did not want to see an independent Kurdistan, but he reminded the Americans that "our only lever over the Iraqi Government is the Kurds." It was vital, the shah argued, to keep the Kurds from joining the national front. When Kissinger asked if this was feasible, the shah assured him that Barzani had "promised not to do anything without our okay." In exchange, Barzani had asked for "the moral support of the U.S." and the shah had told him, "we could provide that." The shah's audacity in giving a commitment to the Kurds on behalf of the United States is an indication of the extent to which Nixon and Kissinger now deferred to him on regional matters. The shah told the Americans that the Kurds were "a trump card that we do not want to let go." Helms was nervous that any major escalation in support for the Kurds might blow the operation's cover. He emphasized that the US role must stay "totally out of the public domain. Our problem is that when something like this gets into the public domain, then the pressure mounts in the Senate."[138]

The shah met again with Kissinger and Helms on July 27, at the end of his visit to Washington. He knew that the Americans were aware of his talks with Baghdad, so he played down the prospects of any deal between Iran and Iraq. The Iraqis felt "weak," the shah explained, and he knew that they were simply negotiating "to gain time." He told Kissinger that he had told Barzani "absolutely not to participate in a coalition government. I told them to stop receiving Soviet representatives or the Baath representatives from Baghdad. But if we are going to ask that of them," the shah argued, "we will have to give them some more money." Kissinger assured the shah, "you can count on it in principle."[139] Soon after the shah's departure, Saunders and Kennedy from the NSC staff met with John H. Waller, the chief of the CIA's Near East Division, to discuss what additional support the United States could provide the Kurds. Waller proposed doubling the level of US financial aid to the Kurds, but was not in favor of giving Barzani any heavy weapons for offensive military operations.[140] But after a week of deliberation, the Agency's recommendation to Kissinger was much less generous. Clearly reluctant to risk exposing the operation through any dramatic escalation, William Colby, a career intelligence officer who had replaced Schlesinger as director of the CIA, recommended maintaining the annual subsidy for the Kurds at its current level, while making a one-off additional payment and replenishing the CIA's stockpile of ordnance for the Kurds, which was running low. If this was not sufficiently responsive to the shah's demands, then the most that Colby considered advisable was a 50 percent increase in the CIA's monthly cash payments to the Kurds.[141] After consulting with Helms, Kissinger agreed to increase the cash payments for the Kurds by 50 percent.[142] The shah received news of the US decision on August 24 and decided to vastly increase Iran's support for the Kurds to nearly $30 million per year.[143]

Kissinger had relayed his decision to increase US support for the Kurds just days after a beleaguered Nixon had nominated him to replace Bill Rogers as secretary of state, while allowing him to retain his post as the president's national security advisor.[144] Now at the helm of both the NSC and the State Department, Kissinger managed to keep the Nixon-Kissinger-Pahlavi partnership on track despite the rising tide of Watergate. Helms reported that the shah was "impressed and gratified" by how quickly the White House had responded to his request. This decision was "symbolic" of Washington's continuing support for the shah, Helms told Kissinger, "and he likes this reassurance too."[145] Kissinger had once again deferred to the shah on the Kurdish operation, despite the misgivings of the CIA. He was convinced by the shah's argument that the battle in Kurdistan was not just between the KDP and the Ba'th, or between Iran and Iraq, but in fact was a Cold War struggle between the United States and the Soviet Union. Kissinger hoped that the war in Kurdistan would become a "bottomless pit" and an "open wound" for the Soviets. He also wanted Moscow's Arab clients to understand that "they cannot get a free ride by linking up with the Soviet Union.[146] Kissinger was confident that "if we could get the Soviets to suffer a misadventure in Iraq it would curb the Soviet appetite in the Middle East."[147]

Kissinger's wholesale acceptance of the shah's portrayal of a Soviet-backed Iraq brushed aside dissenting views within the State Department on the nature of the Ba'th's relationship with Moscow. As early as April 1973, Arthur Lowrie was reporting from Baghdad on Iraqi efforts to "demonstrate their independence" from the Soviet Union.[148] Iraq was not only pursuing détente with Iran, but had also reached a deal in March with the Western oil companies for compensation for the nationalization of the Iraq Petroleum Company the previous year and had expressed interest in purchasing American-manufactured Boeing aircraft for its national carrier.[149] Lowrie credibly argued that the shah's self-serving analysis that Iraq was becoming a "Soviet satellite" was in fact a "self-fulfilling prophecy." "If Iran resists Iraqi overtures for détente, continues to give military assistance to [the] Kurds, maintains [its] uncompromising position on Shatt al-Arab, and intensified [sic] anti-Iraqi propaganda," Lowrie wrote, then the "Baath regime will continue to strike out against Iran through subversion and propaganda and continue to rely on USSR for arms and protection."[150] Unaware of the covert CIA role in the Kurdish conflict, Lowrie advised Washington in July that the United States should "disassociate" itself from the Kurds and instead pursue détente with Iraq. This would serve Kurdish interests, as Barzani would be encouraged to seek a settlement with Baghdad, and it would also serve US interests, as an end to Iraq's civil war would reduce the Ba'th's dependence on the Soviets. Reading Lowrie's cables in Tehran, Helms warned the White House that Lowrie advocated these subversive views at "any and all occasions" and if the shah got whiff of them, there would be hell to pay.[151] But Lowrie was not the sole dissenting voice in the State Department. On August 23, the day before the shah was informed of the increase in the US subvention for the Kurds, INR produced a report arguing that Iraq's relationship with the USSR, "though viewed by outsiders such as Iran, Pakistan, and Saudi Arabia as a smoothly functioning partnership for radical penetration and subversion—has actually been long subject to strains and is now becoming increasingly complicated and frustrating for Moscow."[152] Fortunately for the shah, neither these dissenting views from the State Department, nor Colby's concerns about the secrecy of the CIA operation, trumped the Nixon-Kissinger-Pahlavi partnership.

Mohammad Reza Shah had managed to keep a tight grip on the Kurdish operation. Despite the March 1970 accord, he had kept Barzani from joining the Ba'th in the national front government, and he had convinced the United States to increase its assistance to the Kurds at a time when domestic imperatives militated against a bigger American commitment. Periodic clashes between the Pesh Merga and the Iraqi army increased throughout 1973, though the scale of the fighting fell short of a full-scale resumption of the war.[153] By October it was clear that neither the Kurds nor the Ba'th were interested in any kind of mutual accommodation. Barzani issued a new set of demands for what amounted to an independent Kurdish state that would include Kirkuk and its oil. The Ba'th dismissed the Kurds' demands and instead set about drafting an autonomy law for Kurdistan, as per the March 1970 agreement, with or without Barzani's cooperation.[154] Meanwhile, Egypt and Syria launched a coordinated surprise attack against Israel's positions in the Sinai and the Golan Heights on October 6, catching the Israelis off guard. Hoping to keep Iraq out of the war, the Israelis asked Barzani to launch an offensive to keep the Iraqi army tied down in Kurdistan. Barzani relayed the Israeli request to Kissinger in Washington, who in turn asked Helms to seek the shah's advice in Tehran.[155] Helms quickly consulted with Alam and cabled to Kissinger the shah's view that it was a mistake to sacrifice the Kurds on the altar of Israeli security. The shah feared that a Kurdish offensive would upset the status quo and end in disaster for Barzani. The shah made it clear that he did not want the Kurds to be seen as "proxies of Israel and America."[156] Helms concurred and told Kissinger, "We have armed [the] Kurds for defensive purposes and their forces are in no sense equipped to come out of their mountain terrain and attack on the plains. If they were to get chewed up militarily, it would deprive the Shah of his 'Kurdish card' and he does not want to see that."[157] Colby agreed with the view from Tehran and advised restraint. Kissinger was once again swayed by the shah's judgment, writing in his memoirs, "I considered it unwise to tie the Kurds too explicitly to Israel's tactical preferences and thereby bring down on the already beleaguered Kurds the wrath of other Arab states."[158] Kissinger instructed both Helms and Colby to tell Barzani, "We do not repeat not consider it advisable for you to undertake the offensive military action that the Israelis have suggested to you."[159] With Kissinger's help, the shah succeeded in keeping Barzani out of the October War.

The End of the Stalemate in Kurdistan

After the October War, Kissinger began his famed shuttle diplomacy in the Middle East to secure disengagement agreements between Israel and its Arab neighbors. During one of these trips in November 1973, he visited Iran to discuss the regional implications of the conflict with the shah, particularly the Arab oil boycott of the West that had set oil prices soaring. During Kissinger's visit to Tehran on November 9, the shah promised not to join the Arab oil embargo and agreed to intervene with both President Anwar Sadat of Egypt and King Faisal of Saudi Arabia to try to end the energy crisis.[160] While Kissinger was encouraging Egypt to move away from the Soviet camp and make peace with Israel, he was convinced that Ba'thi Iraq was taking Egypt's place as "the principal Soviet client in the Middle East" and "the driving force in the 'rejection front' seeking to block [an] Arab-Israeli peace initiative."[161] This was music to the shah's ears. He told Kissinger that to prevent Baghdad from fomenting trouble in the Middle East, Iran must "keep Iraq occupied by supporting the Kurdish rebellion within Iraq, and maintaining a large army near the frontier."[162] The two men agreed to keep the Kurdish operation going. Kissinger's visit demonstrated that, despite Watergate, the US-Iran partnership would survive under the stewardship of the shah and Kissinger. But the problem they would soon confront was that Iraq's strength was growing, and its leadership was determined to resolve the Kurdish conflict by whatever means necessary.

By the autumn of 1973, the Ba'th were firmly entrenched in Baghdad. A failed coup attempt in June by Nadhim Kazzar, the head of the Iraqi security services, gave Saddam Hussein an excuse to execute over 30 of his rivals in the regime and to reorganize the security services by placing his half-brother, Barzan al-Takriti, in charge. The following month the ICP, with the encouragement of the Soviet Union, joined the Ba'th in a "National Patriotic Front," leaving Barzani's Kurdish forces as the only significant domestic threat to the Ba'th.[163] As oil prices skyrocketed, thanks to the Arab oil embargo, so too did Iraq's revenues, giving Baghdad ample resources to confront both Iran and the Kurds.[164] Between 1972 and 1973 Iraq's oil revenue tripled from $600 million to $1.8 billion. In 1974 it would more than triple again, reaching $5.7 billion.[165] Despite the restoration of diplomatic relations between Iran and Iraq during the October War, tensions between the two countries soon resurfaced, and serious border clashes in February 1974 threatened to escalate into war. The Iraqis did not want a war with Iran, but they hoped that a show of strength would bring the shah to the negotiating table. Saddam Hussein met with the Iranian ambassador to Iraq on March 3 and 6 and reached a "gentleman's agreement" with him for a cease-fire.[166] He assured the ambassador that any Iraqi soldier in violation of the cease-fire would be "executed on the spot" and asked him to convey an invitation to the shah to come to Baghdad to negotiate a "package deal" that would resolve the dispute.[167]

While the Iraqis were signaling their willingness to make a deal, they also needed to convince the shah that the stalemate in Kurdistan was untenable. The shah had kept Barzani from joining the Ba'th in the national front, but the Iraqis had pressed on with drafting a law for limited Kurdish autonomy without him. On March 11, 1974 (the deadline set by the March 1970 accord), Iraq unilaterally promulgated an autonomy law that, according to the British ambassador in Baghdad, "went as far as any previous Iraqi government had gone to meet Kurdish demands. Indeed, it is difficult to see how much further they could have gone without setting in train a process which would have led to the break-up of Iraq."[168] But the law excluded Kirkuk and its oil from Kurdish control and allowed the central government to retain powers that would deny the Kurds any meaningful self-rule. Barzani realized that the conflict was coming to a head and he was confronted with the choice of either capitulating to Baghdad or renewing the war in Kurdistan. He visited Tehran from March 16 to 19, accompanied by Mahmoud Uthman, to consult with the shah as well as the CIA and SAVAK. Barzani tried to convince his sponsors to support a major Kurdish offensive against the Iraqi army by providing him with anti-aircraft and anti-tank weapons. He also wanted them to recognize and finance an autonomous government in northern Iraq, made up of both Arabs and Kurds, with an annual budget of between $180 million and $360 million. Barzani threatened to "seek asylum in Iran, and tell the Kurdish people to make the best deal they can with the Ba'th," unless he got the help he asked for from Iran and the United States.[169] The shah was willing to substantially increase his assistance to the Kurds, but only enough, according to Helms, "to avoid creating a situation where they would have to capitulate to Baghdad."[170] Similarly, Kissinger was unwilling to go beyond what was required to keep the Kurds on their feet, given the domestic weakness of the Nixon administration. Colby, who was facing intense Congressional scrutiny of the CIA following Watergate, opposed any increase in aid to the Kurds. Kissinger tried to steer a middle course, instructing his deputy at the White House, General Brent Scowcroft, to work with Helms to prepare a proposal for a modest increase in US assistance to the Kurds, so as to satisfy Barzani.[171]

With the arrival of the Iranian New Year, Nowruz, in March 1974, the Iraqi Kurds had few reasons to celebrate the coming of spring. The four-year truce that had been established by the March 1970 accord had expired. Barzani had rejected the autonomy law, despite the opposition of a number of KDP leaders, including his own son, Ubayd Allah, who had defected to the central government. Neither Iran nor the United States was willing to support Barzani's idea of establishing an autonomous government in the Kurdish-controlled enclave in northern Iraq. As Scowcroft wrote to Helms on March 26, establishing such a government would only provoke the Iraqis into attacking the Kurds, thereby upsetting the delicate stalemate between the Iraqi army and the Pesh Merga. "Up to now neither the Shah nor ourselves has wished to see matters resolved one way or the other," Scowcroft wrote. Acquiescing to Barzani's demands would mean escalating military support for the Kurds to a level that "would project us beyond the boundaries of a covert operation, making secrecy impossible, and would thus jeopardize other policy equities." Therefore, Scowcroft argued, only the shah could provide Barzani with the support he was asking for. The most that the United States could offer the Kurds was a "token amount" of additional aid as a "symbolic gesture of sympathy."[172]

As the winter snows melted, the CIA reported that skirmishes between Kurdish and Iraqi forces were increasing. The Iraqi army had strengthened its defensive positions in Kurdistan by withdrawing from "exposed out-lying garrisons" and Barzani was expecting a major Iraqi offensive.[173] To make matters worse, SAVAK chief Nasiri had informed Callahan on March 17 that the Turkish military was busy sealing the Turkish border with Iraq to the north of the Kurdish enclave.[174] The Israelis, who had a military and intelligence presence on the ground in Kurdistan, were worried about the Kurds. The Israeli ambassador to the United States, Simcha Dinitz, warned Kissinger on March 21 that the Kurds were in a "desperate situation" and urged him to help Barzani.[175] Neither the shah nor

Kissinger wanted to see the resumption of a full-scale war in Kurdistan, which would upset the delicate stalemate they had so far managed to maintain. They both took the position that Barzani's best strategy was to defend his mountain strongholds, rather than attacking the fortified Iraqi positions. Kissinger secured Nixon's approval on April 11 for a very modest increase in US assistance to the Kurds, which would allow the Kurds to "keep the Iraqi Government tied down and to limit its capacity for adventures abroad." It did not serve US interests, Kissinger argued, to support Barzani's plan for creating a "separatist" government. The CIA's covert support for the Kurds would remain at the levels agreed to in August 1973, but the United States would provide an additional $500,000 to $750,000 for "refugee relief" and would airlift to Iran its remaining stockpile of small arms and ammunition for the Kurds.[176] Kissinger explained to the shah that "[s]upporting a Kurdish government on a long-term basis on the scale which Barzani requests would be beyond our financial resources for this project and could not be carried out [secretly]. We do not feel an open confrontation with [the] government of Iraq would serve US and Iranian interests or the interest of long-term Kurdish survival."[177]

The shah was in complete agreement with Kissinger, but he had to deal with Barzani, who was in Tehran in April, poised to announce the creation of his autonomous government.[178] In consultation with Helms, the shah convinced Barzani not to make the announcement and to continue holding his positions in northern Iraq, by more than doubling Iran's annual assistance to the Kurds from roughly $30 million to $75 million. This was only a fraction of the figure Barzani had asked for, but despite his earlier threats to throw in the towel if Iran and the United States did not meet his demands, he seemed satisfied with this outcome. Callahan met with Barzani in Tehran and reported that the Kurdish leader was "understanding of our position" and expressed his "warm gratitude" for the additional refugee assistance from the United States. Helms was relieved that the autonomy plan had been quashed. The operation had "crossed a difficult political hurdle" and the Kurds' sponsors were now in a "positive and viable position."[179] The shah too was content that Iran's subvention for the Kurds was at "just about the right level for the present situation." He admonished the Kurds to desist with any talk of autonomy and instead "adhere to the line that they consider themselves a part of Iraq and are only defending themselves against an oppressive and illegal regime and are seeking democratic liberties for all the people of Iraq."[180]

Despite the triumphant mood in Tehran, however, the Kurds' situation in northern Iraq looked ominous. It was only a matter of time before the Iraqis launched a full-scale offensive against the Kurds. From Baghdad, Lowrie reported that on April 6 the Iraqi Ministry of Defense had called up reservists to active duty. Lowrie had also been told by the Hungarian military attaché that the Iraqis had deployed two divisions of special mountain troops, one regular infantry division, and two armored brigades to strike the Kurdish positions, supported by four air squadrons.[181] As the Ba'th pressed ahead with a blockade of Kurdish-controlled territory and clashes between the Pesh Merga and Iraqi troops escalated, Saddam Hussein publicly warned Barzani to "raise the white flag before it is too late."[182] At a regular meeting with his senior State Department staff on April 22, Kissinger was advised that a resumption of the war in Iraqi Kurdistan was not "necessarily a bad thing," as it would distract the Ba'th from making mischief elsewhere, so "we can sit back and be fairly relaxed about it." But the secretary of state was far from relaxed. He had kept the State Department in the dark about US support for Barzani, so when the discussion steered toward international support for the Kurds, Kissinger joked, "I don't even know where the place is" and quickly changed the subject to a discussion of a fishing dispute with Ecuador.[183] As the war heated up, he was determined to keep the US role hidden, even from his own officials. The running joke in the State Department was that Kissinger treated the US Foreign Service like mushrooms: "he kept them in the dark, piled manure on them, and in the end, they got canned."[184] In Tehran, the shah assured Helms that despite the Iraqi offensive, he remained committed to the Kurdish operation and would not give up his "Kurdish card" so easily.[185]

As tensions escalated, the United Nations was drawn into efforts to prevent the Kurdish conflict from escalating into a full-blown Iran-Iraq war. Iraq had lodged a complaint against Iran at the UN Security Council back in February, and in March UN secretary-general Kurt Waldheim had appointed a Mexican diplomat, Luis Weckmann-Muñoz, as his special representative to investigate the situation along the Iran-Iraq border.[186] After some shuttle diplomacy between Tehran and Baghdad in April, Weckmann-Muñoz reported privately to Waldheim that he had secured a commitment from both Iran and Iraq to restart diplomatic talks. He told the secretary-general that the central sticking point was the question of the Shatt al-Arab. The Iraqis refused to accept Iran's abrogation of the 1937 Tehran Treaty because, as Saddam Hussein had explained to the UN envoy, the Ba'th Party had taken power "through revolution and not through the democratic process" and therefore any concession on the Shatt would erode their fragile legitimacy at home and would be interpreted as a "sign of weakness" abroad.[187] The shah had also been hawkish, telling the UN envoy that Iran could "easily destroy" Iraq, which was an "artificial" state and "a mere creation of [Winston] Churchill."[188] Nonetheless, Weckmann-Muñoz reported, the Iraqis were eager to strike a deal with Iran on the Shatt as part of a "package deal."[189] This deal, the UN envoy explained, "will, almost inexorably, be at the expense of the Kurds of Iraq."[190] Waldheim presented Weckmann-Muñoz's formal report to the UN Security Council on May 20.[191] A week later, on May 28, the Council adopted Resolution 248, which incongruously "welcomed the determination on the part of Iran and Iraq to de-escalate the prevailing situation," at the same time that the Iraqis were preparing their offensive against the Kurds, and the shah was escalating his support for Barzani.[192] In Tehran, the British ambassador asked the shah if the Security Council resolution meant that Iran was seeking a *quid pro quo* with Iraq, whereby the shah would drop his support for Barzani in exchange for Iraqi concessions in the Shatt. The shah "replied unhesitatingly that he could not let down the Kurds." But the British were convinced that the shah would "abandon them [the Kurds] to their fate if he calculated that there was a chance of a genuine accommodation with the government in Baghdad."[193]

As the shah pondered a deal with Iraq, Kissinger continued with his shuttle diplomacy in the Middle East. During his frequent visits to Jerusalem, his Israeli hosts pressed him to do something to reverse the tide of the Kurdish war. On May 7, 1974, Prime Minister Golda Meir handed Kissinger a report on the situation in Kurdistan, warning him that the Kurds were in "trouble" and asking the Americans to help provide Barzani with anti-aircraft and anti-tank weapons to defend themselves against the coming Iraqi offensive. The CIA station in Tehran continued to receive similar requests from the Kurds, but the Americans remained determined not to risk exposing their hand in the Kurdish operation by escalating their support for the Pesh Merga beyond the level that had been agreed in April.[194] In June, Nixon authorized a continuation of US support for the Kurds totaling $8.06 million per year.[195] The shah, too, maintained his support at roughly $75 million per year, but he worried that with hundreds of thousands of Kurdish refugees pouring into Iran, he would have a humanitarian disaster on his hands when winter arrived.[196] The pressure on the shah to reach a deal with Iraq was mounting. Despite the massive injection of additional Iranian arms and money, the Kurds' position in northern Iraq looked vulnerable. To compound the shah's worries, the US House of Representative's Judiciary Committee passed the first of three articles of impeachment against Nixon on July 27, charging the president with obstruction of justice. Four days earlier, Helms had sent a telegram to Washington warning that Watergate had made the shah "somewhat restive and in a bit of quandary" about his relations with the United States.[197] The shah had confided to Alam on July 14 that Nixon's downfall was a conspiracy orchestrated by powerful business interests and the CIA. The same people who had assassinated President Kennedy, he believed, were now after Nixon for some unknown reason. In any event, the shah hoped this was the case, because if Nixon's fate was a mere twist of fortune, then it boded ill for the future of the free world.[198] Three trends now converged to push the shah toward a settlement with Iraq: the weakening of the United States because of Watergate; a vigorous diplomatic effort by Iraq; and the launch of the Iraqi offensive against the Kurds.

Five years after having seized power in Baghdad, the Ba'th were making progress in the summer of 1974 toward rehabilitating Iraq's international position. They had normalized relations with Western Europe, and there were signs of a thaw in their relations with the United States.[199] Baghdad was also continuing its efforts to draw Iran to the negotiating table by asking Egyptian president Anwar Sadat, with whom the shah enjoyed a warm friendship, to communicate an offer of diplomatic talks to Tehran. Sadat had told the shah that Iraq genuinely wanted to distance itself from the Soviet Union and end its isolation in the Arab world. But the shah was still unconvinced that the Ba'th had really turned over a new leaf. In late July, after talks with both Barzani and King Hussein of Jordan, the shah told the Americans that Iraq's diplomatic initiative was a "tactical move to divert attention from Iraq's serious internal problems."[200] But there was an increasing "divergence" of views between the shah and some in the State Department, who regarded the Iraqi approach to Iran as a credible element of Iraq's larger move to distance itself from Moscow.[201]

Despite his suspicions, the shah was in no position to dismiss the Iraqi offer. He suffered a major blow on August 9, when Nixon resigned the presidency of the United States. That same month, the Iraqis launched their long-awaited seventh offensive against the Kurds. From Tabriz, US Consul Robert E. Neumann reported that eight regular Iraqi divisions and several independent battalions were trying to punch through the Kurdish defenses and seal the Iranian border. The Iraqi air force, armed with

Soviet MIGs and Tu-22 bombers, provided air cover for the Iraqi armored columns, armed with Soviet T-55 tanks, as they slowly pushed the Kurds deeper and deeper into their mountain strongholds. The Kurds claimed that they could hear Soviet advisors on the radio, directing the Iraqi forces, and that Soviet pilots were flying the Iraqi Tu-22s. Rather than trying to hold on to his positions at all costs, Barzani's strategy was to fight a delaying action. The Kurds calculated that if they could "bleed [the] Iraqis at [a] minimum rate of 30 killed per day" then they would "eventually undermine [Iraq's] will to fight and bring about [the] fall of [the] Baghdad government."[202] The Iraqis were well aware that on the other side of the border, the Iranians had amassed three armored divisions, two infantry divisions, and two infantry brigades. They feared that Iran might attack Iraq in order to prevent a Kurdish defeat.[203] As the war in Kurdistan escalated dangerously, the shah decided to test Iraq's willingness to make a deal and avert a full-blown Iran-Iraq war. He authorized low-level preliminary diplomatic talks with the Iraqis in Istanbul from August 12 to September 1.[204] Meanwhile, the Israelis provided Kissinger with a report on August 23, bearing the grim news that "[t]he present Iraqi offensive is liable to become a turning point in favor of the Iraqis in this war." The Israelis warned that the Iraqi army might be able to capture Barzani's headquarters and reach the Iranian border, cutting off the supply lines from Iran.[205] The next day, Mordechai Shalev, a diplomat at the Israeli Embassy in Washington, read to Scowcroft a cable from Jerusalem that described the Kurds' military position as "critical." The Kurds had no long-range artillery or anti-tank weapons with which to stop the Iraqi advance and "they may collapse and be destroyed as a political entity."[206] The Israelis proposed that they could provide Soviet anti-tank missiles to the Kurds, if the United States would then resupply Israel with American-made missiles.[207] The Americans had, in fact, already agreed to reallocate some of the money budgeted for providing the Kurds with AK-47 rifles to procuring heavier anti-tank weapons for the Pesh Merga. But delivering large anti-aircraft weapons to the Kurds' positions in northern Iraq would be both prohibitively expensive and logistically difficult.[208]

The shah desperately wanted to prevent a Kurdish collapse, which would destroy whatever leverage he had over Baghdad. Iranian troops, dressed in Kurdish mufti, had been conducting covert missions across the border into Iraq since July. However, on August 23, Iran stepped up its support for the Kurds by sending 120-mm mortar platoons on 48-hour missions across the border. Furthermore, a battalion of Iran's long-range

175-mm artillery began hitting Iraqi positions from across the border.[209] The Israelis were also stepping up their delivery of arms. General Nasiri informed Helms on August 25 that Iran was shortly expecting delivery of 300 tons of ordnance from Israel for the Kurds.[210] The following day, Kissinger took the Israeli resupply proposal to Nixon's successor, President Gerald Ford, for his approval. Ford had known nothing of the Kurdish operation when he was vice president, so Kissinger brought him up to speed, warning him that if these anti-tank weapons did not reach the Pesh Merga, "the Kurds will collapse." The shah was going to send Iranian troops into Iraq to reinforce the Kurds, which Kissinger supported, but he told Ford, "I hate to be on record because of all the leaks." The president authorized the military resupply arrangement that the Israelis had proposed and asked Kissinger if the Kurds would prevail. Kissinger replied, "Yes. It is their existence at stake."[211] But by the end of the summer, the Iraqis held more Kurdish territory than at any time since 1961. The CIA's assessment was that Iraq was willing to sustain "heavy casualties" in order to "end the Kurds' organized military resistance" before the winter of 1974–1975.[212] The question now was whether the Kurds could hold on during the autumn until the annual lull in the fighting that the cold Kurdish winter would impose.

With President Ford's approval, the Israelis agreed in September to provide the Kurds with 82 "Strela" shoulder-fired anti-aircraft missiles and 507 "Sagger" portable guided anti-tank missiles, both of Soviet manufacture, in exchange for which the United States would resupply Israel with American-made "Redeye" anti-aircraft missiles and TOW (tube-launched, optically-tracked, wire-guided) anti-tank missiles.[213] These weapons would help the Kurds to slow the Iraqi advance and allow them to survive until winter. With the pressure easing on the battlefield, the shah was in no hurry to make a deal with the Iraqis. He continued to see the Ba'th as a "bunch of thugs and murderers implacably hostile to him" and Iraq's attempts at détente as nothing more than "tactical moves to ease internal and external pressures."[214] The Iraqis were also deeply suspicious of Iranian intentions. Iraqi foreign minister Shathel Taqa warned Lowrie on August 26 that "if [the] Shah or anyone else has [any] idea of [a] new Bangladesh in Iraq he is very mistaken."[215] There were those in the State Department, like Lowrie, who were eager to improve relations with Iraq so that American companies could benefit from Iraq's oil bonanza, but the secretary of state stuck to the shah's hard line.[216] Kissinger advised Ford in early September that "Iraq has recently hinted to other countries that it would like to end its isolation and its dependence on the Soviet Union; the Shah and Ambassador Helms feel the pressure should be kept on Iraq, to bring a more responsible government into power."[217] Helms had warned Kissinger to keep an eye on his staff at Foggy Bottom: "In our own government there appears to be confusion as to where our own interests lie up to a significant level in the Department of State."[218]

The steps that Iran, Israel, and the United States had taken to strengthen the Kurds slowed the Iraqi advance, and by October it looked as if Barzani's forces would survive until the annual winter lull in the fighting.[219] Nonetheless, the Kurds' situation was extremely precarious. According to reports that the British Embassy in Baghdad was receiving, the morale of the Iraqi army was high and, unlike previous Iraqi offensives, there was no sign that the Iraqis would be withdrawing from the Kurdish mountains for the winter. Instead, they were fortifying their positions and stockpiling supplies, in order to finish off the Kurds in the spring.[220] Barzani traveled to Tehran in late October and again pleaded with the shah for more help.[221] He also gave the CIA station in Tehran a letter for Kissinger, saying that the Kurds had suffered 1,200 casualties and were estimating Iraqi casualties at 6,000. Barzani wrote that his headquarters were coming under direct fire from Iraq's long-range artillery and he was in desperate need of arms and ammunition for his Pesh Merga, as well as food for the hundreds of thousands of displaced Kurds who sought his protection from the advancing Iraqi forces.[222] The shah responded to Barzani's appeal by ordering a unit of Soviet-made 130-mm Iranian artillery to cross into Iraq to defend Barzani's headquarters in the Hajj Umran–Rawanduz area, just across the border from the Iranian city of Piran Shahr. By November, another artillery unit, armed with American-made 155-mm and 8-inch guns followed. To protect the Iranian artillery from Iraqi air raids, 23-mm and 35-mm air defense batteries, as well as two units of British-made "Rapier" surface-to-air missiles, were also deployed by the Iranians across the border.[223] The Iranian 23-mm anti-aircraft guns shot down an Iraqi fighter-bomber on November 12, and a month later Iran's Rapier missiles shot down another two Iraqi jets.[224] As Alam confided to British ambassador Anthony Parsons, Iran could use its superior military strength to reverse the Iraqi advance, but this was extremely risky, as it would trigger an all-out war with Iraq that would also draw in the Soviet Union. Furthermore, the Iranians were hosting more than 100,000 Kurdish refugees from Iraq and with the winter fast approaching, something would have to be done to allow these Kurds to return to their homes across the border. Parsons predicted that the shah could not stomach either a Kurdish defeat or a Kurdish victory so, before the fighting erupted again in the spring, he was likely to reach a settlement with Iraq.[225]

As the Iraqis signaled their willingness to negotiate a deal with Iran, the policies of the Kurds' sponsors slowly began to diverge. The shah was concerned that Iran's covert war in Kurdistan was escalating into an overt war with Iraq. INR concluded in November that "Iran's support for the Kurdish rebellion in Iraq has recently reached a level comparable to that of Indian involvement with the Bengalee [sic] rebels in East Pakistan just prior to the 1971 war."[226] The shah's only choice was to use the winter lull in the fighting to secure a deal with Iraq, while the Kurds were still on their feet. As Iran continued talks with Iraq, Kissinger and the Israelis pressed ahead with the supply of sophisticated anti-tank and anti-aircraft weapons to the Kurds. In Jerusalem on October 13, Kissinger told Israeli prime minister Yitzak Rabin that there had been some "improvement" in the position of the Kurds. When he returned to Washington, the Israelis provided him with a list of $24 million worth of weapons that they wanted to supply to the Kurds, for which they asked to be reimbursed by the United States.[227] Ambassador Dinitz gave Kissinger the list on October 19, but Kissinger insisted on consulting with the shah before agreeing.[228] Kissinger flew to the region and met with the shah in Tehran on the evening of November 1, 1974 at Saadabad Palace. Their five hours of talks were dominated by the continuing energy crisis, but the shah did raise the Kurdish issue. In an ominous statement, the shah told Kissinger that "even if the Iraqis succeeded in destroying the Kurds, they will still be nailed down on the Iranian border where they would in any event prefer to be as against facing the Israelis on the Syrian front."[229] The shah's faith in the Kurds' fighting ability was clearly wavering, but he nonetheless approved the Israeli re-supply proposal, as it would buy him more time to negotiate with Iraq.

After speaking with the shah in Tehran, Kissinger met again with Rabin in Jerusalem on November 7, where the Israelis informed him that the Kurds had successfully used the Sagger missiles to destroy a number of Iraqi tanks. Kissinger assured the Israelis that both he and the shah continued to support the Kurdish operation. When Rabin complained that "the Kurds are very disappointed about the US attitude," Kissinger told him that because of Watergate there was little more that he could do.[230] Just getting the CIA and the Pentagon to agree to the secret arms resupply that the Israelis wanted had been a "bureaucratic nightmare," Kissinger later recalled. Colby, for example, had opposed any augmentation of the Kurdish operation and had suggested that the shah should pick up the bill.[231] By November, however, Kissinger had secured authorization to resupply the Israelis.[232]

While Kissinger and the Israelis were busy arming the Kurds with more sophisticated weapons, the shah continued to explore the idea of a deal with Iraq. He had authorized Khalatbari to meet with Taqa on the sidelines of the UN General Assembly in New York in October, but the Iranian foreign minister described their two meetings as "tough and certainly not smooth."[233] In Tehran, Alam told Helms that the shah was very eager to resolve the Shatt dispute with Iraq, which he described as the "basic ingredient of any Iranian-Iraqi settlement." Alam explained that the shah saw the 1937 Tehran Treaty, signed by his father, as a British "colonialist" diktat. The shah wanted to improve his dynasty's image by revising this historical injustice and moving the border to the *thalweg* of the Shatt.[234] King Hussein had been working throughout 1974 to mediate between the shah and Saddam Hussein, but the shah remained skeptical that the Iraqis were serious about an agreement.[235] The Egyptians had relayed a message from Hussein to the shah in mid-November, warning that Iraq would conduct air strikes inside Iran unless the Iranians ceased their artillery attacks.[236] That same month, Iraqi information minister Tariq Aziz traveled to Amman with a message containing Iraq's terms for a deal with Iran, but the offer failed to satisfy the shah.[237] After a visit by the shah to Amman in January 1975, Jordanian prime minister Zaid al-Rifai concluded that the issue was not simply the Shatt. The shah also worried about the political vacuum that would be created in Kurdistan if Barzani were defeated. Would the Iraqi Communists, now allied with the Ba'th and backed by the Soviet Union, take over the region? Rifai relayed to Washington the shah's comment that the "Iraqis should be pleased to have Barzani in the north rather than [a] Kurdish Communist Party."[238]

As the bitter winter cold enveloped the Zagros Mountains between Iran and Iraq, the Kurds were under a constant barrage of air and artillery fire from the Iraqis. Their only lifeline remained the Iranian border.[239] According to reports reaching the US Consulate in Tabriz, roughly 40,000 Kurdish Pesh Merga were holding out against 200,000 Iraqi troops, thanks to the Iranian artillery units along the border that were firing up to 300 rounds per day at the Iraqi positions.[240] With the Kurds facing an Iraqi onslaught in the spring, the shah began to make contingency plans for the Iranian forces deployed inside Iraq. In December, he instructed Alam to liaise with SAVAK and Iran's top military brass to develop a plan to prevent Iran's artillery pieces from falling into Iraqi hands if the Kurdish positions were overwhelmed.[241] Helms, who had been involved in the Kurdish operation from its inception, tried to put a brave face on the situation. He advised Kissinger that "[i]t is not necessary for the Kurds to take Baghdad 'to win.' If they succeed in bringing down the Baathist government or, at a minimum, in forcing it to come to acceptable terms with them, then the Kurds will have 'won.' "[242] But these goals were now completely unrealistic for a Kurdish movement that might not survive beyond March. Ambassador Parsons provided the Foreign Office with a far more realistic assessment from Tehran: "I have a feeling that we are all—including the Shah—becoming uneasily aware that certain assumptions which we have hitherto been inclined to make about the Kurdish problem may no longer be entirely valid; and that a reassessment may be required which, on the Iranian side at least, could be painful." The Kurds would not survive without "the direct commitment of major Iranian fighting formations," which would mean war between Iran and Iraq. This was a path that the shah was unwilling to go down. Instead, Parsons predicted that the shah would help the Kurds to survive the winter, while looking for a deal with Iraq that would "enable him to avoid plunging deeper into the Kurdish morass when the campaigning season re-opens."[243] The Israelis had come to the same conclusion as Parsons. On January 16, 1975, Israeli foreign minister Yigal Allon told Kissinger that "we're losing the winter" and warned him that "[t]o abandon the Kurds is a crime."[244]

The very next day Khalatbari began three days of talks with his Iraqi counterpart, Foreign Minister Sa'dun Hammadi, in Istanbul. The US Embassy in Ankara reported to Kissinger the basic demands of both parties: the Iraqis wanted Iran to end its support for the Kurds, while the Iranians wanted Iraq to concede on the Shatt.[245] The two foreign ministers agreed that the shah and Saddam Hussein would meet on the sidelines of the Organization of the Petroleum Exporting Countries (OPEC) meeting in Algiers in March for talks that would be hosted by Algerian president Houari Boumediène.[246] Iran had managed to prevent a Kurdish collapse in 1974, but the Iranians were convinced that a Kurdish defeat in 1975 was now inevitable. Both the chief of SAVAK, Nasiri, and the chief of Iranian military intelligence, General Naser Moqaddam, told Parsons that the Kurds could no longer resist the Iraqi army without drawing Iran into a war with Iraq.[247] Iran, not the United States, was bearing the biggest financial and military burden in the Kurdish operation, so the Kurds' fate rested in the shah's hands. The Americans, who had been drawn into the Kurdish war by the shah, could do little more than wait for his decision. As

Kissinger explained in his memoirs, the United States could neither cut off support to the Kurds, which would have led to a precipitous Kurdish collapse, nor could it escalate its role "in a war so logistically difficult, so remote, and so incomprehensible to the American public."[248] In late January, Kissinger received a letter from Barzani asking for more Sagger anti-tank missiles, with which the Kurds could "change the total impact of our military operations." Barzani also asked to come to the United States to discuss the situation directly with Kissinger.[249] Colby advised against allowing Barzani to visit Washington, given that his presence would expose the US role in the operation, and that the United States was in no position to meet his demands for increased aid.[250] Kissinger did not reply to Barzani's letter. Instead, he traveled to Switzerland to meet with the shah, who was on his annual skiing vacation.

During their four hours of discussions in Zurich on February 19, the shah told Kissinger that the Kurds "have no guts left" and that he was planning to meet with Saddam Hussein in Algiers. The shah was clearly worried that Barzani would capitulate and join the national front with the Ba'th and the ICP. He told Kissinger that "he cannot accept an autonomous Kurdish state which would be under the dominance of a Communist Iraqi central government." Kissinger reported to Ford that the shah was "tempted to try to move in the direction of some understanding with Iraq regarding the Kurds, but is understandably skeptical that much is possible. In the meantime, he intends to continue his support for the Kurds."[251] In his memoirs, Kissinger writes that he vigorously argued against abandoning the Kurds. He told the shah that any agreement with Saddam Hussein was "worthless" and that Barzani's defeat would "destabilize the entire area." He also worried that the Soviets would "view Iran's retreat as symptomatic of the growing weakness of the West," thereby encouraging their "adventurism." The shah shared Kissinger's mistrust of Hussein, but he had reluctantly come to the conclusion that it was impossible to continue supporting Barzani without sparking an Iran-Iraq war. His country's interests were best served by securing a deal with Iraq before the Pesh Merga were defeated. Returning to Washington, Kissinger finally replied to Barzani's letter from January, asking for a face-to-face meeting in Washington. He had little choice but to tell Barzani not to come, but to send an emissary instead. Kissinger also warned the Israelis that the shah was considering abandoning the Kurds, telling Ambassador Dinitz on February 22 that, "[the shah is] afraid the Kurds have had it. He may begin a negotiation with the Iraqis if they meet at OPEC, in exchange for a veto over whom they put in if Barzani gets driven out. I warned him strongly against it."[252]

The Algiers Agreement

Despite Kissinger's warnings, the shah went ahead with his meeting with Saddam Hussein in Algiers and on March 5 signed a communiqué announcing that Iran and Iraq had agreed to demarcate their land borders; to set the *thalweg* as their border in the Shatt; and to "maintain strict and effective control over their joint borders in order to put a final end to all acts of subversion wherever they may come from."[253] The basic elements of the agreement were already on the table before the Algiers meeting, but the shah had waited to meet Hussein face-to-face to judge if he was really willing to concede on the Shatt. In exchange for cutting off Iran's assistance to the Kurds, the shah had secured Iraq's recognition of Iranian sovereignty over the eastern half of the Shatt, an elusive goal of Iranian diplomacy throughout his reign. The shah had not consulted with any of his civilian or military advisors, not even Alam, before making this deal in Algiers.[254] Had he done so, Alam might have warned him that he would go down in history as having used and betrayed the Kurds. But the shah was oblivious to such concerns. Returning to Tehran, he told Alam that the negotiations had been so intense that he had not slept for more than two hours a night in Algiers and had lost weight during the trip. He was proud of his achievement and was glad to have finally rid himself of the 1937 Tehran Treaty that his father had signed under pressure from the British. When Alam asked him what would happen to the Kurds, the shah replied, "nothing." He explained that "[t]hese people who have been defeated so many times, they know very well that they cannot survive ten days without our support in the face of the Iraqi offensive; what can they say now?" The shah recalled that in his four and a half hours of talks with Saddam Hussein, the Iraqi leader had told him that on several occasions Iran's troops and artillery were all that stood between the Iraqi army and victory. Hussein had told the shah, "your unsparing sword cut down the flower of Iraqi youth." Alam did not share the shah's triumphalism. He worried that international opinion would blame his boss for whatever atrocities the Iraqis committed against the Kurds. He reminded the shah that he had told Barzani to reject a settlement with Baghdad just a year earlier. The shah replied, "both the Kurds and the Iraqis knew that it was all an act and that the Iraqis had every intention of taking over Kurdistan." The next day Alam reported to the shah that the Western newspapers were accusing Iran of selling out the Kurds. The shah replied, "We couldn't station our troops there indefinitely and keep fighting forever." But when Alam saw the shah the next morning, he found him in poor spirits and deep in thought. He suspected that the accusations of betrayal weighed heavily on the shah's mind.[255]

As the ink on the Algiers communiqué was still drying, General Nasiri was dispatched to inform Barzani that the Iran-Iraq border would be sealed in a few weeks' time. Barzani and his Pesh Merga could either surrender to the Iraqis or go into exile in Iran, where they would be given safe haven if they agreed to disarm.[256] According to David Kimche, then a senior Mossad official, the Israelis stationed in Kurdistan watched with dismay as the Iranian artillery units that were holding the Iraqis at bay withdrew across the border.[257] Kimche claims that the Israeli government had no warning of the Algiers agreement, but this seems unlikely given Kissinger's conversation with Dinitz on February 22. However, it appears that this information never filtered down to the Israelis on the ground in Kurdistan. Eliezer Tsafrir, the Mossad liaison with Barzani, had to quickly flee across the border into Iran to avoid being captured by the Iraqis. He later recalled, "I was cursing Iran all the way to Tehran. I was terribly disappointed."[258] The shah had to explain to his partners in the Kurdish operation why he had made the decision to abandon the Kurds without consulting them. He took the line that he saw Iraq's willingness to negotiate on the Shatt as a historic opportunity to both resolve the border dispute and to draw Iraq away from the Soviet Union. He told Parsons that he had been "astonished" by Hussein's willingness to make concessions on the Shatt, particularly at a time when the Kurds were "ready to admit defeat."[259]

Through Helms, the shah conveyed a message to Kissinger outlining the background to his decision. On March 2, the shah explained, he had received an Egyptian envoy, Ashraf Marwan, who had just come from Baghdad with a message from Saddam Hussein saying that Iraq would move away from the Soviet camp if Iran ended the war in Kurdistan. When he met with Hussein in Algiers, he struck a deal with the Iraqi strongman, who promised that Iraq would observe a cease-fire until March 31 to give Barzani and his troops enough time to surrender or go into exile in Iran. SAVAK and the Iraqi security services would then cooperate to ensure that Kurdish Communists did not fill the vacuum left by Barzani in Kurdistan. "How it will work out," the shah conceded, "I obviously do not know. But

I feel that I had to take a chance since otherwise the Kurdish cause would be hopeless in the relatively near future and I might be accused of having destroyed a chance for getting the Iraqis out of the Soviet orbit."[260] The shah sought to justify his actions to his American partners in Cold War terms, arguing that it was his intention to draw Iraq away from the Soviet camp. In reality, the shah had little choice but to make a deal with Hussein over the Shatt in 1975. Undoubtedly, he would have preferred to continue with the Kurdish operation, but the stalemate between the Pesh Merga and the Iraqi army had collapsed in 1974, so when the shah was presented with a major concession by the Iraqis on the Shatt, he took it. Helms, for one, saw the agreement as a *fait accompli* and advised Washington to send the shah a congratulatory message.[261]

News of the Algiers agreement reached Kissinger while he was preparing for one of his regular shuttle diplomacy trips to the Middle East. He would later recall that he was "stunned" by the news, but it is difficult to understand why it came as such a shock to him. Just a month earlier he had described the shah to President Ford as a "cold-blooded realist," and the shah himself had floated the idea of an Algiers agreement with Saddam Hussein during their meeting in Zurich.[262] Kissinger had been kept informed of the ongoing Iran-Iraq talks by the State Department since 1973, and almost every observer of these discussions had concluded that a *quid pro quo* on the Shatt and the Kurds was likely.[263] Yet Kissinger maintains that "[t]he Shah had not mentioned that a deal was imminent or that he would acquiesce in total Iraqi control of the Kurdish era." The most likely explanation for this lapse in Kissinger's judgment was that the secretary of state simply had too many domestic and international fires to extinguish to pay much attention to Kurdish affairs, so he placed his faith in the shah. In his memoirs, Kissinger writes, "Only outsiders are in a position to reflect on events freed of the constraints of time.... There was very little time available for any systematic review of the options in faraway Kurdish areas."[264] The evidence suggests that the Algiers communiqué did indeed come as a surprise to Kissinger, who hurriedly cabled Scowcroft on March 9 to cancel arrangements for a scheduled visit by Kurdish emissaries to Washington later that month.[265] Scowcroft later recalled that Kissinger's reaction to the news of the Algiers agreement was "much less emotional than mine was." His boss had quickly resigned himself to the reality that "this is power politics and our stake in the region is the shah, so we can't afford to be undercutting him."[266]

Kissinger was scheduled to fly to Israel on March 9 from Damascus, where he had met with Syrian president Hafez al-Assad. On the way to the airport, Syrian foreign minister Abd al-Halim Khaddam told him that the end of the war in Kurdistan was good news for the Arabs: "solving that problem has left a lot of satisfaction with us."[267] With the diminished Iranian threat, the Iraqi army could turn its attention to Israel. Arriving in Jerusalem, Kissinger got an earful from Rabin, who complained that the shah had "sold out the Kurds" and, by extension, Israel. Kissinger replied, "I warned the Shah against it and he did it anyway." Rabin worried that the Algiers Agreement reflected "a whole different outlook" by the shah toward the Middle East, as Iran moved closer to the Arabs and distanced itself from Israel.[268] These Israeli concerns were well founded, given that Iran had extended nearly $1 billion in loans and aid to Egypt in 1974. "As Iran's ties with the Arabs deepen," the CIA had concluded in a January 1975 assessment, "its Israeli connections will probably become an increasing liability."[269] Kissinger sympathized with the Israelis' anger, telling Rabin, "I was shaken too by the Iranian decision. Because we had participated in it too. The brutality of it." He told Rabin that he had warned the shah, "it was a bad idea—particularly the idea that he believed the assurances that no Communist would be put in [Kurdistan]."[270]

Barzani sent a message to Kissinger on March 10, pleading with the secretary of state to help the Kurds: "our hearts bleed to see that an immediate by-product of this agreement is the destruction of our defenseless people in an unprecedented manner.... Our movement and people are being destroyed in an unbelievable way with silence from everyone."[271] Droves of Pesh Merga and their families were trying to flee Iraq to safety in Iran before the border was sealed on March 31, swelling the numbers of Kurdish refugees already there.[272] Kissinger was angry at the shah's "deceptive methods" and considered Iran's actions "brutal and indefensible." But ever the political realist, he accepted that "in terms of a cold-blooded assessment of Iran's security, the Shah's decision was as understandable as it was painful." The shah had left Kissinger with little choice but to acquiesce to the abandonment of the Kurds. Colby explained to Kissinger that without Iranian participation, the CIA had neither the resources nor the logistical capability to carry on the Kurdish operation. The CIA planned to make one last monthly payment to Barzani, in the hope of preventing "undesirable indiscretions" by the angry Kurds.[273] Kissinger was keenly aware that at a time when Congress was cutting off assistance to beleaguered

US allies in Indochina, the American public was hardly likely to support a massive increase in US assistance for a guerrilla war in Kurdistan. He ignored Barzani's desperate appeals because, as he would later explain, "there was nothing I could say." Crucially, at no point did Kissinger consider threatening Iran with any curb on arms sales to pressure the shah to resume supplies to the Kurds: "Our commitment to the defense of Iran had not been a favor to be withdrawn when we were displeased but an expression of our own geopolitical interest."[274] Instead, he meekly sent a message to the shah, saying, "This is obviously a matter for Your Majesty to decide in the best interests of your nation. Our policy remains as always to support Iran as a close and staunch friend of the United States."[275]

Barzani refused to give up the fight and sought an audience with the shah, who, according to Alam, was not eager to receive him. Alam sensed that the shah was embarrassed to speak to Barzani, even though he felt that "in truth we were the ones doing the fighting." The shah finally received Barzani on the afternoon of March 11, 1975, exactly five years after the Kurdish leader had defied the shah by signing a peace accord with Saddam Hussein in March 1970. The shah told Barzani in no uncertain terms that the Algiers agreement was vital to Iran, but promised to give him and his Pesh Merga sanctuary in Iran.[276] As Barzani returned to Kurdistan, both Helms and Callahan feared that the angry Kurds might reveal the CIA's covert role in the Kurdish war.[277] Helms warned Kissinger that something must be done to placate the "distressed and disconsolate" Barzani if Kissinger wanted to avoid a "batch of unpleasant publicity."[278] But all that the secretary of state could offer Barzani, in a message that was relayed through a Kurdish representative in Tehran on March 17, was his "great admiration" and "prayers" for the Kurds and a promise to intervene with the Iranians. Kissinger instructed Helms to "find a tactful way" to make the shah understand how embarrassing it would be "if there is a massacre and Barzani charges that he has been let down."[279] The next day, the shah received Callahan and agreed that the CIA and SAVAK would pay out the Kurds' monthly subvention for March.[280] The fighting in Kurdistan continued as some Pesh Merga refused to surrender, while Barzani remained near the Iranian border, paralyzed by indecision in his moment of defeat.[281] Finally, on March 21, he ordered an end to all Kurdish resistance and on the night of March 27–28 he and his entourage crossed into exile in Iran. As the cease-fire expired on April 1, the Iraqi army pushed forward into the heart of Kurdish territory, meeting very little resistance, and reached the Iranian border for the first time since 1961. The Iraqis granted amnesty to all Kurds, except those closely associated with Barzani. Some 70,000 Kurdish refugees returned to Iraq by May, but almost 100,000 remained in Iran. The displaced Kurds were resettled in southern Iraq, as the Ba'th sought to "Arabize" the north and establish a *cordon sanitaire* along their border with Iran and Turkey.[282] For Barzani, this was a repeat of the events of December 1946, following the fall of Mahabad. Nearly three decades later, he once again found himself defeated and in exile.

Kissinger and the Kurdish Fallout

While the dust was still settling on the battlefields of Kurdistan, the foreign ministers of Iran and Iraq met in Tehran on March 15, 1975, to begin negotiations on a treaty that would codify the Algiers communiqué. The détente between the two countries proceeded, with official visits by Hoveyda to Iraq in March and by Hussein to Iran in April.[283] Finally, on June 13, the Baghdad Treaty was signed, dividing the Shatt al-Arab between Iran and Iraq along the *thalweg*. As thousands of Kurdish refugees returned to Iraq from Iran to face an uncertain future, Barzani remained in exile in Iran. The shah was assailed in the American press for leaving the Kurds to be "obscurely hanged," as C. L. Sulzberger wrote in the *New York Times*.[284] The opinion page of the *Washington Post* concluded that, after the Algiers agreement, "[j]ust about everyone comes out ahead except the Kurds, who are mourning their ravaged hopes and their dead."[285] The shah tried to explain his actions to the American public by drawing an analogy with the US decision to withdraw its support for South Vietnam. He told Joseph Kraft, a sympathetic columnist, that the Kurds "were making no progress in the war. They were running, not as fast as the South Vietnamese but nearly as fast. We Iranians would have to do the fighting. I decided I didn't want a war with Iraq at time when the Near East was a powder keg and the Russians supported Iraq and the United States suffered from a Watergate complex."[286]

Despite the public criticism of the shah in the United States, Kissinger remained committed to the US-Iran partnership that had been forged under the Nixon Doctrine. Preparing Ford for his first meeting with the shah in May 1975, Kissinger advised the president, "I see the Shah as playing an increasingly important role in the Persian Gulf, the Middle East, South Asia, and further afield. He may have some excessive ideas of his importance and some people consider him arrogant, but there is no gainsaying the sharply rising economic and military strength of which he disposes."[287] Ford met with the shah in the Oval Office on May 15 and 16, 1975, making him the sixth US president to welcome the shah to the White House. The shah was angry with the American media's portrayal of his decision at Algiers, telling Ford, "I have to say this in the face of all the press reports that I abandoned them. They weren't fighting—we were. The Kurds weren't fighting. Sadat, Hussein, Boumediène said 'Give them [Iraq] a chance to cut loose from the Soviet Union and adopt a more independent policy.' So at Algiers I had talks which settled the border and opened the way for Iraq to be more independent of the Soviet Union."[288]

When reports emerged during the shah's visit that Iraq had executed some captured Kurds, Kissinger shrugged off the news by telling his senior staff, "In fact, it's inevitable, sooner or later. It doesn't surprise me."[289] But public sympathy, stoked by the media, was with the Kurds. For example, shortly after the shah's visit, Ford received a letter from George Meany, president of the AFL-CIO, the largest federation of trade unions in the United States, and a long-time supporter of the Kurdish cause, asking the president to intervene to help the Iraqi Kurds. Kissinger dismissed the appeal, advising Ford that "the Iraqis are making an effort to treat the Kurds humanely."[290] But recriminations over the plight of the Kurds continued, and the blame would soon be directed at Kissinger himself. Watergate had shattered the public's trust in government, particularly the CIA, and Congress took the opportunity to assert greater oversight over the intelligence community.[291] The CIA's covert Kurdish operation had been officially terminated on June 4.[292] However, much to Kissinger's fury, the US House of Representatives' Select Committee on Intelligence, led by Congressman Otis Pike, was conducting an investigation into a variety of recent CIA activities, including its assistance to the Kurds. Kissinger did his best to prevent the release of classified documents to the Pike Committee's staff, citing executive privilege.[293] When preparing to testify before the hostile Committee in October, he told Ford that exposing the Kurdish operation would "infuriate the Shah" and he worried that the Committee was determined "to show I am the evil genius."[294]

As Kissinger feared, his closed-door testimony to the Pike Committee quickly leaked to the media. On November 1, journalist Daniel Schorr broke the story on the *CBS Evening News* broadcast, revealing that the United States had been secretly helping Iran to arm the Kurds. The story hit the headlines the next morning.[295] The shah had just returned to

Tehran on November 2 from a visit to Ankara, when he received former Senator J. William Fulbright, a southern Democrat who had retired as the long-serving chairman of the US Senate Foreign Relations Committee. When Fulbright asked the shah if he had seen the *CBS News* report on the CIA's Kurdish operation, the shah "reacted with a smile rather than a frown and commented, 'Yes, that story was the first thing my government mentioned to me when I alighted at the airport a few minutes ago.' " If the shah was resigned to the public exposure of the Kurdish operation, Helms was livid. Although he realized that Kissinger was "painfully aware. . . of [the] damage these leaks do," he nonetheless warned the secretary of state "to keep Department cables away from Congressional committees."[296]

But the worst was yet to come. Some of the Kurds in Barzani's entourage, angry at Kissinger's treatment of Barzani in exile, began publicly pointing the finger at the secretary of state for the Kurds' defeat.[297] The leaks from the Pike Committee continued, including embarrassing details of the gifts that Barzani had sent Kissinger, including Persian carpets and a gold necklace as a wedding present for Kissinger's bride, Nancy Maginnes.[298] Then, on February 5, 1976, William Safire attacked the secretary of state in his column in the *New York Times*, accusing Kissinger of being "callous" and "amoral" for advising Ford to remain silent in the face of the shah's "unconscionable sellout" of the "Shah-forsaken" Kurds. Quoting from the leaked final report of the Pike Committee, Safire claimed that Kissinger had told Committee investigators, "Covert action should not be confused with missionary work."[299] As the White House and the State Department denied the accusations, a furious Kissinger worked the phones to limit the damage to his reputation.[300] At 2.50 p.m. he spoke with journalist John Osborne: "The assumption has to be when people are in high office they are trying to do the right thing for their country. The picture that this paints of the senior officials has to be destructive of public morality." When Osborne told him that he thought the Kurds had been "let down," Kissinger responded that "[o]nce the Iranians stopped supporting them, there was no technical means for us to get in there. It would have cost $500 million to do it as a unilateral effort."[301] At 3 p.m. Kissinger called Israeli ambassador Dinitz to ask him to pressure Safire to back off. Kissinger asked Dinitz, "Do you think you could get your friend under some sort of control. What we did for the Kurds was not exactly against the interests of Israel." Dinitz said that Safire had a grudge against Kissinger, and he doubted that he could exert much influence over the *Times* columnist.[302]

Safire had worked with Kissinger in the White House as Nixon's speechwriter and had been recruited by the *New York Times* in 1973 to refute charges that the newspaper was biased against Nixon and the Republican Party. But when Safire learned that his White House phone had been bugged since 1969, allegedly on Kissinger's orders, he became a trenchant critic of the secretary of state.[303] Safire was unrelenting in his attacks and hit back at Kissinger's denials on February 12, citing specific documents mentioned in the Pike Report.[304] At a press conference that day, Kissinger was confronted with the question of whether he was considering resigning. He lashed out at the Pike Committee, accusing them of a "new version of McCarthyism."[305] The story, however, would not go away as the final report of the Pike Committee was leaked to the media, despite efforts by House Republicans to suppress its release.[306] Daniel Schorr had obtained a copy of the report and passed it to the *Village Voice*, which published it in full on February 16, giving Kissinger's critics even more ammunition.[307] When Safire launched another salvo at Kissinger on April 12, this time over the removal of classified documents from the White House, Ford told Kissinger, "That Safire article is the damndest thing I ever saw" and asked, "Why is Safire so vicious?" Kissinger replied, "He thinks I was responsible for tapping him. . . . I didn't even know he was being tapped, as is the case with several others."[308] Safire's accusation that Kissinger had cynically betrayed the Kurds would continue to dog the secretary of state.[309] Ford joked with Kissinger that "[y]ou have a real friend in Safire," while Kissinger's long-time journalist friend Ted Koppel asked if Safire "is going to write that on your tombstone."[310]

And so the abandonment of the Kurds was added to the litany of charges arrayed against Henry Kissinger by his critics, though this was neither the first nor the last time that the Kurds would fall victim to great power politics.[311] Barzani, suffering from cancer, was allowed to secretly visit the United States in the summer of 1975 for medical treatment and to finally settle in Washington's Virginia suburbs the following year, where he lived a life of exile.[312] Barzani was a living reminder to Kissinger that he had steered the United States into the war in Kurdistan at the shah's behest in 1972 and that he had been forced to accept the shah's abandonment of the Kurds in 1975, for which he was now being held responsible. Kissinger complained to his senior State Department staff that the charges against him of abandoning the Kurds were unfair: "What do they say we should have done without the Iranians? How could we have supported him if we had had the means?" He asked if Barzani was "running around town telling people that the fault really ends up here at the Department of State?" Notoriously thin-skinned when it came to criticism, Kissinger stuck to the line that the Kurdish operation "couldn't have been sustained without the introduction of Iranian regular forces there at that point. This is what I recall the judgment was."[313] Twenty-three years later, in the last volume of his memoirs, he wrote that the same critics who had called for the US to abandon South Vietnam had then "salved their conscience" by attacking him for abandoning the Kurds. He accepted no responsibility for the fate of the Kurds, writing instead that their tragedy was "imposed" by history, geography, and the weakening of the United States, thanks to the Vietnam War and Watergate. He begrudgingly acknowledged the lessons of the Kurdish episode for the United States: "the need to clarify objectives at the outset; the importance of relating goals to available means; the need to review an operation periodically; and the importance of coherence among allies."[314] Implicit in these "lessons" was an acknowledgment that the Iranian tail had wagged the American dog.

In 1975 the Pike Committee concluded that the partnership forged between the United States and Iran under the Nixon Doctrine meant that "[o]ur national interest had thus become effectively meshed with his [the shah's]." The report characterized Nixon and Kissinger as the shah's "junior American partners" in the Kurdish episode, and concurred with Kissinger's judgment that the Ford administration had "no choice but to acquiesce" to the shah's decision to abandon the Kurds.[315] With declassification 30 years later, the documentary record confirms the findings of the Pike Committee report and provides an interesting window into the nature and dynamics of US-Iran relations during this period of the Cold War. The shah's paramount role in Nixon and Kissinger's decisions to initiate, escalate, and then end the US intervention in Kurdistan demonstrates the extraordinary influence he enjoyed in the Nixon White House as a Cold War partner of the United States. As a consequence of the shah's lobbying, the Nixon administration broke with a long-standing US policy of non-intervention in Kurdistan to back Barzani in 1972. The decision to intervene was taken at the behest of the shah and against all the advice that the White House was receiving from the State Department, the CIA, and the NSC staff. Nixon and Kissinger had embraced the shah as their regional partner and deferred to his judgment on the need to maintain a stalemate in the war between Barzani's Pesh Merga and the Iraqi army. When the shah told Nixon and Kissinger in Tehran in May 1972 that it was vital to prevent a Kurdish collapse in order to contain Soviet influence in the region, they readily agreed, regardless of what their own advisors were telling them. The shah had persuaded Nixon and Kissinger that the Iran-Iraq confrontation in Kurdistan was in fact a battle in the global Cold War, thereby drawing the United States into the conflict alongside Iran.

The purpose of the American role in Iran's Kurdish effort was to assure Barzani that the shah would not abandon the Kurds once they came close to achieving their goal of autonomy. But Washington never enjoyed sufficient leverage over the shah, or played a big enough role in the operation, to be able to provide Barzani with such a guarantee. From its inception, the CIA's planning focused on a limited operation intended to serve the Iranian goal of maintaining the stalemate in Kurdistan, rather than achieving Barzani's aim of Kurdish autonomy. As Kissinger later acknowledged, "the lesson to be learned concerns the original commitment, not the final outcome. The United States should have determined from the start how far it could reasonably go in helping the Kurds, and should have made these limits unequivocally clear before offering assistance."[316] The question then arises: Why did Barzani accept such hollow assurances from the United States? While he might appear naïve for trusting Nixon and Kissinger, the evidence suggests that he was fully aware of the risk he was taking by siding with the shah, but he trusted Saddam Hussein and the Ba'th even less. In his 1973 interview with journalist Jim Hoagland, he had asked for a public commitment from the United States, a year after the private assurances that Helms had given his envoys.[317] Off the record, Barzani told Hoagland, "We do not trust the Shah. I trust America. America is too great a power to betray a small people like the Kurds." Barzani's mistake was that he did not understand the dynamics of the US-Iran relationship. He thought that the shah was a client of the United States, who would never act without a green light from Washington. As one of his lieutenants recalled, Barzani "believed nothing was done in the Middle East, or most of the world, without the support of the US."[318] By underestimating Iran's autonomy, he overestimated Nixon and Kissinger's leverage over the shah.

It was the shah, not Nixon and Kissinger, who controlled the ebb and flow of the Kurdish operation throughout 1973 and 1974. At his request, the United States agreed to escalate its support for the Kurds in August 1973, at the same time that the shah was exploring the idea of a settlement with Iraq. When the shah vetoed the Israeli request for the Kurds to launch an offensive during the October War, Kissinger readily concurred. Unlike a relationship between a superpower patron and a Third World client, all of these decisions were made by the shah without any real consideration for how these choices would impact American interests. Furthermore, throughout the Kurdish episode the shah's direct access to the White House allowed him to cut the naysayers in the State Department out of the loop, a task in which Kissinger was happily complicit. The shah and Kissinger directed the secret operation through SAVAK and the CIA, with Helms as their intermediary. The extreme secrecy surrounding the operation prevented any dissenting views from reaching Presidents Nixon or Ford, which might have caused them to think twice before meddling in Iraq's civil war. This secrecy also allowed Kissinger to keep the operation going at a time of profound domestic opposition to any expansion of America's overseas commitments. The shah's decision to abandon the Kurds at Algiers, despite Kissinger's objections, and Washington's inability to do anything other than to acquiesce to this *fait accompli* exposed how little leverage the United States enjoyed over Iran in 1975. Kissinger later wrote, "I thus had to bear witness to the enslavement of yet another friendly people, aware that, while the Shah's conduct could be used as an alibi, our paralyzing internal crisis had been a contributing cause." As the media heaped scorn on Kissinger, it must have been apparent to the secretary of state that the shah had used not only the Kurds, but also the United States, to pursue Iran's interests in Iraq. There is no evidence that the shah, for his part, was much concerned about the mess he had landed Kissinger in. When Alam had once spoken to the shah of Kissinger's bad press, the shah had replied, "this is what happens to someone who is so arrogant."[319] Despite Kissinger's public humiliation, he nonetheless remained committed to the shah and the US-Iran partnership.

4

A Ford, Not a Nixon

THE UNITED STATES AND THE SHAH'S
NUCLEAR DREAMS

RICHARD NIXON'S RESIGNATION in 1974 heralded the decline of the
Nixon-Kissinger-Pahlavi partnership. While the shah and Nixon had mutual esteem for one another as grand geo-strategic thinkers, the shah had
little respect for Gerald Ford, who had a reputation as an honest but simple
man.[1] Alam recorded in his diary that the shah once described Ford as "a
real idiot" who says whatever his advisers tell him to say and signs whatever
they put in front of him.[2] The personal relationship between the president
and the shah, which had played such a crucial role in US-Iran relations,
was now missing. The strongest force for continuity in Iran policy between the two administrations was Henry Kissinger, whom Ford retained
as both secretary of state and national security adviser, though he lost the
latter post in November 1975 to General Brent Scowcroft. At the same time
that Kissinger was fighting to preserve Nixon's legacy of détente with the
Soviet Union, he also found himself defending the partnership that he
and Nixon had forged with the shah against attacks from both Democrats
in Congress and Republican critics within the Ford administration.

The Vietnam War and Watergate had profoundly impacted public attitudes in the United States regarding America's role in the world. A growing concern with human rights reflected the desire of many Americans
both on the political Left and the Right to pursue a more "moral" foreign
policy guided by American values, in contrast with Nixon and Kissinger's
realpolitik policies of pursuing détente with the Soviet Union and partnerships with anti-communist Third World autocrats like the shah.[3] Critical

views of the shah began to appear more frequently in the mainstream American media, highlighting his role in raising oil prices, the vast amount of US arms he was purchasing, and his poor record on human rights. In October 1974, an unflattering exposé on Iran in *Newsweek* magazine warned that whereas the shah's "grandiose visions were once considered absurd daydreams," his role in raising oil prices meant that he could no longer be dismissed as "an object of ridicule." "Now, with visions of Persia's grandeur dancing in his head, the Shah has set out to convert his immense oil wealth into geopolitical clout." The article quoted an anonymous "Washington observer" who described the megalomaniacal shah as a "Frankenstein monster."[4] This palpable shift in public attitudes threatened to unravel the shah's partnership with the United States. After the Democrats increased their majority in both houses of Congress in the November 1974 mid-term elections, they passed a new Foreign Assistance Act that tried to restrict US arms exports to states like Iran that violated the human rights of their citizens. Much to Kissinger's chagrin, the State Department was now required to provide annual human rights reports on countries that received security assistance from the United States, including Iran.[5]

This cultural shift in the United States coincided with the radicalization of Iranian politics in the 1970s, as skyrocketing oil prices fueled the corruption and brutality of the shah's regime. In March 1975, the shah made a sudden announcement that the handful of toothless state-sanctioned political parties in Iran would be replaced with a single Rastakhiz-e Melli (National Resurgence) Party. When questioned about his decision to establish a one-party state, the shah simply replied, "What's wrong with authority? Is anarchy better?"[6] He expected all eligible voters to join the Rastakhiz Party and advised anyone who did not want to join to leave the country.[7] By May, the CIA station in Tehran reported an "alarming degree" of opposition in Iran to the shah's rule, "even though superficially everything appears normal on the surface."[8] In the United States, human rights groups like Amnesty International and the International Commission of Jurists, as well as the increasingly radical Confederation of Iranian Students, publicized the torture and execution of the shah's opponents in Iran's prisons.[9] Although some Iranian opposition groups were violently anti-American, reports of their brutal treatment at the hands of SAVAK nonetheless hurt the shah's public image in the United States.[10] These trends culminated in the first Congressional hearings on the status of human rights in Iran in the autumn of 1976.[11]

While the shah could still depend on support from a significant "Pahlavi lobby" in the United States in the mid-1970s, including Vice President Nelson Rockefeller and many senior Republican members of Congress, such as Senators Barry Goldwater and Jacob Javits, the political tide was clearly turning against the shah in Washington.[12] Kissinger fought tenaciously against attempts by Congress to investigate the commitments that Nixon had given the shah in Tehran in May 1972, whereby nearly all restrictions on Iranian conventional arms purchases from the United States had been lifted. Kissinger denied Congressional staff access to two key memoranda that he had issued in the summer of 1972, one of which stated that "in general, decisions on the acquisition of military equipment should be left primarily to the government of Iran."[13] Both the State Department and the NSC staff advised Kissinger not to block requests for access to these documents from the House Appropriations Committee and the Senate Foreign Relations Committee.[14] But Kissinger denied that Nixon had given the shah a blank check on arms sales and was unwilling to make these potentially embarrassing memoranda available to his Democratic opponents in Congress. He instructed his staff to simply ignore the requests.[15]

Kissinger also parried attempts by members of the Ford administration to dismantle the Nixon-Kissinger-Pahlavi partnership. The most vociferous criticism from within the administration came from the Department of Defense, which had long expressed concern over Iran's ability to absorb the huge volume of sophisticated arms that the shah was purchasing from the United States. Many in the Pentagon feared that the growing number of US military personnel in Iran, on whom the Iranians depended to operate their American-made weapons systems, threatened to embroil the United States in any military adventure on which the shah might embark.[16] Defense Secretary James Schlesinger sought to steer Ford away from Nixon's policy of Iranian primacy. In September 1975 he warned the president that "US interests and the Shah's perception of his interest could easily collide, and soon."[17] Although this clash between Kissinger and Schlesinger was not limited to the question of Iran policy and was driven to some extent by a long-standing rivalry between the two men, the Pentagon's objections to Iranian primacy would continue under Schlesinger's successor, Donald Rumsfeld.[18] Kissinger also faced opposition on Iran policy from Treasury Secretary William Simon, who was working closely with Saudi oil minister Sheikh Ahmad Zaki Yamani to pressure the shah to lower oil prices.[19] In an Oval Office briefing for the new president in August 1974 regarding the ongoing energy crisis, Kissinger warned Ford not to listen to Simon's advice to abandon the policy of Iranian primacy and tilt toward Saudi Arabia in the Persian Gulf. Kissinger described the Saudis as "the most feckless and gutless of the Arabs," whereas "[t]he Shah is a tough, mean guy." He reminded Ford that the shah "is our real friend. He is the only one who would stand up to the Soviet Union. We need him for balance against India. We can't tackle him without breaking him."[20] Kissinger was largely successful in fending off these attacks on the partnership with the shah. Schlesinger later recalled that despite a "difference in tone" in US policy toward Iran under the new administration, "President Ford tended to follow the commitments of his predecessor and the advice of Secretary Kissinger."[21] Although Ford agreed to continue US support for Iran's covert operation in Kurdistan and US arms sales to Iran, when it came to new commitments to the shah, Ford was far more responsive than Nixon had been to critics of the shah within his administration and in Congress. Kissinger's influence, however substantial, was ultimately not enough to make up for the absence of an intimate friendship between the president and the shah (Figure 4.1).

This chapter explores the dynamics of US-Iran relations during this period of decline through a history of the negotiations between the shah

FIGURE 4.1   Kissinger, the shah's chief ally in the Ford administration, warmly greets the Iranian monarch in the Oval Office on May 15, 1975. Courtesy of the Gerald R. Ford Presidential Library.

and the Ford administration for an agreement on American nuclear exports to Iran.[22] The negotiations began with much enthusiasm in May 1974 in the final months of Nixon's presidency, but ultimately failed to produce an agreement by the time Ford and Kissinger were preparing to leave office in December 1976. The main obstacle to a nuclear accord was the unwillingness of the United States to allow Iran to reprocess spent nuclear fuel, a sensitive nuclear technology that would also allow Iran to stockpile plutonium for a nuclear weapons program. Driven largely by domestic political considerations, the Ford administration tried to impose stringent nuclear safeguards on Iran, which went beyond Iran's commitments as a party to the 1968 Nuclear Non-Proliferation Treaty (NPT). The shah rejected these additional safeguards as a violation of Iranian sovereignty and instead turned to suppliers in Europe for Iran's nuclear energy program. Ultimately, the US-Iran nuclear talks failed because the Ford administration reverted to treating Iran as a client, rather than a partner, of the United States. However, Washington's inability to impose additional safeguards on Tehran suggests that, although the US-Iran partnership faltered under Ford, the shah's autonomy from the United States endured.

The Origins of Iran's Nuclear Program ╲

As in many developing countries, Iran's nuclear program began in the 1950s thanks to assistance from the United States under the "Atoms for Peace" program, which sought to redirect the use of nuclear technology away from the nuclear arms race and toward peaceful civilian applications.[23] In December 1953, President Eisenhower pledged to the United Nations that his country would "devote its entire heart and mind to find the way by which the miraculous inventiveness of man shall not be dedicated to his death, but consecrated to his life."[24] The United States would encourage the spread of civilian nuclear energy, which would be safeguarded by a new International Atomic Energy Agency (IAEA). The United States and Iran signed an agreement on the civil uses of atomic energy in 1957, which would permit private American firms to build a small research reactor in Tehran and would allow Iran to lease up to 6 kilograms of enriched uranium to fuel this reactor. Under Article IX of the agreement, Iran pledged that its nuclear program would not "be used for atomic weapons or for research on or development of atomic weapons, or for any other military purposes."[25] In 1964 a trilateral agreement was signed in Vienna between Iran, the United States, and the IAEA, placing Iran's nuclear facilities and materials under IAEA safeguards.[26] The 5 MW Tehran Research Reactor (TRR), built by a subsidiary of the General Dynamics Corporation, went online in 1967, and a year later Iran signed the NPT, which was then ratified by Iran's Majlis in 1970.

Despite growing international concern about nuclear proliferation in the 1960s following the French and Chinese nuclear tests, Iran's modest program of nuclear research attracted little attention. Iran was not considered a significant proliferation risk; the shah was spending huge sums on conventional weapons for national defense, and his nuclear facilities and materials were fully safeguarded by the IAEA under the NPT. He frequently assured visiting American dignitaries that Iran had no interest in provoking a nuclear arms race in the Middle East. But this assurance always came with the caveat that "should a country such as India develop [a] nuclear weapons capability at some future time, perhaps with Soviet assistance having China in mind, Iran would have to reconsider its present policy and would probably itself wish to develop a similar capability."[27] Disregard for Iran's nuclear ambitions also reflected the Nixon administration's general lack of concern with nuclear proliferation. Nixon and Kissinger were deeply skeptical that the NPT, which their Democratic predecessors had worked so hard to construct, would prevent the spread of nuclear weapons.[28] They doubted that any pledge or treaty would ultimately inhibit states like India or Israel from going nuclear, given their intense security dilemmas, and they were unwilling to spend political capital on defending the global nonproliferation regime.[29] In the case of Iran, this meant that concerns about nuclear proliferation rarely intruded into the administration's deliberations of Iran policy during Nixon's first term in office.

Iran's Great Leap Forward

Washington's quiet complacency about Iran's nuclear program was shattered in 1974 when the shah announced plans for a dramatic expansion of Iran's nuclear energy program, financed by soaring oil prices. The Arab oil boycott, launched in the midst of the October 1973 Arab-Israeli War, followed by OPEC's decision in Tehran in December 1973 to raise oil prices, meant that Iran's annual oil revenues more than quadrupled in a single year from $4.4 billion in 1973 to $17.8 billion in 1974.[30] Consequently, the total amount of public and private sector investment in Iran's Fifth Development Plan (1973–1977) was increased from roughly $36.8 billion to $69.6 billion.[31] In his March 1974 *Nowruz* message, the shah announced that "[w]e shall, as fast as we can, enter the age of using the atom and other sources of energy in order to save oil for production of chemical and petrochemical products. We shall not use oil, this noble substance, as common fuel."[32] The shah launched what was, in effect, a crash program of nuclear energy production. A Swiss-trained nuclear physicist, Akbar Etemad, was quickly selected as the president of a new Atomic Energy Organization of Iran (AEOI) and was charged with rapidly building a full-scale civilian nuclear energy program.[33] The shah's reasoning for this decision, Etemad recalled, was that Iran's petroleum reserves were finite and that in order to meet the long-term energy needs of Iran's rapidly growing economy, the country would have to begin investing in a variety of alternative energy sources. The shah set a national goal of 70,000 MW of electricity production by the 1990s. While most of this capacity was to come from Iran's vast reserves of natural gas and its hydroelectric dams, roughly 23,000 MW was to come from nuclear power plants.[34] Instead of burning oil as a fuel, the shah wanted to use this "noble substance" to manufacture and export petrochemical products, which would be of far greater value to Iran's balance of payments than the crude oil they were made from.[35]

Few in the Iranian government were privy to the shah's thinking on nuclear matters. Given that the country was both awash in petroleum and still struggling to establish more elementary industries, some wondered if atomic energy was an extravagance divorced from Iran's economic realities. Khodadad Farmanfarmaian, the highly regarded director of the body responsible for drafting the Fifth Development Plan, later recalled that nuclear energy was one of the many white elephants that he could not cut from the Plan because it was "very dear and close to his [the shah's] heart."[36] Etemad, however, shrugged off these concerns, telling himself, "they must know something I don't know."[37] The rationale behind the massive increase in expenditure in the Fifth Plan was that, with one "Big Push" to industrialize Iran's economy, financed by the oil windfall, Iran could break out of the "vicious circles" of underdevelopment and join the ranks of the world's leading industrialized economies.[38] Iran would have to move quickly, because although the resources existed for a crash program in nuclear energy in 1974, it was not clear if in four or five years' time those same resources would still be available. Etemad understood that the shah expected quick results; otherwise the monarch would lose both his interest in atomic energy and his faith in AEOI. "My duty was to convince the government," Etemad recalled, "from His Majesty on down, that atomic energy was achievable, and in this way to secure His Majesty's future support."[39]

Thanks to the shah's patronage, within three years AEOI rapidly grew into a bureaucracy of over 1,000 employees with an annual budget of more than $1 billion. In November 1974, Iran reached preliminary agreements with Kraftwork Union, a subsidiary of the German firm Siemens, to build two 1,200 MW nuclear reactors near Bushehr, to be completed in 1981 and 1982, and with Framatome of France to build another two 900 MW reactors on the Karun River between Ahvaz and Khorramshahr by 1983 and 1984. The enriched uranium that would fuel Iran's nuclear reactors would be provided by EURODIF, a European conglomerate that was building an enrichment plant in France. After agreeing to help finance the construction of the plant with a $1 billion loan, Iran would receive a 10 percent share in EURODIF and a similar share of the nuclear fuel that the plant would produce. Iran also looked to a variety of African countries as sources of uranium ore and signed a secret agreement with South Africa in October 1975 to purchase enriched uranium.[40]

The dubious economic rationale for Iran's nuclear program points to considerations of prestige and security behind the shah's quest for nuclear technology. The late 1960s saw a boom in the use of nuclear power in Europe, North America, and Japan.[41] Furthermore, by 1971 all five permanent members of the UN Security Council possessed nuclear weapons.[42] In this context, the shah's dream of Iran achieving military and economic parity with the great powers implied that Iran must also be a member of the nuclear club, with the capacity to produce nuclear energy and, if necessary, nuclear weapons. Although there is no evidence that the shah ever decided to actually build nuclear weapons, his advisers suspected that this was his ultimate goal. His closest confidante, Court Minister Asadollah Alam, recorded in his diary in November 1975, "His Majesty has a grand plan for Iran and I am sure that he is also thinking of developing the atomic bomb (although he repeatedly denies this)."[43]

Etemad worried that the shah might not be aware of the technical barriers to using a civilian nuclear program for military ends. After giving the shah six months of weekly tutorials on the technical aspects of the nuclear program, he finally summoned the courage to ask whether AEOI should plan for a military program. The shah replied that he saw no place for nuclear weapons in Iran's defense doctrine. A regional nuclear arms race would only neutralize Iran's conventional military superiority over its neighbors, while a small nuclear arsenal would not deter the Soviet Union. But the shah gave Etemad his usual caveat that if a hostile regional power developed nuclear weapons, then Iran would have no choice but to develop its own nuclear deterrent. Etemad recalled that nuclear weapons were a "taboo" subject in the AEOI, never to be openly discussed. However, he and his colleagues understood that it was their patriotic duty to develop the scientific know-how for a nuclear weapons program, in the event that it ever proved necessary to build such weapons. Etemad quietly approved budget allocations for dual-use projects, such as research into uranium enrichment, which might later prove useful for a weapons program.[44]

The Long Shadow of India's Nuclear Test

After the dramatic acceleration of Iran's nuclear plans in 1974, American firms were conspicuous by their absence in Iran's nuclear program. The United States was the world's principal nuclear supplier, and there was certainly no lack of interest on the part of Iran in securing access to American nuclear technology and materials. During an audience with the shah on February 21, 1974, World Bank president Robert McNamara "overheard" the shah telling one of his ministers that Iran was interested in purchasing a 10,000 MW nuclear reactor and wondered if any American company was capable of building it.[45] Again, in early March, Fazlollah Akbari, deputy minister of science and higher education, approached the US Embassy in Tehran, asking for American help with the organizational and management aspects of Iran's nuclear program.[46] Kissinger responded enthusiastically to the Iranian overtures and established a task force in the State Department to plan for a US-Iran Joint Commission that would institutionalize economic cooperation between the two countries in a variety of areas, including atomic energy.[47] Kissinger was eager to take advantage of Iran's oil boom to benefit the US balance of payments. Furthermore, the CIA's economic analysts suspected that the secretary of state was also trying to "develop close US tie-ins with Iranian economic development which will give the US leverage in future oil-policy deliberations."[48]

The shah's keen personal interest in Iran's nuclear program meant that nuclear cooperation quickly took on great importance in the US-Iran relationship. Helms reported that when he had first broached the subject of a US-Iran Joint Commission with the shah on March 14, 1974, "I had difficulty getting beyond the subject of nuclear power, because he wanted to get down to brass tacks on that right away." He reported to Kissinger that "there is no mistaking his preoccupation with satisfying his considerable ambitions in the nuclear field." Helms recalled that the shah's "eyes visibly brightened" when the ambassador mentioned some of the industrial applications of nuclear technology.[49] Unfortunately for the shah, the dramatic expansion of Iran's nuclear program was announced just months before India's "peaceful nuclear explosion" on May 18, 1974, which caused a panic in Washington about nuclear proliferation. It appeared that India had carried out its nuclear test with plutonium from a research reactor supplied by Canada, which used heavy water provided by the United States. It was a source of embarrassment for the Nixon administration that the Indian test had been carried out with American materials. Embroiled in the death throes of Nixon's presidency, and not wishing to inflate India's newfound nuclear status, Kissinger's public condemnation of the test was muted. His tempered reaction further enraged critics in Congress, who accused the administration of gross nuclear negligence and worried that the Indian test was the death knell of the nuclear non-proliferation regime. Belatedly and begrudgingly, Kissinger was compelled to respond to the outcry by ordering an interagency study of the implications of the Indian test in NSSM 202.[50] The result of these deliberations was an order from Nixon in June to begin consultations with other nuclear supplier countries on common rules for nuclear exports that would prevent further nuclear proliferation. This ultimately led to the convening in early 1975 of the London Suppliers Group, consisting of Britain, Canada, France, West Germany, Japan, the Soviet Union, and the United States.[51]

The Indian nuclear test could not have come at a worse time for Iran. The news broke just as a delegation from the Atomic Energy Commission (AEC), led by its chairman, Dixy Lee Ray, had arrived in Tehran to discuss Iran's interest in American participation in its nuclear program.[52] A biologist by training, Ray was an outspoken advocate of the Nixon administration's mercantile approach to nuclear energy. Lacking foreign policy credentials, she was a strong advocate for the American nuclear industry and showed little sensitivity to the dangers of nuclear proliferation.[53] Her views on nuclear exports were increasingly at odds with the growing fear, both within the administration and in Congress, that the Indian nuclear test would set off a cascade of nuclear proliferation in conflict-prone regions like the Middle East and South Asia. Etemad recalled that he was having lunch with Ray and Helms at the US Embassy when an aide brought the news of the Indian test. Much to his surprise, her reaction was muted and the visit proceeded unperturbed.[54] Ray and her team met with Iran's "best trained minds in nuclear energy" to discuss how the AEC could help the AEOI select nuclear projects and choose American firms to build them. In addition to her talks with Etemad, she also met with Iraj Vahidi, Iran's energy minister, and was received by the shah in a private audience on May 21. Over a total of seven hours of talks in Tehran, Ray urged the Iranians to press ahead with the selection of sites for their planned nuclear reactors and briefed them on the various commercially available reactor designs. The Iranians responded enthusiastically and asked the AEC to prepare a draft bilateral agreement, covering the supply of both nuclear reactors and nuclear fuel, which would replace the original 1957 agreement.[55]

Despite Ray's enthusiasm for nuclear cooperation with Iran, India's "peaceful nuclear explosion" dramatically changed American perceptions of Iran's nuclear program. In the immediate aftermath of the Indian nuclear test, the American media speculated that Prime Minister Indira Gandhi had given the shah advance notice of the test and that India was helping Iran to plan for its own nuclear test in a barter agreement for oil.[56] According to the US Embassy in Tehran, the Iranians were "calm if somewhat ambivalent" about the Indian test. When the issue came up in conversation between Hoveyda and Helms, the Iranian premier "seemed very relaxed about the event," and ascribed the test to domestic political motives on the part of Gandhi.[57] The shah had frequently said that if India ever developed nuclear weapons, then Iran might have to follow suit. Therefore, the Iranians had every interest in downplaying the significance of India's test and the likelihood that it would prompt Iran to build its own bomb. But the mood in Washington was now firmly against nuclear exports to unstable regions of the Third World. During a trip to the Middle East in June 1974, just a month after the Indian test, a beleaguered Nixon had offered to provide Egypt and Israel with civilian nuclear technology, even though neither country was a party to the NPT.[58] The news had been greeted with dismay by many members of Congress, despite assurances by the State Department that nuclear exports to Egypt and Israel would be covered by stringent safeguards that went far beyond those mandated by the NPT.[59] Alfred Atherton, the assistant secretary of state for Near Eastern affairs, advised Kissinger to impose the same additional safeguards on Iran, a party to the NPT, as the United States was imposing on Egypt and Israel. Atherton worried that if the shah's regime were toppled, the nuclear materials stored in Iran might fall into the hands of "domestic dissidents," "foreign terrorists," or "an aggressive successor." Furthermore, he hoped that additional safeguards could head off the likely press and Congressional criticism of the deal. But he acknowledged that the shah was likely to object to Iran being treated as "a potential regional trouble spot" and to any discrimination against Iran as a party to the NPT.[60]

American fears about Iran's nuclear ambitions were again heightened in June when the press picked up on comments by the shah on the eve of a state visit to France, where he planned to sign a nuclear agreement with French president Valéry Giscard d'Estaing. In an interview with the French business news magazine *Les Informations*, he was asked if Iran would one day have nuclear weapons. He replied, "Without any doubt, and sooner than one would think."[61] The Iranian Embassy in Paris was quick to deny the comments, and the shah denied ever having given the interview.[62] The next day *Le Monde* published an interview with the shah in which he was asked if he would consider withdrawing Iran from the NPT. He replied, "certainly not yet," and reiterated his long-standing position that the Middle East should be declared a nuclear-weapons-free zone. He insisted that nuclear weapons were useless for Iran. A small nuclear arsenal would not give Iran parity with the great powers and would only invite proliferation by its regional rivals. While he considered a nuclear arms race to be "ridiculous," he warned that if any country in the region went nuclear "then perhaps the national interests of any country at all would demand that it do the same."[63] Meanwhile, in Tehran, both Information Minister Gholam Reza Kianpour and Court Minister Alam denied that the shah had indicated a desire to develop a nuclear arsenal. Instead, they clarified the official Iranian position that Iran would only consider withdrawing from the NPT if another country in the region, like Egypt or Israel, introduced nuclear weapons into the Middle East. Helms was satisfied with this explanation and advised Washington that the shah had no intention of building nuclear weapons, regardless of "whatever he may have said off the cuff to French journalists."[64]

Despite the Iranian denials, the shah's comments in Paris on nuclear weapons further heightened fears in Washington about his nuclear ambitions. James Noyes, the deputy assistant secretary for the Near East in the Pentagon's Office of International Security Affairs (ISA), prepared a memorandum for Secretary Schlesinger, warning that a US decision to provide Iran with nuclear reactors and fuel would be widely interpreted as "assistance toward a weapons capability."[65] However, the media coverage of the shah's trip to France also drew attention to the reality that Washington's trepidation about nuclear exports to Iran was costing American firms lucrative Iranian nuclear contracts, which were going to their European competitors. At the conclusion of his visit, the shah and Giscard d'Estaing signed letters of intent for a multibillion dollar nuclear deal that would include the sale of five 1,000 MW nuclear reactors, as well as a nuclear research center to train Iranian scientists.[66] At a time when Europe was struggling to deal with soaring oil prices, the agreement was characterized by the *Washington Post* as an "economic coup" for France.[67] Noyes's comments reflected a broader concern in the Pentagon that the White House was downplaying the proliferation risk posed by Iran in order to placate the shah and secure Iranian nuclear contracts for American industry. Colonel Donald Marshall wrote to his boss, Donald Cotter, the special assistant to Schlesinger on nuclear policy, expressing his concern "that *nowhere* can I find that the military, or anybody with political-military background, is being plugged into the nuclear energy relationship with Iran."[68] Schlesinger later recalled that he was deeply sympathetic to these concerns and opposed the "excessive closeness" in US-Iran relations under Nixon.[69] Having served as chairman of the AEC during Nixon's first term, he was also familiar with the issues surrounding nuclear proliferation. Under Schlesinger's leadership, and that of his successor Donald Rumsfeld, the Defense Department would remain the most forceful advocate within interagency debates for stringent bilateral safeguards on Iran's nuclear program.

The shah was aware of the suspicions about his nuclear intentions, particularly after his comments in Paris. He launched a diplomatic initiative in the summer of 1974 to reassure the international community that Iran was not seeking nuclear weapons by reviving the idea of declaring the Middle East a nuclear-weapons-free zone. He told Helms on July 2 that Iran would sponsor a resolution to this effect at the United Nations. Although he did not expect it to pass, he thought that this would be "a good and reassuring gesture" to the international community.[70] The Iranian Foreign Ministry scrambled to put together a draft resolution that would "have maximum psychological effect on world opinion."[71] Iran's ambassadors around the world were instructed to secure backing for the resolution, with the hope that this would "reassure" Iran's neighbors and promote an image of Iran as a "constructive and responsible" emerging power.[72] A message from the shah was delivered at the opening of the plenary session of the UN General Assembly in September, in which he warned that nuclear proliferation in the Middle East "might mean more than a mere involvement of adversaries in a senseless and wasteful nuclear arms race." As part of this public relations exercise, copies of the shah's message were distributed by the Iranian Embassy throughout Washington, including to the White House and Congress.[73]

Daryoush Bayandor, then the political counselor at the Iranian Mission to the UN in New York, was charged with steering the resolution through the General Assembly. He recalled that "[n]obody believed it was implementable; it was thus some sort of posturing and propaganda for us." The chief obstacle was Israel, the sole state in the region with an (undeclared) nuclear arsenal. Bayandor conducted discreet discussions with his Israeli counterpart at the UN, in order "to prevent them from voting 'no' or make a pernicious campaign in Washington to torpedo the whole idea."[74] After months of negotiations, the Iranians were able to convince the Israelis to abstain on the vote, and with the help of Egypt, were also able to enlist the support of the Arab League. They agreed to an American demand that the resolution should not permit non-nuclear states to conduct "peaceful nuclear explosions," as India had done.[75] Resolution 3263 was adopted by the General Assembly on December 9, 1974, calling on all states in the region to "proclaim solemnly and immediately their intention to refrain, on a reciprocal basis, from producing, testing, obtaining, acquiring, or in any other way possessing nuclear weapons."[76]

Iran's rather transparent diplomatic efforts in 1974 did little to convince the opponents of nuclear exports to Iran that the shah could be trusted with nuclear technology. In an estimate prepared in August, the US intelligence community acknowledged that Iran's nuclear program was "entirely in the planning stage" and saw little likelihood that Iran would withdraw from the NPT while its nascent nuclear program was under construction. But the estimate also warned of "the Shah's ambition to make Iran a power to be reckoned with" and outlined a series of conditions under which Iran would likely build nuclear weapons in the 1980s: "if Iran has a full-fledged nuclear power industry and all the facilities necessary for nuclear weapons, and if other countries have proceeded with weapons development, we have no doubt that Iran will follow suit."[77] In Congress, more alarmist predictions of a nuclear-armed Iran were being made. In September, retired Rear Admiral Gene R. La Rocque, founder and director of the Center for Defense Information, told a public hearing of the Subcommittee on Military Applications of the Joint Committee on Atomic Energy that "one of the early contenders now for nuclear weapons is certainly Iran, with the experience of India." The Subcommittee's chairman,

Senator Stuart Symington, replied that the Committee's staff had calculated that with the nuclear reactors supplied by France, "the Iranians could build a minimum of 200 Hiroshima bombs a year."[78] In Tehran, Helms knew that the Indian test was eroding any chance of a nuclear deal with Iran. He cabled the State Department "to emphasize personally that there has been no change in Iran's declared policy not to acquire nuclear weapons." But Helms's efforts to keep the US-Iran nuclear negotiations on track were complicated by an announcement in July 1974 that the AEC was imposing a moratorium on US exports of enriched uranium reactor fuel because of a domestic supply shortage.[79] After Ray's visit to Tehran, Iran had asked the AEC to approve eight contracts for the supply of enriched uranium for its planned reactors. Because of the moratorium, the AEC approved only two of these contracts as a "political concession" to Iran. Helms reported that both Alam and Foreign Minister Khalatbari had told him that the shah was "very upset" with the AEC's decision.[80]

Undeterred by the growing concerns about the shah's nuclear ambitions, Kissinger pressed ahead with his plans for nuclear cooperation with Iran. In November 1974 he traveled to Tehran for the first meeting of the US-Iran Joint Commission, which he co-chaired with Iranian Minister of Economy and Finance Hushang Ansary.[81] During the Commission's formal session on the morning of November 2, Ansary told Kissinger that Iran wanted to discuss cooperation with the United States on nuclear reactors, uranium enrichment, and training for its nuclear engineers. "Already an extensive dialogue is going on," Ansary said, "and we can iron out the difficulties." Etemad, who was present at the meeting, recalled that Ansary spoke of purchasing as many as eight nuclear reactors from the United States. Such a staggeringly large order was exorbitant even for oil-rich Iran, but the AEOI chief kept silent, as he understood that Ansary's pledge had been made for the sake of political "atmospherics."[82] Kissinger responded cautiously, telling the Iranians that "[w]e have a concern to prevent the spread of nuclear weapons" and joked that thankfully "the weapons are now in the hands of countries who are either responsible or cowardly [Laughter]—one or the other." Kissinger assured Ansary that these concerns would not inhibit Iran's "peaceful uses" of atomic energy. "We strongly support your program," Kissinger declared. It was simply a matter of ensuring that the right "safeguards" were in place.[83]

The Nuclear Fuel Reprocessing Problem

The Ford administration's initial deliberations on nuclear exports to Iran were heavily influenced by a December 1974 report on nuclear proliferation, produced by the NSC's Under Secretaries Committee (NSC/USC) in response to the study memorandum that Kissinger had issued in May. The report made two crucial recommendations that would prove to be major stumbling blocks in the nuclear negotiations with Iran. First, it stated that the United States should "[s]eek to limit the number of independent reactor fuel reprocessing facilities and attempt to control the spread of independent uranium enrichment plants and technology." These two elements of the nuclear fuel cycle were the most sensitive in terms of proliferation risk. Uranium ore can be processed through a variety of enrichment methods in order to separate the denser isotope U-238 from the lighter U-235. Low-enriched uranium (LEU), containing 2–3 percent of U-235, is fabricated into fuel rods for use in reactors. However, the same enrichment technologies can be used to manufacture highly enriched uranium (HEU), containing 90 percent or more U-235, for use in nuclear weapons. Once the LEU fuel rods have been irradiated in a nuclear reactor, the spent nuclear fuel still contains uranium and a small amount of plutonium, which can be chemically separated from the waste and reprocessed into nuclear fuel. In theory, such enrichment and reprocessing technology could allow a country to stockpile HEU or plutonium for use in nuclear weapons. Instead of permitting the recipients of US nuclear exports to conduct enrichment or reprocessing in national facilities on their own territory, the NSC/USC advocated either the construction of "regional multinational plants," whereby a number of neighboring countries would make use of the same reprocessing plant, or a US offer of favorable terms to reprocess nuclear fuel in the United States. This would prevent the recipient countries from covertly stockpiling these fissile materials away from prying foreign eyes.[84]

Second, the report suggested "[o]btaining agreement to place special conditions on nuclear exports to nations in sensitive regions." These "special conditions" went beyond the regular IAEA safeguards that applied under the NPT. They specifically precluded any reprocessing of spent fuel on the soil of the recipient country and gave the United States the option to "buy back" spent fuel derived from American-supplied nuclear materials or facilities. The NSC/USC pointed to the additional safeguards in the agreements that the United States was negotiating with Egypt and Israel as a model that could be applied not only to "other Middle East states, but also to countries in other troubled or unstable areas of the world to be addressed on a case-by-case basis."[85] The difficulty confronting the Americans in denying Iran the right to master the complete nuclear fuel cycle or imposing additional safeguards on an agreement with Iran, along the lines of the NSC/USC report, was that the shah would interpret such conditions as discriminatory and an American vote of no confidence in his leadership and Iran's stability. Unlike Egypt and Israel, Iran was a party to the NPT, so the shah would never agree to restrictions that the United States had not imposed on nuclear exports to other NPT signatories. The shah would simply turn to alternative nuclear suppliers like France or West Germany, which had already secured lucrative contracts to provide Iran with nuclear reactors, while the United States would lose a multibil-lion dollar deal, including a proposed Iranian investment in a uranium enrichment plant in the United States.[86] Etemad had implied as much to Helms when he told the ambassador in October 1974 that the AEOI had been "flooded" with so many offers of sales for its nuclear program that his organization "simply does not have the staff to respond to all its mail."[87] However, without any additional safeguards, the US Senate was unlikely to ratify any nuclear agreement with Iran.

Shortly after the NSC/USC report was issued, the State Department's Near East Bureau sent its recommendation to Kissinger for a draft nuclear agreement with Iran, which had been stalled since Ray's visit to Tehran in May. Kissinger's staff presented him with options ranging from impos-ing no additional safeguards on Iran's nuclear program beyond those con-tained in the NPT, to asking Iran to agree to the same stringent safeguards contained in the agreements with Egypt and Israel. Kissinger opted for a middle course whereby Iran would be asked to agree to additional physical security measures to protect nuclear materials from falling into the hands of terrorists, and would also consent to an American right to veto Iranian reprocessing of spent nuclear fuel. The United States would consider allowing reprocessing of spent fuel in either a foreign facility or a multi-national facility in Iran, thereby diminishing the Iranians' ability to secretly separate plutonium from its spent fuel and stockpile it for a weapons pro-gram. But the secretary of state was less than pleased with these additional safeguards, which were designed to placate a hostile Congress rather than strengthen US-Iran relations. He was particularly unhappy that his offi-cials had tied his hands by already briefing key members of Congress that any nuclear agreement with Iran would contain additional safeguards.[88]

The first meeting of the US-Iran nuclear energy committee, under the rubric of the Joint Commission, took place in Tehran on January 21 and 22, 1975. Negotiations began on a nuclear agreement that the Americans hoped would be signed in March during the scheduled second meeting of the Joint Commission in Washington. Little of substance was achieved in these talks, but the mood of the discussions between Etemad and Ray, who had since moved to the State Department as assistant secretary for oceans and international environmental and scientific affairs, was "unusually frank and amicable."[89] The Iranians wanted American help to train their nuclear cadre, they expressed interest in diversifying their supply of enriched uranium fuel by signing contracts with American firms, and they hoped to award the Americans contracts for constructing dual-use nuclear reactors that could desalinate water in Iran's arid southern coastal regions.[90] But after studying the draft agreement that the Americans had brought with them to Tehran, Etemad quickly registered his displeasure with both the US veto on Iranian reprocessing and the notion that nuclear exports to Iran would be treated no differently from those to Egypt and Israel.[91] Etemad later recalled that the AEOI had made no decision as to whether Iran would reprocess its spent fuel, or would simply rely on imports of nuclear fuel. Such a decision was premature, given that Iran would not be producing any nuclear energy for at least another decade. But the Iranians refused to rule out the possibility that they might wish to build the entire nuclear fuel cycle on their own soil at some point in the future.[92]

The State Department insisted that Iran was, in fact, being given preferential treatment as a party to the NPT, but in reality the difference between the proposed agreement with Iran and those with Egypt and Israel was negligible. Whereas in the Egyptian and Israeli cases the United States flatly refused to allow any national reprocessing and insisted on the right to "buy back" the spent fuel, in the Iranian case the Americans promised to "take into account" Iran's adherence to the NPT when deciding whether or not to exercise their veto over reprocessing.[93] This distinction provided little assurance to the Iranians that they would be allowed to reprocess their own spent fuel on their own soil. Not surprisingly, the negotiations ground to a halt as Iran refused to accept such discriminatory treatment. The second meeting of the US-Iran Joint Commission came and went on March 3–4, 1975, during Hushang Ansary's visit to Washington, without any discussion of nuclear matters. All Etemad would agree to do was to send his comments on the US draft to Washington and to invite the American negotiators back to Iran in late April to continue the negotiations.[94]

Hoping to find a way to break the deadlock, Kissinger ordered an interagency review of the US-Iran nuclear negotiations in NSSM 219 of March 14, 1975.[95] The issue of nuclear exports to Iran was gaining domestic saliency in the United States and would have to be handled delicately to balance the concerns of both the shah and Congress. Earlier that week, the editorial page of the *Washington Post* had warned that the French deal with Iran could lead to an Iranian nuclear bomb, as France had not signed the NPT and "French officials will have virtually no control over the [o]reactors or the enriched uranium that will be supplied to Iran." In the proposed US nuclear deal with Iran, the *Post* editors argued, the Ford administration should "induce Iran to agree that spent nuclear fuel will be shipped abroad for reprocessing, and not left in Iran where it might be used to make nuclear weapons." They acknowledged that this safeguard is not required by the NPT and that the United States was in a "ticklish position" when making such demands. Nonetheless, "everything must be done to ensure that the nuclear club does not expand."[96] The shah responded to these American fears in an interview with a sympathetic newspaper columnist, Joseph Kraft. The shah said that he had seen "the concern registered in newspapers that were partial to Israel" and he repeated his view that the prospect of a nuclear Iran was "ridiculous" and insisted that "[o]nly a few silly fools believe it." He argued that the best evidence for Iran's lack of interest in nuclear weapons was the vast sums he was spending on conventional arms: "I want to be able to take care of anything by nonnuclear means." The shah insisted that Iran could never have a credible nuclear deterrent. "How many do you think it would take to count against the Russians? Or the United States? How much would they cost? Then we would have to buy all the equipment for launching missiles. It's ridiculous." When asked about additional safeguards, the shah replied, "I think it will not be difficult to come up with a formula so long as it is not an American *diktat*."[97]

Kissinger's Opening Gambit

With US negotiators set to return to Tehran on April 21, and a scheduled visit by the shah to Washington in May looming, the pressure on the Ford administration to reach a nuclear agreement with Iran was mounting. An ad hoc interagency working group quickly delivered its response to NSSM 219 on April 15. The working group recognized that any discrimination against Iran as a party to the NPT would be interpreted by the shah as "a reflection on Iran's stability and the integrity of its commitments as well as an indication that the U.S. cannot be relied upon because of the uncertainties of our political process." The key stumbling block was the issue of nuclear fuel reprocessing, but the Americans were very reluctant to give up their right to veto reprocessing. The US position was that in deciding whether to exercise their veto, they would "look sympathetically" on Iran's request, as long as the reprocessing was to take place in a properly safeguarded multinational facility where officials from other countries would be present. This would make it much more difficult for Iran to secretly divert and stockpile plutonium for a weapons program. The NSSM 219 report presented the Ford administration with five options for a US negotiating position. Option 1 was to maintain the current US policy of opposing reprocessing in Iran; Option 2 was to retain the veto on reprocessing, but to give Iran a firm assurance that US approval would be forthcoming if Iran agreed to a multinational facility; Option 3 was to retain the veto, but give up the demand for multinational reprocessing in exchange for bilateral safeguards; Option 4 was to give up the US veto on reprocessing in exchange for "categorical assurances" from Iran that it would establish a multinational facility; and Option 5 was to give up any demand for additional safeguards beyond those imposed by the NPT. The American negotiators sensed that the shah was less opposed to the idea of bilateral safeguards or multinational reprocessing than to accepting a US right to veto reprocessing in the text of the agreement. The report also suggested that the idea of a multinational reprocessing facility in Iran, supplying nuclear fuel to other states in the region like Pakistan, might appeal to the shah's ambitions for regional leadership.[98]

In Tehran, Helms's primary concern was maintaining the partnership with the shah under the Nixon Doctrine, so he pushed Washington toward an accommodation of Iran's position. He recommended abandoning the US veto over reprocessing, which would be seen in Iran as "an affront to the Shah's integrity, an encroachment on national sovereignty and a lack of good faith which could bring into question the whole range of our close and mutual advantageous ties with Iran." Aside from reiterating the familiar arguments about Iran's adherence to the NPT and the availability of alternative nuclear suppliers, Helms suggested moving toward a bilateral, rather than multilateral, solution to the reprocessing problem.

He made the case that by becoming Iran's principal nuclear supplier, the United States could enhance its leverage over Iran by being in a position to threaten a cutoff of nuclear fuel, maintenance, and spare parts if Iran moved toward building a bomb. "Such a sanction," Helms argued, "affecting Iran's most vital interests in a situation in which a substantial part of its economy was dependent on the continued operation of its nuclear energy plants, would complement and reinforce the other deterrents built into NPT, IAEA and the bilateral agreement." Helms suggested that if the opposition in Washington to a nuclear agreement with Iran was simply too great to overcome in the span of a few months, it was "sufficient to his and our purposes that we reach agreement privately" during the shah's visit to the United States in May, and then sell the agreement to the public and Congress afterward.[99]

None of the agencies in Washington were willing to go as far as Helms and abandon the US veto on reprocessing in Iran. Given the ongoing American effort to convince the other members of the London Suppliers Group to place limits on their own exports of reprocessing technology, and the opposition to a nuclear deal with Iran in Congress, it was vital to retain the US veto. The most that the State Department was willing to concede, as a fallback position, was an assurance that the US would approve reprocessing in Iran if the Iranians constructed a properly safeguarded multinational reprocessing facility, in which the United States might participate along the lines of Option 2 in the NSSM 219 report.[100] Both the US Arms Control and Disarmament Agency (ACDA) and the newly created US Energy Research and Development Administration (ERDA) concurred with the State Department's position.[101] Schlesinger, the most hawkish opponent of reprocessing in Iran, also weighed into the debate, recommending not only a retention of the US veto, but also a bilateral safeguards agreement for any Iranian reprocessing facility, in case Iran ever withdrew from the NPT and blocked IAEA inspections. In exchange, the US would give Iran a vague commitment that "barring unforeseen developments we would expect to give Iran our specific approval for reprocessing at a time consistent with the Iranian power reactor program's need for fuel reprocessing in the mid-1980s."[102]

Kissinger proceeded cautiously, issuing NSDM 292 on April 22, 1975, laying out a negotiating position very similar to the consensus around Option 2 in the NSSM 219 report, but also incorporating Helms's idea of a smothering American embrace of the Iranian nuclear program and Schlesinger's advice to include bilateral safeguards. The United States would retain its veto over the reprocessing of spent fuel in Iran, but would consider Iran's willingness to establish a multinational reprocessing plant an "important factor" in deciding whether to approve such reprocessing. As a "fallback" position, the United States would still retain its veto, but would give Iran a categorical assurance that it would approve reprocessing in a multinational facility on Iranian soil, "if the country supplying the reprocessing technology or equipment is a full and active participant in the plant and holding open the possibility of US participation." In case Iran ever withdrew from the NPT and refused IAEA inspections, a "standard provision requiring mutual agreement as to safeguardability shall apply." The distinction between being "favorably disposed" toward multinational reprocessing in Iran in the original US position (Option 1) and firmly agreeing to "approve" such reprocessing in the fallback position that Kissinger had authorized (Option 2) was a fine one. David Elliott, a PhD in high energy physics from Cal Tech who was director for science and technology on the NSC staff, hoped that this formula would allow the United States to retain its veto on reprocessing, thereby giving the administration "a fighting chance of obtaining Congressional approval," while not precluding reprocessing on Iranian soil, thereby satisfying "most of Iran's legitimate concerns."[103] Kissinger instructed the American negotiators to express US willingness to help Iran construct a joint reprocessing facility "at an appropriate time should Iran so desire."[104] By supplying Iran with nuclear fuel, nuclear reactors, and potentially a reprocessing facility, the United States would become the principal supplier of Iran's nuclear program, as Helms had suggested, and would then be in a position to monitor the implementation of safeguards as a full partner in Iran's nuclear program.

Armed with these new instructions, the American negotiators returned to Tehran for more talks on April 26 and 27, 1975. They presented the Iranians with the fallback position that Kissinger had authorized in NSDM 292, and a new draft agreement was transmitted to the AEOI in early May.[105] Although the United States had tried to assure Iran that reprocessing on Iranian soil would not be precluded by the agreement, the AEOI was uncomfortable with the idea of agreeing to a multinational reprocessing facility as a precondition for American approval. The Iranians argued that they might not be able to secure supplier participation in their reprocessing facility. They wanted assurances that the United States would agree to reprocessing in a national plant on Iranian soil, if Iran made a "strenuous effort" to secure supplier participation and failed. But Washington was unwilling to acquiesce to a national reprocessing facility, where Iran could divert plutonium for a weapons program undetected. The United States would agree only to "give great affirmative weight" to Iranian efforts to secure supplier participation, when deciding whether to invoke their veto. From the Americans' perspective, "the added assurances against non-proliferation which accompany supplier involvement depend on its *actually* being achieved, and not merely on an effort to achieve it, however strenuous." But for the Iranians, agreeing to supplier participation as a precondition for reprocessing would give the foreign supplier tremendous leverage over Iran. By being able to suspend participation in the multinational facility, the supplier would enjoy an effective veto over Iran's ability to reprocess its spent fuel on its own territory. The Iranians complained that they "should not be penalized if, through no fault of their own, it [supplier participation] is not achievable." It was clear to Etemad that no agreement would be reached before or during the shah's visit to Washington in May, so he told the Americans that the shah would simply use the trip as an opportunity to seek resolution of any "major problems."[106]

The shah's May 1975 visit came at a time when Congress was trying to place firmer controls on nuclear exports and as tensions in the US-Iran relationship were simmering to the surface. A bill had been introduced in the Senate that year for an "Export Reorganization Act" that would only allow nuclear exports to countries with nuclear safeguards that were "at least substantially comparable" to those in the United States.[107] One of the sponsors of the bill, Senator Abraham Ribicoff, a liberal Democrat who had served in the Kennedy administration, believed that Iran should give a "binding commitment" to forgo enrichment or reprocessing on its own soil, in exchange for an assurance from the supplier countries of a "reliable supply" of nuclear fuel.[108] This Congressional concern with Iran's nuclear ambitions also reflected a growing unease with the shah in the United States, where he was often portrayed as a megalomaniac or the "emperor of oil," as *Time* magazine dubbed him in November 1974, leading the charge for higher oil prices in OPEC.[109] The shah bristled at criticism that he was bankrupting the economies of the West by driving up oil prices in order to finance extravagant arms purchases and maintain his grip on power. He delighted in the leverage that oil gave him over the same Western powers that had once bullied Iran and he berated the West for its "permissive undisciplined society" where "you work not enough."[110] Much to the chagrin of Israel's friends in the United States, the shah had normalized Iran's relations with Ba'thi Iraqi and had established close ties with Egyptian president Anwar Sadat, a moderate Arab leader who had taken Egypt out of the Soviet camp.[111] This shift in Iran's policy toward the Arabs was largely rhetorical, aimed at cultivating moderate Arab support for Iran's regional primacy.[112] Nonetheless, questions were being raised in Congress about the shah's ambitions and the wisdom of unrestricted American arms sales to Iran. Democratic Congressman Clarence Long worried that Iran's growing military power would "increase the peril to the friendly state of Israel."[113]

These two factors—nuclear proliferation and the shah's supposed megalomania—combined in the American popular consciousness to render the idea of nuclear exports to Iran deeply unpalatable. After the shah's sudden decision to abandon the Kurds in March 1975, Senator Henry "Scoop" Jackson wrote to Kissinger, questioning the wisdom of nuclear exports to Iran, given "the disturbing evidence that the Government of Iran is capable of policy shifts so precipitous as to border on the quixotic."[114] A month later, students and faculty at the Massachusetts Institute of Technology (MIT) organized a sit-in at the Department of Nuclear Engineering to protest a special training program there for Iranian graduate students in nuclear engineering.[115] A letter from graduate student Bonnie Burrati to fellow members of a university committee studying the agreement reveals the intense emotions that the shah evoked for some Americans in this period. She first wrote that it "seems suspicious that the Shah has chosen nuclear energy when he is wallowing in oil," and then went on to suggest that nuclear exports to Iran were part of a secret plan engineered by Kissinger to use a nuclear Iran to threaten other Persian Gulf oil-producing countries, "if the oil were shut off." Buratti asked if MIT should "get its hands dirty by doing dictators' dirty work?" She warned that "many of the entering Iranian students will be agents of SAVAK" and suggested that a nuclear Iran might be a threat to Israel, as "Iran itself is not what we might call a philosemitic nation" and the shah is "behind Egypt 100%."[116]

The same skepticism and opposition to Iran's nuclear ambitions that were palpable among the public (Figure 4.2) and in Congress were also reflected within the Ford administration. Those who saw the shah as a "nut," as Treasury Secretary Simon had crudely put it the previous summer, were convinced that nuclear weapons were a logical extension of the shah's plan to make Iran a "superpower."[117] In the summer of 1975, Helms's deputy chief of mission in Tehran, Jack Miklos, cabled

FIGURE 4.2 Cartoon in the *Washington Post*, March 20, 1975, "Explain slowly—what does he need all those weapons for, and why does he need nuclear reactors?" A 1975 Herblock Cartoon, © The Herb Block Foundation.

Washington his concern that Iran's nuclear program had more to do with the shah's grandiose ambitions for Iran to achieve parity with the great powers than with sensible economic planning. The nuclear reactors that the shah wanted were "symbols of arrival among the industrialized nations of the world." Miklos warned that "we cannot, of course, completely rule out the possibility that, in the event of further nuclear proliferation in the region, Iran might feel that it too must acquire nuclear weapons." The shah was resisting the idea of a multinational reprocessing facility, Miklos argued, because he was keeping open the option of stockpiling plutonium for a weapons program. While the Iranians protested that a multinational reprocessing facility would be "unworkable," Miklos suspected that "lurking unspoken in the background may be an unwillingness to submit their plant to foreign surveillance."[118]

Even Kissinger, who was deeply committed to the US-Iran partnership, suspected that the shah's nuclear ambitions went beyond a civilian energy program. In the briefing materials that he prepared for Ford in anticipation of the shah's arrival in Washington, he advised the president that the Indian nuclear test was "probably giving the Shah second thoughts about Iran's renunciation of nuclear weapons." Kissinger noted that Iran was far from having the capacity to build a nuclear arsenal, but he warned that the shah

> probably would like to move toward a position where he could eventually produce weapons on short notice if he believed it necessary. We can expect, therefore, that Iran over the next decade will continue present major efforts to acquire civilian nuclear facilities and develop the know-how and technology to manufacture nuclear weapons, but without taking a firm decision to undertake actual production. The Shah would hope that by avoiding a definite program to produce nuclear weapons he would forestall problems with the US and others over his nuclear intentions.

In case the shah raised the issue of the stalled nuclear deal during his visit, Kissinger advised Ford to say only that he would give Iran's objection to multinational reprocessing "further consideration," but to remind the shah that "we must weigh it carefully in light of general public and Congressional concerns over proliferation."[119] In any event, the shah made no mention of nuclear fuel reprocessing during his meetings with Ford and Kissinger in Washington in May 1975 (Figure 4.3). Instead, he used the visit to reassure the Americans of his good intentions by condemning India's nuclear test. "The Indians try to tell me they are peaceful," the shah told Ford and Kissinger on May 15, "but if they are, why do they need the atom bomb?" He argued that it was "hard to believe" that India needed a nuclear deterrent against China and Pakistan. Rather, he feared that Hindu nationalism was behind the Indian drive for a nuclear bomb.[120] Returning to Tehran, the shah continued to express his interest in a nuclear deal, including Iranian investment in a uranium enrichment plant in the United States, in the hope of enticing the Americans to move the talks forward.[121]

FIGURE 4.3 With the US-Iran partnership in decline, the shah meets with Ford and Kissinger in the Oval Office on May 15, 1975. Courtesy of the Gerald R. Ford Presidential Library.

Searching for a Washington Consensus

Rather than creating momentum for a nuclear deal, the shah's visit to Washington seemed to only provoke the shah's critics to further poison the well of public opinion against the US partnership with Iran. That summer, acerbic criticism of the shah and his close relationship with Kissinger began appearing regularly in Jack Anderson's widely syndicated column in the *Washington Post*, frequently based on anonymous leaks from Simon and other critics of the shah within the Ford administration and in Congress.[122] In one particularly vitriolic column on July 11, Anderson cited a CIA psychological profile that described the shah as a "dangerous megalomaniac, who is likely to pursue his own aims in disregard of US interests." The CIA analysts had reportedly portrayed the shah as a "weak, retiring personality" who suffered from deep insecurities and complexes as a result of his "overbearing father," his "lack of royal lineage," his "fear of impotence," and the "ignominy of being a puppet monarch" early in his reign.[123] Although such profiles were prepared regularly by the CIA, this particular document has never surfaced.[124] Nonetheless, these views reflected the thinking of many in Washington who opposed giving nuclear technology to Iran.

In this tense political climate, a US negotiating team led by ERDA ad-
ministrator Robert Seamans met with Etemad in Vienna in September
1975 for further discussions on the American draft that had been transmitted to the Iranians in May. Etemad firmly rejected any US veto over
Iranian reprocessing of spent fuel and showed little enthusiasm for the
idea of a multinational reprocessing facility in Iran. He told Seamans that
Iran "could not tie its own hands for 30 years" by agreeing to the additional safeguards that the United States wanted to impose. Etemad made
it clear that Iran's negotiations with other nuclear suppliers were "going
smoothly," in contrast with the stalled talks with Washington. Tehran was
quite happy to leave the agreement with the United States "undecided
for the time being," unless the Americans stopped treating Iran like a
"second class citizen" by insisting on safeguards that did not apply to US
nuclear exports to other countries that were party to the NPT. While he
did not rule out the idea of a multinational reprocessing plant, Etemad
was very clear that the "final decision on [re]processing in Iran must rest
with Iran—not [the] U.S." The American negotiators decided to float the
idea of a "U.S. government presence" at Iran's reprocessing facility, if
the Iranians could not secure participation by either a European supplier
country or an American private partner, but Etemad was "non-committal."
He warned his American interlocutors that the shah was "unhappy with
[the] U.S. position" and that his boss was likely to summon Helms for
discussions on the issue.[125]

While in Vienna, Etemad also met with representatives of the American
nuclear industry, including Dwight Porter, a former American diplomat
who was vice president of the Westinghouse Corporation. Porter, who had
known Etemad when he had been posted to the US Mission to the IAEA in
Vienna, was surprised by the "unusual vehemence" of Etemad's remarks,
considering the Iranian nuclear chief's "normally mild manner." Etemad
confided that the shah had repeatedly instructed him that "under no circumstances" was he to agree to the additional safeguards that the United
States was demanding. Etemad feared that the issue had become "entirely
political" and was "driving a deep wedge" into the US-Iran partnership.
Iran would never agree to give any nuclear fuel supplier "the power to turn
off the pipeline whenever it wished, for whatever reason."[126] So a nuclear
agreement with Iran was nowhere in sight and, according to the Embassy
in Tehran, Etemad "was not seized with a great sense of urgency" to break
the deadlock.[127]

The State Department, in consultation with David Elliott from the NSC staff, set about trying to devise some new options to move the negotiations forward. They developed an options paper in later October, which in turn formed the basis of an interagency study issued in November by the NSC Verification Panel's Working Group on Non-Proliferation (VPWG).[128] Ostensibly, the VPWG study addressed various options whereby the United States could move away from its veto on Iranian reprocessing in order to satisfy the shah. However, the report also reflected a palpable frustration within the Ford administration with Iran's refusal to compromise, particularly after Etemad's performance in Vienna. Some in the administration wondered if Iran really wanted US involvement in its nuclear program, and the VPWG study asked "whether it is appropriate for the U.S. to offer any concessions to Iran, in the absence of further assurances that the GOI is, indeed, prepared to proceed with significant nuclear purchases from the United States."[129] The VPWG study was distributed among the agencies for their comments, in the hope that a new consensus might emerge within the administration on how to proceed in the talks with Iran.

While the agencies prepared their responses to the study, Kissinger sent Helms a set of instructions for dealing with the shah in the interim. He instructed the ambassador to tell the shah that Iran was not being singled out for unfair treatment as a party to the NPT. Rather, Iran was subject to a new broad policy of safeguards that the United States would impose on all future nuclear exports. Kissinger also told Helms to suggest to the shah that a regional multinational facility in Iran, which could reprocess spent fuel for neighbors like Pakistan, would remove the need for national facilities in those countries. In this way, Iran's multinational facility would help reduce the risk of Pakistani nuclear proliferation and was thus "directly related to security and stability in the region, Iranian regional leadership and advancement of [the] Iranian economy."[130] But these attempts to appeal to the shah's ambitions for regional leadership did not address his concerns about a double standard when it came to questions of nuclear exports. In November 1975 the shah gave an interview to *Business Week* in which he said that the safeguards the Americans were demanding were "incompatible with our sovereignty" and that the French or Germans "would never dream" of making such demands.[131]

Administration officials in Washington viewed the issue of nuclear exports exclusively in terms of balancing the risk of nuclear proliferation with the commercial interests of American industry. They gave no weight in their deliberations to the political sensitivity in Iran of foreign control over national resources, particularly in the context of Mosaddeq's nationalization of Iranian oil in 1951 and the subsequent Anglo-American-sponsored coup that toppled the popular premier in 1953. The Americans showed no understanding of the damage that would be done to the shah's already precarious legitimacy if he were seen to acquiesce to American "nuclear apartheid," despite Iran's adherence to the NPT and the billions of dollars that Iran would be paying to American firms for this technology.[132] Furthermore, what kind of message would it send to the shah's supporters and detractors, both at home and abroad, if the United States determined that Iran was either too unstable to properly safeguard nuclear materials, or that the shah could not be trusted with nuclear technology? From Tehran, Helms wrote that "Iranian sensitivities in this area of nuclear cooperation run deeper than we had earlier thought." He warned of a "backlash" against other US economic interests in Iran and Iranian investment in the United States and bluntly asked if there was "a clear understanding in Washington of how serious a problem the nuclear deadlock has become."[133]

As the agencies delivered their responses to the VPWG study in the winter of 1975, it was clear that no progress had been made on reaching a consensus.[134] At one end of the spectrum was Helms, who felt that additional safeguards would do little to deter Iran from going nuclear if its national interests dictated such a move, and that the shah simply would look to other nuclear suppliers if Washington continued to drag its feet. The present US policy would only damage the US-Iran relationship and would result in the loss of the lucrative Iranian nuclear market to European competitors. He advised Kissinger that "circumstances will not force Iran into America's arms" and suggested that Washington abandon the idea of a regional multinational reprocessing facility, which the Iranians felt was "ridiculous in the Middle East setting." Instead, the United States should propose a binational facility, jointly run by Iran and the United States "under stringent safeguards." Helms was resigned to the reality that Iran, like India, could "construct a nuclear explosive device if it so desired" and that "whatever commitments Iran may have made to the US or under the NPT is likely to fall by the wayside if Iran's perception of its national interests dictate."[135] At the other end of the spectrum was the Pentagon, now led by Secretary of Defense Donald Rumsfeld, who continued to resist the idea of allowing Iran to reprocess spent fuel in a national facility. Rumsfeld recommended making no further concessions on reprocessing "pending clarification of the totality of Iran's demands."[136]

Comments made by Etemad in New Delhi in late December 1975, during a visit to India by the Iranian nuclear chief, seemed to confirm American suspicions that Iran was following India down the path to nuclear proliferation. After discussions with Prime Minister Gandhi and Indian nuclear officials, Etemad told a press conference that "Iran has not yet considered peaceful nuclear explosions but will not rule them out altogether," though he insisted that "Iran is not interested in establishing facilities for recovery of plutonium from spent fuel from her reactors."[137] These statements caused alarm and confusion in Washington, where Charles Robinson, the State Department's under secretary for economic affairs, immediately sent a cable to Helms in Tehran asking for clarification.[138] When Jack Miklos met with Etemad in early January to clarify his statements in New Delhi, the Iranian nuclear chief said that Iran was not ruling out the use of "peaceful nuclear explosions" (PNEs) for large development projects such as building canals or cutting through mountains. However, he insisted that "it is not a move Iran intended to make unilaterally and outside of the commitments it had undertaken under the NPT and IAEA agreements." Such PNEs would only be conducted "with material and technical assistance provided by outside sources," or in other words, with the knowledge and consent of Iran's nuclear suppliers. Furthermore, Etemad's point about reprocessing was that no decision had been taken to reprocess spent fuel in Iran, but he refused to rule it out altogether.[139] Reflecting the shah's bigger concern, Etemad suggested to Miklos that they take steps to combat the perception that the holdup in the nuclear negotiations was "somehow related to the overall quality of US-Iran relations."[140]

Those in the Ford administration who favored some sort of compromise to break the deadlock recognized that this would mean moving away from multinational reprocessing and toward a binational US-Iran reprocessing arrangement. Robert Seamans, the ERDA chief who had been leading the negotiations with Etemad, argued that the United States should neither abandon its veto over reprocessing, nor give up on the idea of a regional multinational reprocessing facility. But he advised the president that the United States should limit its veto by assuring the shah that if Iran failed to secure supplier participation in a multinational facility, "despite vigorous good faith efforts," and if the United States also declined to participate in a binational plant, then the United States would consent to reprocessing in a national facility in Iran "subject to a joint US-Iranian determination that (1) the plant is safeguardable and (2) the IAEA safeguards as they are to be applied to the plant will be effective."[141] Seamans's proposal to drop supplier participation as a precondition for US approval of reprocessing in Iran was a major concession and represented a significant departure from the established US position in NSDM 292.

The State Department also felt that compromise was necessary to move the negotiations forward, but like the Pentagon, they were unwilling to make any further concessions until the shah's views were clarified. They suggested sending a high-level delegation to Tehran for "exploratory" talks with the shah "to ascertain directly the Shah's views" on whether Iran was open to any kind of additional safeguards. Implicit in this suggestion for "direct" talks with the Iranian monarch was a strategy of going over the head of the troublesome Etemad, in the hope that the shah might be more amenable to compromise in the greater interest of US-Iran relations. It might still be possible to "moderate or overcome" the shah's opposition to additional safeguards beyond the NPT, the State Department argued, by asking him to join the United States as a partner in efforts to curb nuclear proliferation. By appealing to his self-image as a responsible world statesman, they hoped to "enlist Iran's positive support rather than cause it to feel that we seek to impose our will on them."[142] But convincing the shah that the United States regarded Iran as a non-proliferation partner, rather than a proliferation risk, was a tall order. The shah deeply resented the discriminatory treatment that Iran was being subjected to as a party to the NPT and viewed with suspicion the secretive London Suppliers Group, which was seen in Tehran as a cartel or club of nuclear powers for controlling the price of nuclear fuel, a sort of "nuclear OPEC."[143]

The options presented in the VPWG study for abandoning the US veto on Iranian reprocessing were unacceptable to the State Department, which had one eye on the ongoing talks in the London Suppliers Group and another on the mounting concern in Congress about nuclear proliferation. The administration could hardly make major concessions to Iran on reprocessing at the same time that it was asking other nuclear suppliers to withhold reprocessing technology from their clients and trying to assure Congress that nuclear exports to Iran posed no risk of proliferation. Like Helms and Seamans, they suggested retaining the US veto on reprocessing, but shifting away from the idea of a multinational reprocessing facility and toward some sort of binational arrangement between Iran and the United States. If Iran was ultimately unable to secure supplier participation in a multinational or binational plant, then the Americans could offer Iran two alternatives. First, Iran could sign a bilateral safeguards agreement with the United States, whereby it could reprocess spent fuel in a national facility in Iran, "subject to the *continuing* requirement that we be satisfied that the safeguards applied to these activities by the IAEA are effective." Under this bilateral agreement, the United States would always be able to withdraw consent for reprocessing and it would also be allowed to station American personnel in the Iranian facility. Alternatively, Washington could ask Iran for a "buy-back option," whereby it would have the right to purchase Iran's irradiated fuel rods. If the United States chose not to exercise this option, then Iran would have the right to reprocess the spent fuel in a national facility, "subject to a mutual determination that such facilities can be effectively safeguarded."[144]

Despite the willingness of Seamans and the State Department to consider national reprocessing, the only thing that all the agencies agreed on was the need for further "exploratory talks" with the shah. Both the Pentagon and ACDA remained firmly opposed to any further compromise on the issue. Fred C. Iklé, the director of ACDA under both Nixon and Ford, took very seriously the risk of nuclear proliferation and had frequently clashed with Kissinger on the issue.[145] He insisted that the American negotiators "should avoid any statements that would lead the Shah to believe that we would be prepared to settle for a formula which concedes that there are circumstances under which we *will* consent to a [sic] reprocessing in a national plant in Iran."[146] But the shah and Etemad had already made it abundantly clear that Iran would never agree to a US veto over reprocessing. These "exploratory talks" were not intended to bridge the gap between the Iranian and US positions, but rather to buy time for the administration to build some kind of consensus in Washington on how to move forward. Critics within the administration were already busy sabotaging the nuclear deal with Iran, leaking to journalists their concerns that "the Shah's nuclear plans are overambitious—that the kingdom does not have the technology to support a rapid expansion of nuclear generating power."[147]

A political battle over nuclear exports to Iran was being waged on three fronts: the diplomatic negotiations between the United States and Iran; the policy debate within the Ford administration; and the legislative contest between the administration and Congress. Scowcroft complained to Ford that "[w]e have, most recently, not been negotiating with Iran but with ourselves." Under Nixon, decisions on Iran policy had been largely insulated from bureaucratic infighting and domestic political considerations because of the intimate relationship between the president and the shah and the White House's obsession with secrecy. Nixon had strong opinions on the shah and all decisions relating to Iran were made by him, with Kissinger's advice, in the White House. The shah's critics within the administration were either sidelined or bypassed through backchannels, while Congress was left in the dark. But Ford had taken office without a popular mandate, forcing him to govern by consensus.[148] He had no relationship with the shah and no strong views on Iran. Ford's passivity and political weakness meant that the circle of decision-making on Iran expanded beyond the White House, to include critics within the administration and in Congress who were uncomfortable with the leverage that Iran had exercised over the United States under Nixon. The shah's influence no longer trumped the views of his critics, particularly on the sensitive issue of nuclear reprocessing, as it might have done under Nixon. With this lack of consensus in Washington, Scowcroft cautiously advised Ford to put off any decision on Iranian reprocessing: "to resolve that problem now would require a detailed, controversial decision by you on a US position that might not be acceptable to the Shah." Instead, he counseled the president to move ahead with the exploratory talks that the agencies had recommended.[149] Ford duly ordered Seamans to return to Tehran to speak with the shah, accompanied by Carlyle E. Maw, a lawyer who was Kissinger's under secretary for international security affairs at the State Department. In a February 4 memorandum, Scowcroft notified all the relevant agencies of the president's decision and told them that Ford would "reserve his judgment" on the final US position, as long as there was still hope that the shah might be willing to agree to multinational reprocessing. If, as expected, the shah refused to shift his position, Seamans and Maw were authorized to "explore with Iran other techniques for achieving the same objective."[150]

With few cards left to play, the president's envoys could do little more than flatter the shah and appeal to his vanity, as the State Department had suggested. They carried with them a letter from Ford for the shah, in which the president praised Iran's "leading role in supporting the Non-Proliferation Treaty and other efforts to abate the spread of nuclear weapons." Referring to spent fuel reprocessing, Ford called on the shah to help "ensure that the sensitive aspect of the nuclear fuel cycle evolves in a manner that reassures the world."[151] The US strategy was to convince the shah that he would be making a "major act of nuclear statesmanship" by forgoing national reprocessing on Iranian soil.[152] This was a desperate move by the Americans, with little chance of success. Just weeks earlier, the *New York Times* had quoted the shah as saying: "We gave them [the Americans] guarantees that these reactors will be used only for peaceful purposes, and not for nuclear weapons. But they asked unnecessarily for additional guarantees that we won't give."[153]

A Compromise on Reprocessing

The shah received Seamans and Maw in Tehran on February 23, 1976. After reading Ford's letter, he asked them, "What more do you want me to do?" Iran was a party to the NPT and the shah could not understand "why the US does not trust Iran to develop fully its peaceful nuclear power program." Despite the shah's exasperation, the overall mood of the meeting was positive, and he agreed to send Etemad to Washington in April for further talks. He was still interested in purchasing reactors from the United States and in investing in a uranium enrichment plant in the United States, and he acknowledged "a shared responsibility to assure the proper use of US supplied nuclear facility [*sic*] and materials." But as Seamans reported to the president, the shah "never indicated, however, that he would accept US conditions on reprocessing or whether or not he would accept reprocessing solely on a multinational scale."[154]

Not only did the exploratory talks in Tehran fail to elicit any hint of compromise from the shah, they also seemed to confirm that the gap between the American and Iranian positions could not be bridged. In reply to Ford's letter, the shah wrote on March 4 that Iran would have to be reassured of the United States' reliability as a nuclear supplier if the talks were to move forward. The shah hoped that Ford's "non-proliferation policy would remain flexible enough to allow a fruitful and meaningful cooperation to prevail between our two countries in the field of nuclear energy."[155] The clear implication of the shah's message was that if the United States continued to drag its feet, Iran would look to other, more reliable, nuclear suppliers. Seamans recognized the lack of American leverage and reiterated to Ford his earlier proposal that if Iran tried and failed to secure foreign participation in its reprocessing facility, then Washington should agree to Iranian reprocessing in a national facility, as long as the Americans were "satisfied the safeguards applied to these activities by the IAEA are effective" and as long as Iran allowed the United States "to assign staff to the facility if in the U.S. judgment this is necessary to supplement IAEA safeguards."[156] The Iranians had consistently resisted the idea of a multinational reprocessing facility and it was now clear that this demand would have to be dropped if Washington wanted a deal with the shah.

As the Americans prepared for Etemad's visit in April 1976, the administration debated Seamans's proposal to allow national reprocessing in Iran. The State Department was reluctant to make such a big concession to Iran, but they were willing to accept national reprocessing as a fallback position. Kissinger's staff reiterated the idea they had put forward in January of first exploring an option to "buy back" the spent fuel that Iran produced from reactors or nuclear material supplied by the United States. If Iran failed in its efforts to secure international participation in its reprocessing facility, and if the United States decided to forgo the option of buying back Iran's spent fuel, only then should the Americans consent to national reprocessing subject to the same safeguards that Seamans had proposed. This proposal had the benefit of at least delaying national reprocessing because of Iran's obligation to first exhaust efforts to secure international participation in its facility. However, the State Department begrudgingly recognized that additional safeguards could not be imposed on the shah. Under Secretary Joseph Sisco concurred with the Policy Planning Staff, directed by Winston Lord, that it might be "counterproductive" to introduce new proposals like the buy-back option, which were not "realistic" given how determined the shah was to preserve for Iran the option of mastering the full nuclear fuel cycle.[157] Kissinger's instinct was to accommodate the shah and he shared Sisco and Lord's skepticism that the shah would agree to this new proposal. He had initially asked for a meeting with his senior staff to discuss their proposal, but with time running out before Etemad's scheduled arrival in Washington on April 20, he reluctantly approved the Department's recommendation to seek a US buy-back option, with national reprocessing as a fallback position.[158]

The exploratory talks in Tehran had clarified for many in the Ford administration that they could not preclude national reprocessing, at least in principle, in any nuclear agreement with Iran. Kissinger, Seamans, and even Iklé all acknowledged this reality.[159] The only holdout was Rumsfeld, who was still insisting on multinational reprocessing in Iran.[160] Scowcroft put his weight behind the State Department's recommendation, advising the president to ask the shah for a US option to buy back Iran's spent fuel, while also assuring him that the United States would agree to national reprocessing if Washington decided not to exercise this option. If Iran rejected the buy-back proposal, then the US negotiators would agree to national reprocessing under the safeguards that Seamans had proposed. Scowcroft argued that insisting on a multinational facility as a precondition to reprocessing "seems pointless and possibly counterproductive." The State Department's proposal still held open the possibility of either full US participation, or at least an American presence, in an Iranian national reprocessing facility, thereby satisfying Congressional non-proliferation concerns.[161] On the eve of Etemad's arrival in Washington, President Ford signed NSDM 324, adopting a new US negotiating position. The United States would try to retain its veto on spent fuel reprocessing in Iran, but would consent to reprocessing in a national facility on Iranian soil, if Iran failed in its efforts to establish a multinational facility. While the US negotiators were instructed to seek a spent fuel buy-back option, NSDM 324 authorized them to drop this demand if they deemed it "essential" to reaching an "ad referendum" agreement with Iran.[162]

The United States' acquiescence to national reprocessing represented a significant diplomatic victory for Iran. Over nearly two years of negotiations, the shah had evaded every American attempt to pin him down on additional safeguards beyond Iran's obligations under the NPT. Meanwhile, the Ford administration had first conceded fuel reprocessing on Iranian soil in April 1975 and, a year later, it also conceded a multinational facility as a precondition to such reprocessing. Kissinger tried to justify these concessions to his State Department staff. He told them that he was very skeptical that any group of countries would ever agree to cooperate in a regional multinational reprocessing plant: "in any region you look at it is a fraud."[163] He noted that Pakistan would never agree to a regional reprocessing plant in Iran, nor would the shah consent to a multinational facility in Pakistan. The shah was not about to sacrifice Iran's right to reprocess spent fuel on its own territory, for the sake of preventing Pakistan from going nuclear. The shah was resisting American attempts to enlist him in a campaign to pressure Pakistani prime minister Zulfikar Ali Bhutto, his CENTO ally, to pull out of a nuclear deal with France that included the transfer of reprocessing technology. As both the shah and Etemad had intimated to the Americans on a number of occasions, the best way for Washington to prevent Pakistani nuclear proliferation was to sell Pakistan the conventional arms it needed to defend itself against India and to provide Islamabad with a meaningful security guarantee.[164]

Initially, it appeared that this American compromise on national reprocessing might break the deadlock in the nuclear negotiations with Iran. Although there were no major breakthroughs during the April 20–21 talks in Washington, Etemad had assured the Americans that "Iran was sincerely interested in reaching agreement with [the] U.S." The US negotiators had "the definite impression that this was so and that Etemad was probably under high-level instructions to try and overcome differences."[165] But Kissinger was also well aware that Iran could easily turn to France or West Germany for its nuclear needs, and he worried that US insistence on additional safeguards was jeopardizing lucrative nuclear contracts. The United States had lost its monopoly in the global nuclear market, as Canadian and European firms aggressively lobbied for contracts in emerging markets, including Iran.[166] A comprehensive German nuclear deal with Iran was already being negotiated in the spring of 1976.[167] Kissinger fumed that "we are the only country which is fanatical and unrealistic enough to do things which are contrary to our national interests. The Europeans are not so illogical."[168] The revelations the previous summer that the Germans had agreed to sell the entire nuclear fuel cycle to Brazil, including enrichment and reprocessing technology, while France was negotiating similar deals with Pakistan and South Korea, had infuriated Congress.[169] In response, Congress passed the Symington Amendment to the Foreign Assistance Act in June 1976, which blocked US economic and military assistance to any country engaged in nuclear trade, unless all transferred nuclear materials and facilities were placed under strict multilateral safeguards. As the 1976 presidential elections went into full swing, the Democratic candidate, Governor Jimmy Carter of Georgia, had made nuclear proliferation an election issue. In a speech at the United Nations in May, he had called for "a voluntary moratorium" by all nuclear supplier countries on transfers of enrichment and reprocessing technology.[170] The growing domestic political saliency of nuclear proliferation in the middle of an election year increasingly narrowed Ford's options in the nuclear negotiations with Iran.

Agreeing to Disagree

In the summer of 1976, after more than two years of negotiations, the Ford administration was still clinging to the hope that it could impose additional safeguards in a nuclear agreement with Iran, which would be crucial for ratification of the agreement by Congress. That hope evaporated when West Germany signed a broad nuclear cooperation agreement with Iran which, like their controversial deal with Brazil, included the eventual transfer of reprocessing technology. Bonn had kept Washington apprised of its negotiations with Tehran and looked to Kissinger for his blessing for the deal, but the secretary of state worried that the Germans were trying to make him the "fall guy" for an agreement that would be deeply unpopular in Congress.[171] After seeing the text of the agreement, an angry Kissinger reminded West German ambassador Berndt von Staden that "we had strongly urged that the FRG [Federal Republic of Germany] not transfer reprocessing to Iran. You know our position in this matter. I don't want anyone in the FRG to say he didn't know." Von Staden tried to defend the agreement by arguing that it contained strict safeguards that were "breaking new important ground" and would serve as a "useful precedent." Regardless of these safeguards, Kissinger was convinced that "It will still look like Brazil." He warned the ambassador that "we cannot avoid saying that we did not approve of this agreement" and to "be under no illusion as to what will happen when the agreement is announced."[172] Von Staden was right that the German-Iranian deal set a new precedent, but it was hardly a useful one from Kissinger's perspective. By agreeing to supply Iran with reprocessing technology, the Germans had undercut the US demand for a veto on Iranian reprocessing and a right to buy back Iran's spent nuclear fuel.

The State Department had delivered a revised draft of the US-Iran nuclear agreement to Etemad in June, hoping that the Iranians might respond positively to the compromise language on reprocessing, in accordance with NSDM 324. The draft agreement actually consisted of two documents. One was a new bilateral agreement between the United States and Iran to replace the original 1957 agreement on the civil uses of atomic energy, which the Americans hoped would be a template for future nuclear export deals. The other was a separate diplomatic note that elaborated the arrangements for managing Iran's spent nuclear fuel. Together, they constituted an agreement whereby the United States would only allow Iran to reprocess spent fuel in a national facility on Iranian soil, under strict bilateral and IAEA safeguards, if the Iranians made a good faith effort to secure international participation in their reprocessing plant, and if the United States chose not to buy back the spent fuel from Iran's reactors. Article XI of the American draft allowed the United States to review the design of any reactors or other equipment purchased by Iran for its nuclear program and gave American officials access to "all places and data" in order to keep track of nuclear material exported to Iran.[173]

The likelihood that the shah would agree to such intrusive and onerous safeguards, given the favorable terms of the German-Iranian deal, was very low. The Iranians were simply unwilling to forgo the option of national reprocessing of spent fuel, lest they leave themselves at the mercy of foreign nuclear fuel suppliers. Etemad sent the US Embassy in Tehran a lengthy response to the revised American draft on July 21, which left little hope that a US-Iran nuclear deal could still be reached. Iran was willing to agree to "active participation" by the United States in its reprocessing facility, but Etemad wanted to amend the American text to make such participation "commensurate with the respective United States economic and financial contribution to the facilities on the basis of reasonable economic practice." In other words, the United States would have to invest in the reprocessing facility if it wanted a say in its management. "Otherwise," he wrote, "Iran alone would be footing the bill for the non-proliferation objectives." Totally rejecting any US veto over Iranian reprocessing, he insisted that "Iran considers reprocessing an important 'downstream' activity, and for obvious security of supply and economic reasons seriously intends to have it performed in facilities established in Iran." The Iranians would maintain "effective control of the management and operation of the reprocessing facilities," while the United States would have a "minority voting right without a veto power" in the operation of the plant. Etemad all but repudiated the buy-back option as well, when he wrote that "Iran should have [the] full right to decide whether to reprocess or otherwise dispose or treat the materials provided under the agreement," subject to the agreed safeguards. He had transformed an American right to buy back Iran's spent fuel into an Iranian option to reprocess its spent fuel in the United States, if Iran decided "at any given time, that reprocessing in Iran is not advisable."[174]

This uncompromising Iranian response posed a serious problem for Kissinger, who was scheduled to visit the country in August 1976 for a meeting of the US-Iran Joint Commission. While a host of contentious issues were on Kissinger's agenda, with a proposed arms-for-oil barter agreement at the top of the list, the American media focused on a report in a Tehran newspaper that Kissinger would sign a deal for the sale of eight nuclear reactors to Iran worth $26 billion. American officials downplayed expectations that any deal would be reached during Kissinger's visit.[175] Robert Oakley, who had succeeded Harold Saunders as senior director for the Middle East and South Asia on the NSC staff, had consulted with his colleagues in the White House and the State Department, and they agreed that Etemad's July 21 reply was "a major set-back, returning our negotiations to the starting point." Oakley advised Scowcroft that "[w]e are now so far apart that it may be better for the Secretary to discuss this exclusively with the Shah and not have a meeting of the Nuclear subcommittee of the Joint Commission."[176] Kissinger's staff had to save him from the impossible task of negotiating a nuclear agreement with Iran that would not be seen by the shah as discriminatory, but would also satisfy Congress.

To make matters worse, on the eve of Kissinger's departure, the Foreign Assistance Subcommittee of the Senate Foreign Relations Committee published a scathing report on US arms sales to Iran, which was indicative of the prevailing attitude in Congress. The report concluded that because of the commitments Nixon had made to the shah in Tehran in 1972, "U.S. arms sales to Iran were out of control." The subcommittee was chaired by Senator Hubert Humphrey, a senior Democrat who had served as vice president under Lyndon Johnson and had lost the 1968 presidential election to Nixon. In an indictment of Nixon's policy of Iranian primacy, Humphrey wrote that Washington had "ignored the substantial and far-reaching foreign policy implications which result from our deep involvement in sales, training and logistical supply programs with Iran."[177] A *Washington Post* editorial lamented that Nixon's tilt toward Iran "was never debated within the administration, let alone in public" and labeled it "high-handed and irresponsible." The shah was portrayed as a dangerous megalomaniac who might draw the United States into a regional conflict in the Middle East or South Asia.[178] The Humphrey Report echoed increasing calls for the United States to distance itself from the shah because of human rights violations in Iran. Human rights organizations, as well as vocal Iranian dissidents, had brought the shah's human rights record to the attention of the national press.[179] Jimmy Carter had already given notice that he would block the sale of nuclear reprocessing technology to countries like Iran if he were elected to the White House. Now, Humphrey was also indicating that a Democratic administration might impose limits on US arms sales to Iran.

Kissinger hoped that his visit to Iran would shore up the United States' partnership with the shah, which was under withering fire from the Democrats in Congress and critics within the administration. He complained to Ford, "It couldn't be a worse time. Treasury and Defense are going after the Shah. Simon is going around saying the Shah is dangerous and shouldn't have exotic weapons." He warned Ford that, with this "vicious campaign" against the shah, "[w]e are playing with fire."[180] Perhaps sensing that his closest ally in Washington was under siege and that the US-Iran partnership was in peril, the shah eased the pressure on Kissinger in anticipation of his arrival in Iran. As Oakley had suggested, Kissinger would not attend the meeting of the joint nuclear energy committee. Instead, mid-level American officials attended the meeting with Etemad in Tehran on August 3 and 4, before Kissinger's arrival. Helms reported that in those meetings, Etemad "retreated" from the position he had taken in his July 21 letter: "While contending [that the] U.S. has [an] obligation to assist Iran in all areas of nuclear technology, Etemad acknowledged this was impractical for [the] U.S. under current conditions, and Iran would not press [the] point." The American negotiators insisted on framing the buy-back option as a US right to purchase Iran's spent fuel, rather than an Iranian option to reprocess its spent fuel in the United States. Some of the AEOI officials attending the meeting objected, but Etemad, who alone would have been privy to the shah's instructions, overruled them and agreed to the original American formula. Both delegations agreed on a "bottom line" that any agreement would not preclude, at least in principle, national reprocessing on Iranian soil.[181]

The shah received Kissinger on the afternoon of August 6 at his summer palace in Nowshahr on the Caspian Sea for three hours of private discussions. He explained to Kissinger that he could not be seen to acquiesce to any agreement that treated Iran any differently from other parties to the NPT. He insisted, according to Kissinger, that "we avoid doing anything which would appear to be discriminatory against Iran." But as Kissinger intimated to the shah, the political tide in the United States had turned decisively against the nuclear agreement. In the current political climate in Washington, Kissinger explained, "reprocessing in Iran on a purely national basis would not be an acceptable solution." Even American participation in a binational plant in Iran was not feasible "under current and foreseeable conditions." Although the draft nuclear agreement did not preclude the possibility of Iranian national reprocessing, Kissinger insisted that in practice Washington would always exercise its option to either buy back or exchange Iran's spent fuel. The shah "seemed agreeable" to this arrangement, according to Kissinger.[182] He may well have concluded that a nuclear agreement with the United States was impossible and that it was more important to ensure the success of Kissinger's visit in order to buttress the flagging US-Iran relationship. Kissinger reported to Ford that the agreement they had "hammered out should be satisfactory to key Congressional leaders and be useful not only for Iran but as a model for others who wish to buy nuclear reactors." During their discussion, "[t]he Shah repeated his anxiety about America's loss of political will.. . . He is disturbed by Congressional and Democratic attitudes to arms sales, and he fears it will only get worse." Kissinger was confident that his visit "went far to smooth his [the shah's] ruffled feelings" and to "reassure him about our own steadiness."[183]

At a joint press conference following their discussion, the traveling American press corps set about ruffling the same royal feelings that Kissinger had tried to soothe. The shah faced a barrage of hostile questions about the Humphrey Report, oil prices, and the question of torture of political prisoners in Iran's prisons. The shah expressed his frustration that American opinion seemed to be backing away from the central logic of the Nixon Doctrine, whereby the United States was helping Iran to defend itself without direct American military intervention. "I think that you are not pursuing a policy of standing by your friends who are spending their own money and are ready to spend their own blood for the sake of their own country," the shah complained. In exasperation he asked the American journalists, "What alternative do you have? Either all out nuclear holocaust, another Vietnam on your hands, every now and then." When asked about the nuclear negotiations, the shah was conciliatory. He assured the press that "although we are a signatory of the NPT, whatever safeguards that will be given which will not trespass on our national rights and sovereignty, we will give it very easily, willingly." He insisted that "we have absolutely no plans of becoming Atomic—military wise, absolutely none."[184]

With November's presidential elections looming, the August 1976 trip had been Kissinger's last opportunity to secure a nuclear agreement with the shah during Ford's first and, as it turned out, only term in office. Both men had sensed that a window of opportunity for a nuclear deal was closing, and both had compromised in order to try to save the deal. Although progress had been made on the reprocessing problem, with a tentative agreement on the buy-back option, the domestic political environment in the United States ultimately rendered a deal in 1976 impossible. While the Ford administration was busy conducting a major review of its nuclear policy, in response to Carter's challenge in May, the shah was looking elsewhere for the nuclear reactors he had hoped to buy from the United States.[185] In October, during a visit by President Giscard d'Estaing to Iran, France finalized an $8 billion deal to build a total of eight nuclear reactors in Iran, beginning with two 900MW reactors near Abadan, as well as a nuclear research center near Isfahan to train Iranian nuclear scientists.[186] The final nail in the coffin of the US-Iran nuclear deal came three weeks later, when the shah received an advance copy of a major policy statement by Ford on nuclear policy.[187] In an audacious announcement on October 28, the president declared that "the United States should no longer regard reprocessing of used nuclear fuel to produce plutonium as a necessary and inevitable step in the nuclear fuel cycle." Ford ordered a deferral of the commercialization of chemical reprocessing in the United States, as well as a three-year moratorium on US exports of enrichment and reprocessing technology. He called on "nuclear suppliers to provide nuclear consumers with fuel services, instead of sensitive technology or facilities."[188]

Ford's October statement meant that the nuclear deal with Iran would have to be renegotiated from scratch, but that would have to await the outcome of the presidential elections. In the meantime, the US-Iran partnership continued to deteriorate as Ford tried to protect the fragile global economic recovery, following the 1973 oil shock, from another increase in oil prices by OPEC at its scheduled summit in Doha in December 1976. Ford wrote to the shah on October 29, informing him that Kissinger had relayed the shah's "concern about the need to maintain close cooperation between our two countries despite opposition in Congress and other circles." The president warned the shah that "[t]he struggle with certain segments of American opinion on this subject has by no means been won," and any move by Iran to raise oil prices "would play directly into the hands of those who have been attacking our relationship."[189] Ford's letter implied that Iranian defiance on oil prices would harm its chances of winning Congressional approval for further arms sales or the proposed nuclear deal. The shah's reply reached the president soon after he had lost the election to Carter. In perhaps the strongest language ever used by the shah with an American president, he told Ford that Iran was not about to commit economic "suicide" because the West refused to reduce its dependence on oil or lower inflation through painful cuts in spending. He threatened that

> if there is any opposition in the Congress and in other circles to see Iran prosperous and militarily strong, there are many other sources of supply to which we can turn, for our life is not in their hands. If these circles are irresponsible then it is hopeless, but should they

be responsible, they will certainly regret their attitude to my country. Nothing could provoke more reaction in us than this threatening tone from certain circles and their paternalistic attitude.

The tone of this exchange strongly suggests that the decline of the US-Iran partnership was well under way during Ford's presidency, rather than under the Carter administration, as has commonly been thought.[190] Carter would resume the nuclear negotiations with the shah in April 1977, but the rising tide of domestic unrest that engulfed Iran in 1978 prevented the two countries from signing a nuclear agreement before the shah's overthrow in 1979.[191]

The failure of the long and torturous US-Iran nuclear negotiations, from May 1974 to August 1976, laid bare the decline of the Nixon-Kissinger-Pahlavi partnership in the aftermath of Watergate. Mohammad Reza Shah and Henry Kissinger had failed to reach an accord on US nuclear exports to Iran because Ford reverted to treating the shah as a client, rather than a partner, of the United States. In two years of nuclear talks, the Ford administration insisted on a veto over reprocessing of spent nuclear fuel in Iran in order to satisfy Congress that Iran would not be able to use American-supplied nuclear materials and facilities to stockpile plutonium for a nuclear weapons program. The shah considered this veto a violation of Iran's sovereignty and consistently rejected it. The decision on how to dispose of its spent fuel, he insisted, was for Iran, and Iran alone, to make. Throughout the negotiations, Kissinger struggled to build a consensus in favor of a nuclear deal with Iran, especially given the shah's poor public image in the United States. Many in the American political establishment worried that a megalomaniacal shah was following India down the path of nuclear proliferation. Without going so far as to abandon the US veto on reprocessing, Ford and Kissinger made two concessions in the hope of securing a nuclear deal with Iran, first by allowing Iranian spent fuel reprocessing, as long as it was conducted in a multinational facility, and subsequently by dropping the multinational facility as a precondition but insisting on an option to buy back Iran's spent fuel. During Kissinger's visit to Tehran in August 1976, the shah responded positively to these American concessions in the hope of bolstering his faltering relationship with Washington. However, Ford's tough October 1976 statement on nuclear proliferation ended any prospect of a deal during his presidency.

The American demand for a veto over Iranian reprocessing was seen by the shah as discriminatory, given that no such demand had been made of any other signatory to the NPT. From Washington's perspective, this was simply a case of bad timing, as the nuclear negotiations with Iran came just after the Indian nuclear test forced the administration to rethink its policy on nuclear exports. Having grown accustomed to being treated with respect and deference by Nixon, the shah saw Ford's response as a weakening of his partnership with the United States. The notion that the United States would decide for Iran how it could dispose of its spent nuclear fuel was anachronistic in the wake of Nixon ordering his officials not to second-guess the shah's decisions. Kissinger continued to see the shah as a vital Cold War partner and tried in vain to make a deal that would satisfy both parties. But Kissinger could not overcome the opposition from those in Washington who saw the shah as the "emperor of oil" and feared the consequences of placing nuclear technology in his hands, especially after the privileged treatment the Iranian leader had been given under the Nixon administration. Frustrated and disappointed, the shah bargained hard in the knowledge that Washington was in no position to impose additional safeguards that violated Iran's sovereignty, given that the United States had lost its monopoly over the global nuclear supply market. Unable to get the deal he wanted from the United States, he turned to France and West Germany instead.

The dramatic rise in oil prices after 1973 had afforded Iran even greater autonomy from the United States. The shah's decision to rapidly expand Iran's nuclear industry in 1974 had been made without consulting Washington and with Iranian, not American, interests in mind. Nonetheless, the failure to reach a nuclear accord under Ford did not translate into a total repudiation of Nixon's policy of Iranian primacy. Ford honored Nixon's commitments to the shah. Annual US arms sales to Iran nearly doubled during his presidency from just over $1 billion in 1975 to nearly $2 billion in 1976. That figure would reach a peak at more than $2.5 billion in 1977 during the first year of the Carter administration.[192] But when it came to new commitments to Iran, such as a nuclear agreement, Nixon's unelected successor could not build a consensus within his administration and in Congress to preserve the US-Iran partnership, and the discriminatory nuclear agreement that he offered was rejected by the shah. Nixon's successor made light of his simplicity when he joked that he was "a Ford, not a Lincoln." But in the shah's eyes he was a Ford, not a Nixon.

Conclusion

"IS THERE A special relationship between Henry Kissinger and the Shah of Iran?" This was the question posed by veteran journalist Dan Rather in a May 1980 segment of the popular CBS television show *60 Minutes*. Kissinger had been scheduled to appear on the show, which had been delayed in order to accommodate the former secretary of state's schedule. But at the last minute, Kissinger had pulled out, complaining that it would be a "hatchet job."[1] The broadcast included interviews with James Akins, a former US ambassador to Saudi Arabia who had been fired by Kissinger for being too sympathetic to the Saudis, William Simon, the former treasury secretary who had clashed with Kissinger over support for the shah and rising oil prices, and George Ball, a former undersecretary of state in the Kennedy and Johnson administrations who had advised President Jimmy Carter on Iran and had criticized Kissinger for his efforts to secure exile for the shah in the United States. Don Hewitt, the executive producer of *60 Minutes*, wrote to Kissinger, "You may have been—probably were—the best Secretary of State we ever had. But you are not the Statue of Liberty or the Washington Monument, and I think it's unrealistic of you to expect us to treat you like a national shrine."[2] The broadcast accused Kissinger of colluding with the shah to raise oil prices in 1970s, so that Iran could purchase more arms from the United States in order to police the Persian Gulf under the Nixon Doctrine. These arms sales supposedly fueled the shah's megalomania and contributed to the 1979 Iranian Revolution and the subsequent Tehran hostage crisis. As Dan Rather said on air, "we paid one hell of a price for arming the shah."[3]

Nearly six years after Nixon's resignation, three years after Kissinger left office, and more than a year after the overthrow of the shah, the Nixon-Kissinger-Pahlavi partnership still cast a long shadow over US-Iran relations. Although it was journalistic hyperbole to blame the Iranian Revolution and the Tehran hostage crisis on Kissinger, the basic premise of a special relationship was plain for all to see. After Mohammad Reza Shah had fled the revolutionary turmoil in January 1979, Kissinger had worked tirelessly to offer him entry to the United States. Although Carter had initially agreed to admit the shah, he changed his mind during the shah's stay in Egypt and Morocco, fearing the reaction of Ayatollah Khomeini and the revolutionaries in Tehran. Kissinger, with the help of his friend David Rockefeller, found a temporary refuge for the shah in the Bahamas.[4] Then, when the shah was no longer welcome there, Kissinger traveled to Mexico in April and convinced President José López Portillo to offer the shah safe haven.[5] Both Kissinger and Nixon visited the shah during his stay in the resort town of Cuernavaca, south of Mexico City. Nixon recalled that during several hours of discussions in July, tears came to the shah's eyes as the deposed monarch pondered the gruesome fate of his former ministers and generals who had remained in Iran, the shoddy treatment he had received from Carter, and the continuing decline of American power.[6] This was the last time the two men would ever see each other. During an airport news conference, Nixon told the assembled journalists that "[o]ne principle that I have followed is that whether it's in Vietnam or it's in Iran, you don't grease the skids for your friends. If the United States does not stand by its own friends we are going to end up with no friends."[7]

Kissinger relentlessly pressured Carter, both publicly and privately, to admit the shah to the United States. The press reported Kissinger's remarks at a Harvard Business School dinner in New York in April, where he declared that "a man who for 37 years was a friend of the United States should not be treated like a Flying Dutchman who cannot find a port of call."[8] However, Carter feared that admitting the shah would lead to retaliation against Americans in Iran. In a prophetic comment to his national security adviser, Zbigniew Brzezinski, the president said on July 27 that "he did not want the Shah to be here playing tennis while Americans in Tehran were being kidnapped or even killed."[9] The pressure mounted on Carter when the shah's health deteriorated rapidly in October. Carter's chief of staff, Hamilton Jordan, warned the president that "if the Shah dies in Mexico, can you imagine the field day Kissinger will have with it? He'll say that first you caused the Shah's downfall and now you've killed him." An infuriated Carter replied, "To hell with Henry Kissinger. I am the President of this country!"[10]

Nonetheless, given the shah's dire medical condition, Carter relented and allowed the shah to travel to New York for treatment on October 22.[11] In retaliation, a group of radical Iranian students climbed the walls of the US Embassy in Tehran on November 4 and took scores of Americans hostage. Kissinger was savaged in the press for having advocated the shah's entry to the United States. Anthony Lewis attacked Kissinger's "cowardice" in his *New York Times* column. The former secretary of state had "urged the Shah's admission to the United States," Lewis wrote, "but has taken no responsibility for the result."[12] Kissinger remained unapologetic, insisting that "it is incompatible with our national honor to turn our back on a leader who cooperated with us for a generation. Never before have we given foreign governments a veto over who can enter our country as a private citizen."[13] Kissinger saw the shah for the last time on the morning of November 10, during a visit with his wife Nancy to the shah's bedside at New York Hospital–Cornell Medical Center.[14] Under pressure from Carter, the shah would leave the United States in December for Panama and then Egypt, where he succumbed to cancer in a military hospital outside Cairo on July 28, 1980.

***

How, then, are we to remember this partnership among Richard Nixon, Henry Kissinger, and Mohammad Reza Pahlavi? It was undoubtedly the clearest expression of the Nixon Doctrine, which, as historian John Lewis Gaddis argues, marked a return to an "asymmetrical" US strategy of containment, whereby the United States would choose where and when to confront its Soviet adversary. The decline of American power in the era of the Vietnam War meant that the United States had to be more careful about picking "uncongenial" fights in the global Cold War.[15] Yet, as Kissinger recognized, the world had become a "single strategic theater" where even the most obscure local conflict could have far-reaching international consequences.[16] Nixon and Kissinger resolved this dilemma in the Persian Gulf by looking to Iran to fill the vacuum created by the British withdrawal from the region in 1971. For eight years, this strategy seemed to work. The Soviet Union made few inroads into the Gulf; Saddam Hussein's Ba'thi regime in Iraq was cowed, signing the Algiers Agreement with Iran in 1975; and Arab radicals failed to topple conservative Gulf rulers like Sultan Qaboos of Oman, who defeated a rebellion in Dhofar with the help of the shah. Most important, the rivalry between Iran and Iraq for regional supremacy never escalated into war. The worst fears of those who had predicted chaos after the British withdrawal failed to materialize, thanks to Mohammad Reza Shah's leadership. This stability was shattered by the Iranian Revolution, which plunged Iran and the whole Gulf into violence and instability. The fall of the shah, combined with the Soviet invasion of Afghanistan, forced the United States to take up the mantle of regional primacy from Iran. In his January 1980 State of the Union address, Carter declared that "[a]n attempt by any outside force to gain control of the Persian Gulf region will be regarded as an assault on the vital interests of the United States of America, and such an assault will be repelled by any means necessary, including military force."[17] This Carter Doctrine heralded the beginning of direct US military intervention in the Gulf, which continues to this day.[18] In this sense, the Nixon-Kissinger-Pahlavi partnership will be remembered as an Iranian interregnum between *Pax Britannica* and American hegemony in the Persian Gulf.

With the benefit of hindsight, historians are severely critical of Nixon and Kissinger for investing so heavily in the shah's deeply unpopular regime. For example, James Bill writes that "in seeking to wed America's national interests with those of the shah, they never stopped to ponder the actual strength of the Iranian leader. They ignored the domestic forces brewing within Iran and failed to question the results of their policies on Iranian society itself."[19] There is no doubt that in the 1969–1976 period, neither Nixon nor Kissinger paid any heed to the Iranian opposition or expressed any concern about the human rights record of the shah's regime. Yet, this criticism overlooks the fact that the militant opposition to the shah in the 1970s only served to reinforce the logic of US support for the Pahlavi monarchy. The "language of dissent" adopted by the shah's leftist and Islamist opponents was largely borrowed from the global protest movements of the 1960s.[20] From Washington's perspective, the militant opposition to the shah was the local Iranian manifestation of the global disorder that Nixon and Kissinger's grand strategy of détente was designed to combat. The logic of this strategy meant that increasing opposition to the shah necessitated more US support for the shah, as a "bulwark" against disorder, not less. As historian Jeremi Suri writes, "Kissinger understood both the nature of this policy and its shortcomings. It was not unique to his endeavors in the Middle East. He constructed his career around the presumption that in a cruel and violent world powerful leaders, not democratic politics, offered the best protection for life and liberty."[21] The destruction and violence that Iran and its neighbors were plunged into after the fall of the shah, especially during the horrific 1980–1988 Iran-Iraq

War, would seem to vindicate these presumptions. Yet, the stability that the shah provided in the 1970s also came at a steep cost, not only to those Iranians who found themselves imprisoned, tortured, or exiled for daring to oppose the regime's brutality and corruption, but also to the United States, which was forever implicated in the shah's misdeeds.

The Nixon administration's policy toward Iran was not simply a reflection of geopolitical realities. If that were the case, then Nixon and Kissinger would have continued with their predecessors' policy of treating the shah as a client of the United States. This would have meant meddling in Iran's internal affairs, as the Eisenhower, Kennedy, and Johnson administrations had all done from time to time; continuing to second-guess the shah's decisions on arms purchases; and maintaining a balance of power between Iran and Saudi Arabia in the Persian Gulf after the British withdrawal. Breaking with this policy, Nixon and Kissinger instead embraced the shah as a US partner under the Nixon Doctrine. How the shah ran his country was his business. What mattered to the Nixon administration was the contribution that Iran could make to American strategies of containment. This change in policy was not only a function of America's quagmire in Vietnam, or Iran's rising oil revenues, but also of shared ideas among Nixon, Kissinger, and the shah concerning the need to preserve order at a time of revolutionary upheaval. These three Cold Warriors agreed that the threats to Iran's stability, both foreign and domestic, also constituted threats to the United States' interests in this crucial theater of the Cold War. During Nixon's first term as president, the shah relentlessly lobbied the new administration to abandon Johnson's policy of balancing Iran and Saudi Arabia as the twin pillars of the Gulf and to support Iran in its bid to assume the mantle of regional primacy abandoned by the British. Thanks to his long-standing friendship with Nixon, the shah enjoyed a sympathetic hearing in the White House. Unlike his predecessors, Nixon did not see the shah as a megalomaniac, squandering Iran's oil income on useless weapons. Rather, he saw a modernizing anti-communist statesman who shared both his views on the Cold War as well as his disdain for liberal intellectuals.

In Nixon's mind, the question was not whether the shah should assume leadership in the Persian Gulf region, but whether he was up to the task of taking on such an important role. Iran's uncompromising defense of its regional primacy against the challenge from Iraq in the 1969 Shatt al-Arab crisis and its covert support for Pakistan during the 1971 South Asian crisis demonstrated that the shah was more than ready for this newfound role. In National Security Decision Memorandum 92 of November 1970, the Nixon administration had recognized the preponderance of Iranian power in the Gulf, and in their May 1972 meetings in Tehran, Nixon and Kissinger assured the shah that Iran would be able to purchase whatever conventional weapons it wanted from the United States in order to deter any regional adversary. As a US client in the 1950s and 1960s, Iran had been a Cold War battleground where the United States occasionally violated Iran's sovereignty to protect American interests. As a US partner in the 1970s, Iran became an autonomous Cold War actor, working with the United States to keep the oil-rich Gulf out of the hands of the Soviet Union and its Arab clients.

By embracing Mohammad Reza Shah as their partner, Nixon and Kissinger allowed him to shape the Nixon Doctrine according to Iranian interests. This was the price that they willingly paid for the shah's help in preserving regional order. This meant that when the shah asked Nixon and Kissinger to support Iran's secret war in Iraqi Kurdistan in 1972, they readily agreed, ignoring advice from the CIA, the NSC staff, and the State Department. At the same time that the United States was searching for a Vietnam exit strategy, it found itself drawn into another civil war in the faraway mountains of Iraqi Kurdistan. The shah used the United States to keep Barzani and his Pesh Merga fighting, so as to paralyze the Iraqi army and neutralize the Iraqi threat to Iran's oil-rich province of Khuzestan and Iranian shipping through the Shatt al-Arab. But when the shah's faith in the United States was shaken by Watergate, and as the tide of battle turned against the Kurds, the shah made a deal with Saddam Hussein in March 1975 to cut off Iranian aid to Barzani in exchange for Iraqi territorial concessions in the Shatt. Although Kissinger had warned the shah against abandoning the Kurds, he had no choice but to accept the shah's decision and to suffer the domestic recriminations that followed.

As the shah's influence in Washington receded following Nixon's resignation in August 1974, Iran's partnership with the United States steadily declined. There was no longer an intimate relationship between the shah and the White House. The shah's critics in Congress and within the administration were no longer sidelined, as they had been when Nixon and Kissinger conducted the nation's foreign policy behind closed doors. Gerald Ford did not repudiate the Nixon Doctrine, and US arms continued to flow to Iran with little impediment. However, as American criticism of the shah's human rights record, vast spending on arms, and orchestration of painful oil price increases mounted, Washington reverted to treating the shah as a US client. This was apparent in the negotiations for US nuclear exports to Iran, as the Ford administration tried to foist additional safeguards on Iran that went beyond its commitments under the Nuclear Non-Proliferation Treaty. The shah would not tolerate such discrimination, viewing it as reminiscent of America's past meddling in Iran's internal affairs, and he ultimately gave lucrative nuclear contracts to France and West Germany.

By the late 1970s, the shah's public image in the United States had been reduced to that of a megalomaniacal dictator, bent on increasing oil prices to fund his insatiable appetite for arms. In the aftermath of Watergate and the Vietnam War, US partnerships with Third World auto-crats like the shah seemed an anachronistic hangover from the discred-ited Nixon administration. Yet, the shah was a far more complex figure than the caricature his critics drew. He was undoubtedly intoxicated by the oil bonanza of the 1970s, which led him to make a series of disas-trous political and economic decisions at home, not the least of which was the overheating of the Iranian economy with profligate spending in the 1970s and the establishment of a one-party state in 1975. Yet, at the same time, he was extremely calculating in the conduct of Iranian diplomacy, displaying a pragmatism and judiciousness that was entirely absent in his arbitrary domestic leadership. At the same time as the shah cultivated a Cold War partnership with the United States, he pursued a successful détente with the Soviet Union. While he seized the Persian Gulf islands of Abu Musa and the Tunbs, he also relinquished Iran's claim to Bahrain. While he helped funnel US military assistance to Pakistan, he refused to be drawn into an Indo-Pakistan War. While he asserted Iran's sovereignty in the Shatt al-Arab and fought a covert war against Saddam Hussein's Iraq in Kurdistan, he also avoided an Iran-Iraq war. Although Iran's pol-itics imposed few, if any, limits on the shah's power at home, the inter-national system, primarily Cold War bipolarity, imposed firm limits on Iran's power in the global arena that the shah understood and respected.

The shah has been traditionally characterized as a mere instrument of American power, a US client who defended American interests in Iran and the Persian Gulf in exchange for Washington's economic and mili-tary support for his unpopular regime. Amin Saikal, a critical biographer of the shah, writes that Mohammed Reza Shah never managed "to over-come the indignity of his initial reliance on the CIA for wresting power from Mossadeq, nor break free from his initial dependence on the United States, and thus balance Iran's relations with that country on the basis of a symmetrical relationship."[22] The three episodes examined in this book counter this static view of the shah's relationship with the United States. From the 1960s onward, the shah's autonomy from the United States steadily grew, in parallel with Iran's rising oil revenues and military expenditure. Presidents Kennedy and Johnson found it increasingly difficult to treat the shah as a Cold War client of the United States. The turning point came with the Nixon Doctrine, which recognized Iran as a partner of the United States in the global Cold War of the 1970s. Iran was not simply a Cold War battleground, to be won or lost by the United States, but an autonomous Cold War actor that defended the stability of the Persian Gulf and projected its power from the Zagros Mountains to the Bay of Bengal.

The Nixon-Kissinger-Pahlavi partnership is one thread in the global history of the Cold War, which has restored agency to Third World actors like the shah and placed them firmly at the center of the worldwide struggle between the Soviet Union and the United States. This interpretation might suggest that blaming the shah's downfall on the policies of Nixon, Kissinger, or Carter is erroneous. The shah's mistakes, like his triumphs, were his own. Given the shah's autonomy from the United States, could Nixon and Kissinger have pressured him to carry out meaningful domestic political reform? It seems unlikely that they would have had any more success than Kennedy and his "New Frontiersmen" a decade earlier. Alternatively, could Carter have intervened in Iran in 1979 to save the shah, as Eisenhower had done in 1953? Surely the nature and dynamics of US-Iran relations had changed so dramatically during the preceding decade that such a gross violation of Iran's sovereignty was unthinkable.

An acknowledgment of the shah's autonomy from the United States in the 1970s may prompt more interesting questions about the Cold War in the Third World. For example, what does the shah's autonomy say about the notion of Cold War "alignment" in the Third World? The origins of the term "Third World" imply Cold War non-alignment, which would seem to exclude US allies like Pahlavi Iran that attended the 1955 Bandung Conference of Afro-Asian Peoples, but did not show up for the 1961 Belgrade summit of the Non-Aligned Movement (NAM).[23] How meaningful is it to draw a distinction between aligned and non-aligned in the Third World, particularly in the 1970s, when the NAM was in decline? The case of Iran would suggest that the borders between alignment and non-alignment were more fluid and dynamic than previously thought. Few, if any, countries eschewed assistance from one or both of the superpowers during the Cold War. Nor did alignment necessarily imply exploitation or neo-colonialism. What distinguished Third World countries was not the strategies they employed for defending their interests and sovereignty during the Cold War, but the extent to which they succeeded in doing so.

***

In the three decades since the fall of the shah, Iranian-American partnership has turned to enmity. Yet, issues like the stability of the Persian Gulf and nuclear proliferation remain of vital concern to both countries. For Washington, the importance of a partnership with Iran has outlived the Cold War, as the dilemma of limited means and global interests has only intensified after September 11, 2001. After that infamous day, when Iranian president Mohammad Khatami swiftly condemned the attacks on the United States and Iranians held a spontaneous candlelight vigil in Tehran to express their solidarity with America's grief, it appeared that a partnership between the United States and Iran might once again be possible. The two countries worked together quietly and effectively to topple the Taliban in Afghanistan and to establish the Karzai government in 2001.[24] Yet, détente has eluded them ever since President George W. Bush branded Iran a member of the "axis of evil."[25] For enmity to transform once again into partnership, Iranian and American leaders must share a common set of ideas about the nature of the global order, as Nixon, Kissinger, and the shah did some 40 years ago. For the United States, this means accepting that any global order must respect not only Iran's national sovereignty, but also its legitimate interests and aspirations, which remain surprisingly unchanged since the days of the shah. For Iran, this means acknowledging that enmity with the United States is the greatest obstacle to the rise of Iranian power. In doing so, Iranians may come to recognize that, while the Iranian Revolution repudiated the Pahlavi monarchy, the Pahlavi Doctrine of strength through partnership with the United States has even greater saliency in the post–Cold War world, where the United States remains the world's sole superpower, than it did in the 1970s. Through his partnership with Richard Nixon and Henry Kissinger, Mohammad Reza Pahlavi achieved a level of regional primacy and global influence for Iran that no other Iranian ruler has enjoyed in the modern era. While some have referred to the "flawed genius" or "majestic failure" of the shah in light of his overthrow in 1979, perhaps one day he will come to be remembered as the best foreign minister Iran never had.[26]

Notes

INTRODUCTION

1. The shah was styled His Imperial Majesty, the *shah-an-shah* (king of kings) *ary-amehr* (light of the Aryans). Throughout this book he is referred to interchange-ably as Mohammad Reza Pahlavi, Mohammad Reza Shah, and the shah.

2. The United States, like a number of other countries, was represented by its am-bassador to Egypt. See A. O. Sulzberger, "U.S. Quietly Acknowledges Death of Shah," *New York Times*, July 28, 1980.

3. On the Carter administration and Iran, see Christian Emery, *US Foreign Policy and the Iranian Revolution: The Cold War Dynamics of Engagement and Strategic Alliance* (Basingstoke, UK: Palgrave Macmillan, 2013); Mark Gasiorowski, "US Intelligence Assistance to Iran, May-October 1979," *Middle East Journal* 66, no. 4 (2012): 613–627; Gary Sick, *All Fall Down: America's Fateful Encounter with Iran* (London: I. B. Tauris, 1985); Luca Trenta, "The Champion of Human Rights Meets the King of Kings: Jimmy Carter, the Shah, and Iranian Illusions and Rage," *Diplomacy & Statecraft* 24, no. 3 (2013): 476–498.

4. Farah Pahlavi, *An Enduring Love: My Life with the Shah, A Memoir* (New York: Hyperion, 2004), 328–388. See also William Shawcross, *The Shah's Last Ride: The Story of the Exile, Misadventures and Death of the Emperor* (London: Chatto & Windus, 1989).

5. Christopher S. Wren, "Few Ex-Allies Will Attend Funeral of Shah Today," *New York Times*, July 29, 1980. See also Robert Sam Anson, *Exile: The Unquiet Oblivion of Richard M. Nixon* (New York: Simon & Schuster, 1984), 223–225.

6. Bernard Gwertzman, "Carter Emissary Dissuaded Shah from U.S. Exile," *New York Times*, April 20, 1979; "Kissinger Interceded For Shah in Mexico, As Did the State Dept.," *New York Times*, June 12, 1979.

7. "Who Lost Iran?" *Washington Post*, February 26, 1979.

8. "Kissinger's critique (continued)," *Economist*, February 10, 1979; "Letter: Kissinger on Iran," *Economist*, February 17, 1979.

9. See James A. Bill, *The Eagle and the Lion: The Tragedy of American-Iranian Relations* (New Haven, CT: Yale University Press, 1988); Richard W. Cottam, *Iran and the United States: A Cold War Case Study* (Pittsburgh, PA: University of Pittsburgh Press, 1988); Barry Rubin, *Paved with Good Intentions: The American Experience and Iran* (New York: Oxford University Press, 1980).

10. See, among others, James A. Bill and Wm. Roger Louis, eds., *Musaddiq, Iranian Nationalism and Oil* (London: I. B. Tauris, 1988); Mark J. Gasiorowski, *U.S. Foreign Policy and the Shah: Building a Client State in Iran* (Ithaca, NY: Cornell University Press, 1991); Mark J. Gasiorowski and Malcolm Byrne, eds., *Mohammad Mosaddeq and the 1953 Coup in Iran* (Syracuse, NY: Syracuse University Press, 2004); Mary Ann Heiss, *Empire and Nationhood: The United States, Great Britain, and Iranian Oil, 1950–1954* (New York: Columbia University Press, 1997).

11. David R. Collier, "To Prevent a Revolution: John F. Kennedy and the Promotion of Democracy in Iran," *Diplomacy & Statecraft* 24, no. 3 (2013): 456–475; James F. Goode, "Reforming Iran during the Kennedy Years," *Diplomatic History* 15, no. 1 (1991): 13–29; Victor V. Nemchenok, "In Search of Stability Amid Chaos: US Policy Toward Iran, 1961–63," *Cold War History* 10, no. 3 (2010): 341–369; Roland Popp, "Benign Intervention? The Kennedy Administration's Push for Reform in Iran," in *John F. Kennedy and the 'Thousand Days': New Perspectives on the Foreign and Domestic Policies of the Kennedy Administration*, eds. Manfred Berg and Andreas Etges (Heidelberg: Universitatsverlag Winter, 2007), 197–219; April R. Summit, "For a White Revolution: John F. Kennedy and the Shah of Iran," *Middle East Journal* 58, no. 4 (2004): 560–575; Andrew Warne, "Psychoanalyzing Iran: Kennedy's Iran Task Force and the Modernization of Orientalism, 1961–3," *International History Review* 35, no. 2 (2013): 396–422.

12. See Claudia Castiglioni, " 'I Can Start a Revolution but You Won't Like the Result': The United States and Iran in the Decade of Development," in *The Middle East and the Cold War: Between Security and Development*, eds. Massimiliano Trentin and Matteo Gerlini (Newcastle, UK: Cambridge Scholars Publishing, 2012), 105–127; Andrew L. Johns, "The Johnson Administration, the Shah of Iran, and the Changing Pattern of U.S.-Iranian Relations, 1965–1967: 'Tired of Being Treated like a Schoolboy,'" *Journal of Cold War Studies* 9, no. 2 (2007): 64–94; Stephen McGlinchey, "Lyndon B. Johnson and Arms Credit Sales to Iran 1964–1968," *Middle East Journal* 67, no. 4 (2013): 229–247.

13. Bill, *Eagle and the Lion*, 203; Cottam, *Iran and the United States*, 149; Gasiorowski, *U.S. Foreign Policy*, 209; James F. Goode, *The United States and Iran: In the Shadow of Musaddiq* (Basingstoke, UK: Macmillan, 1997), 186; Rubin, *Paved with Good Intentions*, 124.

14. Douglas Little, *American Orientalism: The United States and the Middle East since 1945* (Chapel Hill: University of North Carolina Press, 2004), 145.

15. See Odd Arne Westad, *The Global Cold War: Third World Interventions and the Making of Our Times* (Cambridge: Cambridge University Press, 2007).

16. See Tony Smith, "New Bottles for New Wine: A Pericentric Framework for the Study of the Cold War," *Diplomatic History* 24, no. 4 (2000): 567–591.

17. See Roham Alvandi, "Nixon, Kissinger, and the Shah: The Origins of Iranian Primacy in the Persian Gulf," *Diplomatic History* 36, no. 2 (2012): 337–372; William Burr, "A Brief History of U.S.-Iranian Nuclear Negotiations," *Bulletin of Atomic Scientists* 65, no. 1 (2009): 21–34; Andrew Scott Cooper, *The Oil Kings: How the U.S., Iran, and Saudi Arabia Changed the Balance of Power in the Middle East* (New York: Simon & Schuster, 2011); Jacob Darwin Hamblin, "The Nuclearization of Iran in the Seventies," *Diplomatic History* (forthcoming 2014); Stephen McGlinchey, "Richard Nixon's Road to Tehran: The Making of the U.S.-Iran Arms Agreement of May 1972,' *Diplomatic History* 37, no. 4 (2013): 841–860.

18. Asadollah Alam, *Yad'dashtha-ye 'Alam: Virayish va muqaddamah az Ali Naqi Alikhani* [The Alam Diaries: Edited by Alinaghi Alikhani], Volumes I–VI [1969–1977] (Bethesda, MD: Iranbooks and Ibex, 1993–2007). These diaries were periodically deposited by Alam in a bank vault in Switzerland with instructions that they were not to be made public as long as the Pahlavi dynasty ruled Iran. It seems likely that Alam planned to use his diaries to write a biography of the shah, though he succumbed to cancer in 1978 before he could embark on this project. The Alam diaries are, however, fraught with methodological challenges. A loyal servant of the shah and a protagonist in this history, Alam was hardly a disinterested observer. Nonetheless, these diaries are the most valuable Iranian source on the shah's highly secretive decision-making. See Abbas Milani, "Asadollah Alam," in his *Eminent Persians: the Men and Women Who Made Modern Iran, 1941–1979*, Volume I (Syracuse, NY: Syracuse University Press; and New York: Persian World Press, 2008), 44–55; Helms to Alam, August 15, 1977, 1-3-3, Papers of Richard Helms, Georgetown University Library, Washington, DC. An abridged English edition of Alam's diaries has been published, though all references in this book are to the complete Persian edition unless stated otherwise. See Asadollah Alam, *The Shah and I: The Confidential Diary of Iran's Royal Court, 1969–1977*, trans. ed. Alinaghi Alikhani (London: I. B. Tauris, 1991).

19. See Abbas Milani, "Ardeshir Zahedi," *Eminent Persians*, Vol. I, 327–340.

20. Gasiorowski, *U.S. Foreign Policy*; Victor V. Nemchenok, " 'That So Fair a Thing Should Be So Frail': The Ford Foundation and the Failure of Rural Development in Iran, 1953–1964," *Middle East Journal* 63, no. 2 (2009): 261–284; Roland Popp, "An Application of Modernization Theory during the Cold War? The Case of Pahlavi Iran," *International History Review* 30, no. 1 (2008): 76–98; Cyrus Schayegh, "Iran's Karaj Dam Affair: Emerging Mass Consumerism, the Politics of Promise, and the Cold War in the Third World," *Comparative Studies in Society and History* 54, no. 3 (2012): 612–643; Matthew K. Shannon, "Losing

Hearts and Minds: American-Iranian Relations and International Education during the Cold War," PhD diss., Temple University, 2013.

1   THE UNITED STATES AND IRAN IN THE COLD WAR

1. Geir Lundestad, "Empire by Invitation? The United States and Western Europe, 1945–1952," *Journal of Peace Research* 23, no. 3 (1986): 263–277.

2. See Abraham Yeselson, *United States–Persian Diplomatic Relations 1883–1921* (New Brunswick, NJ: Rutgers University Press, 1956).

3. See T. H. Vail Motter, *The Persian Corridor and Aid to Russia* (Washington, DC: Office of the Chief of Military History, Department of the Army, 1952).

4. On the Roosevelt administration and Iran, see Mark H. Lytle, *The Origins of the Iranian-American Alliance, 1941–1953* (London: Holmes & Meier, 1987).

5. A. H. Hamzavi, "Iran and the Tehran Conference," *International Affairs* 20, no. 2 (1944): 192–203.

6. Louise L. Fawcett, *Iran and the Cold War: The Azerbaijan Crisis of 1946* (Cambridge: Cambridge University Press, 1992), 119.

7. See Justus D. Doenecke, "Revisionists, Oil and Cold War Diplomacy," *Iranian Studies* 3, no. 1 (1970): 23–33.

8. See Stephen L. McFarland, "A Peripheral View of the Origins of the Cold War: The Crises in Iran, 1941–47," *Diplomatic History* 4, no. 4 (1980): 333–352.

9. Fakhreddin Azimi, *Iran: The Crisis of Democracy* (New York: St Martin's Press, 1989), 108–115.

10. Mostafa Elm, *Oil, Power, and Principle: Iran's Nationalisation and its Aftermath* (Syracuse, NY: Syracuse University Press, 1992), 45.

11. Not to be confused with the Azerbaijan Soviet Socialist Republic, with its capital in Baku.

12. Fernande S. Raine, "Stalin and the Creation of the Azerbaijan Democratic Party in Iran, 1945," *Cold War History* 2, no. 1 (2001): 6.

13. "New Evidence on the Iran Crisis 1945–46: From the Baku Archives," *Cold War International History Project Bulletin* 12/13 (2001), Document 2, 311–312.

14. Raine, "Stalin and the Creation," 9.

15. On the 1946 Azerbaijan crisis, see Fawcett, *Iran and the Cold War*; Jamil Hasanli, *At the Dawn of the Cold War: The Soviet-American Crisis over Iranian Azerbaijan, 1941–1946* (Lanham, MD: Rowman & Littlefield, 2006); Bruce R. Kuniholm, *The Origins of the Cold War in the Near East: Great Power Conflict and Diplomacy in Iran, Turkey, and Greece* (Princeton, NJ: Princeton University Press, 1980).

16. Mohammad Reza Pahlavi, *Mission for My Country* (London: Hutchinson, 1961), 114.

17. On the origins of the "Northern Tier" concept, see Nigel J. Ashton, *Eisenhower, Macmillan and the Problem of Nasser: Anglo-American Relations and Arab Nationalism, 1955–59* (London: Macmillan, 1996), 39–42.

18. On British and US policy during the Azerbaijan crisis see Fawcett, *Iran and the Cold War*, 108–176; Lytle, *The Origins of the Iranian-American*, 138–173.

19. State 385 to Moscow, March 5, 1946, *FRUS 1946*, VII, pp. 340–342.

20. Raine, "Stalin and the Creation," 31; Natalia I. Yegorova, *The "Iran Crisis" of 1945–46: A View from the Russian Archives*, Working Paper 15 (Washington, DC: Cold War International History Project, 1996), 3–4.

21. Stalin to Pishevari, 8/5/1946, in Yegorova, *The "Iran Crisis,"* 23–24.

22. Maziar Behrooz, *Rebels with a Cause: The Failure of the Left in Iran* (London: I. B. Tauris, 1999), 19–20; Abbas Milani, *The Shah* (New York: Palgrave Macmillan, 2011), 131–134.

23. On the shah's 1949 visit to the United States, see James F. Goode, *The United States and Iran, 1946–51: The Diplomacy of Neglect* (London: Macmillan, 1989), 52–70.

24. Memorandum by Acheson, November 18, 1949, *FRUS 1949*, VI, pp. 572–573.

25. Memcon, 18/11/1949, *FRUS 1949*, VI, pp. 575–576.

26. See Christopher de Bellaigue, *Patriot of Persia: Muhammad Mossadegh and a Very British Coup* (London: Bodley Head, 2012); Homa Katouzian, *Musaddiq and the Struggle for Power in Iran* (London: I. B. Tauris, 1990).

27. Rouhollah K. Ramazani, *Iran's Foreign Policy 1941–1973: A Study of Foreign Policy in Modernizing Nations* (Charlottesville: University Press of Virginia, 1975), 219–250.

28. See William Roger Louis, "Musaddiq, Oil, and the Dilemmas of British Imperialism," in his *Ends of British Imperialism: The Scramble for Empire, Suez and Decolonisation* (London: I. B. Tauris, 2006), 727–787.

29. See Malcolm Byrne, "The Road to Intervention: Factors Influencing U.S. Policy Toward Iran, 1945–1953," in *Mohammad Mosaddeq and the 1953 Coup*, 201–226.

30. Memcon, October 23, 1951, *FRUS 1952–1954*, X, 117.

31. See Azimi, *Iran*, 257–338.

32. C. M. Woodhouse, *Something Ventured* (London: Granada, 1982), 117.

33. Mark J. Gasiorowski, "The 1953 Coup d'état against Mosaddeq," in *Mohammad Mosaddeq and the 1953 Coup*, 231.

34. One of the CIA's official histories of the coup was made public in April 2000. See Mark J. Gasiorowski, "The CIA Looks Back at the 1953 Coup in Iran," *Middle East Report* 216 (2000): 4–5.

35. Memcon, March 4, 1953, *FRUS 1952–1954*, X, 312.

36. Kermit Roosevelt, *Countercoup: The Struggle for the Control of Iran* (New York: McGraw-Hill, 1979), 199.

37. On the Eisenhower administration and Iran, see Bill, *Eagle and the Lion*, 51–130; Gasiorowski, *U.S. Foreign Policy*; Goode, *The United States and Iran: In the Shadow of Musaddiq*, 154–166; and Rubin, *Paved with Good Intentions*, 54–105.

38. On the United States and Jordan, see Nigel J. Ashton, *King Hussein of Jordan: A Political Life* (New Haven, CT: Yale University Press, 2008); Avi Shlaim,

Lion of Jordan: The Life of King Hussein in War and Peace (London: Allen Lane, 2007). On the Soviet Union and South Yemen, see Fred Halliday, *Revolution and Foreign Policy: The Case of South Yemen, 1967–1987* (Cambridge: Cambridge University Press, 1989); Mark N. Katz, *Russia and Arabia: Soviet Foreign Policy toward the Arabian Peninsula* (Baltimore, MD: The Johns Hopkins University Press, 1986).

39. See Nigel J. Ashton, ed., *The Cold War in the Middle East* (London: Routledge, 2007); Fawaz A. Gerges, *The Superpowers and the Middle East: Regional and International Politics, 1955–1967* (Boulder, CO: Westview Press, 1994); Yezid Sayigh and Avi Shlaim, eds., *The Cold War and the Middle East* (Oxford: Clarendon Press, 1997).

40. Hedley Bull, *The Anarchical Society: A Study of Order in World Politics* (New York: Columbia University Press, 1977), 214–216; Westad, *The Global Cold War*, 4–5.

41. Tehran 436 to State, August 21, 1953, *FRUS 1952–1954*, X, 351.

42. Gasiorowski, *U.S. Foreign Policy*, 94, Table 4.

43. See Heiss, *Empire and Nationhood*, 187–220.

44. Richard Nixon's handwritten notes, Pre-Presidential Papers, Foreign Affairs/National Security (PPS325), 1953, Box 2, RMNL.

45. Richard M. Nixon, *The Real War* (London: Sidgwick & Jackson, 1980), 295.

46. Editorial Note, *FRUS 1952–1954*, X, 398.

47. State 1175 to Tehran, December 13, 1954, *FRUS 1952–1954*, X, 505. See also Milani, *Shah*, 198–200.

48. Gasiorowski, *U.S. Foreign Policy*, 116–118; Ervand Abrahamian, *Tortured Confessions: Prisons and Public Recantations in Modern Iran* (Berkeley: University of California Press, 1999), 88–123.

49. Jernegan to Dulles, December 9, 1954, *FRUS 1952–1954*, X, 504.

50. Ahmad Mirfendereski with Ahmad Ahrar, *Dar hamsayegi-ye khers: Diplomasi va siyasat-e khareji-ye Iran, az 3 Shahrivar 1320 ta 22 Bahman 1357* [Neighbouring the Bear: Iranian Diplomacy and Foreign Policy, 1941–1980] (Tehran: Elm, 2003), 90.

51. Behçet Kemal Yeşilbursa, *The Baghdad Pact: Anglo-American Defence Policies in the Middle East, 1950–1959* (London: Frank Cass, 2005), 110–120.

52. On the United States' refusal to join the Baghdad Pact, see Ashton, *Eisenhower, Macmillan*, 37–60.

53. On the Eisenhower Doctrine, see Salim Yaqub, *Containing Arab Nationalism: The Eisenhower Doctrine and the Middle East* (Chapel Hill: The University of North Carolina Press, 2004).

54. Tehran 1726 to State, February 28, 1959, *FRUS 1958–1960*, XII, 229. See also Mark J. Gasiorowski, "The Qarani Affairs and Iranian Politics," *International Journal of Middle East Studies* 25, no. 4 (1993): 625–644.

55. Tehran 304 to State, August 1, 1958, *FRUS 1958–1960*, XII, 246; Yeşilbursa, *Baghdad Pact*, 211.

56. Pahlavi, *Mission for My Country*, 122.

57. For more detail, see Roham Alvandi, "Flirting with Neutrality: The Shah, Khrushchev, and the 1959 Soviet-Iranian Negotiations," *Iranian Studies* (forthcoming 2014).

58. Wright to Harrison, January 30, 1959, FO 371/140799; Denis Wright, *The Memoirs of Sir Denis Wright 1911–1971 in Two Volumes*, Volume II, unpublished manuscript, Bodleian Library, University of Oxford, 316.

59. SNIE 34–58, August 26, 1958, *FRUS 1958–1960*, XII, 249.

60. Editorial Note, *FRUS 1958–1960*, XII, 248.

61. Memcon, November 13, 1958, *FRUS 1958–1960*, XII, 256.

62. See Frances Bostock and Jeffrey Jones, *Planning and Power in Iran: Ebtehaj and Economic Development under the Shah* (London: Frank Cass, 1989).

63. E. A. Bayne, *Persian Kingship in Transition* (New York: American Universities Field Staff, 1968), 188–189.

64. See Popp, "An Application of Modernization," 89–91.

65. John F. Kennedy, *The Strategy of Peace*, ed. Allan Nevis (New York: Harper & Row, 1960), 107, 219. See also Goode, "Reforming Iran," 15–16.

66. See Robert B. Rakove, *Kennedy, Johnson, and the Nonaligned World* (Cambridge: Cambridge University Press, 2013). On Egyptian-Iranian relations, see Shahram Chubin and Sepehr Zabih, *The Foreign Relations of Iran: A Developing State in a Zone of Great-Power Conflict* (Berkeley: University of California Press, 1974), 140–169.

67. Ali Amini in an interview with Habib Ladjevardi, December 4, 1981, Paris, Tape 3, HIOHP; Iraj Amini, *Bar bal-e bohran: Zendegi-ye siyasi-ye Ali Amini* [On the Wings of Crisis: The Political Life of Ali Amini] (Tehran: Nashr-e Mahi, 2009), 227–230.

68. Record of Action 2427, May 19, 1961, *FRUS 1961–1963*, XVII, 51.

69. Komer to Bundy, October 20, 1962, Presidential Papers: President's Office Files, Box 119, JFKL.

70. See Ali M. Ansari, "The Myth of the White Revolution: Mohammad Reza Shah, 'Modernization' and the Consolidation of Power," *Middle Eastern Studies* 37, no. 3 (2001): 1–24.

71. Homa Katouzian, *The Persians: Ancient, Medieval and Modern Iran* (New Haven, CT: Yale University Press, 2009), 263.

72. State 32 to Tehran, July 16, 1963, *FRUS 1961–1963*, XVIII, 297.

73. Katouzian, *Persians*, 264.

74. See Goode, "Reforming Iran," 27–29; Popp, "Benign Intervention," 213–217.

75. See Johns, "The Johnson Administration, the Shah of Iran"; McGlinchey, "Lyndon B. Johnson and Arms Credit Sales."

76. Roham Alvandi, "The Shah's Détente with Khrushchev: Iran's 1962 Missile Base Pledge to the Soviet Union," *Cold War History* (forthcoming 2014).

77. See Abbas Milani, *The Persian Sphinx: Amir Abbas Hoveyda and the Riddle of the Iranian Revolution* (London: I. B. Tauris, 2000), 158–163; Richard Pfau, "The Legal Status of American Forces in Iran," *Middle East Journal* 28, no. 2 (1974): 141–153.

78. Talbot to Bundy, March 9, 1962, *FRUS 1961–1963*, XVII, 210.

79. See Ramazani, *Iran's Foreign Policy*, pp. 361–363.

80. Tehran 451 to State, October 27, 1964, *FRUS 1964–1968*, XXII, 54.

81. Tehran 404 to State, October 14, 1964, *FRUS 1964–1968*, XXII, 52.

82. Baqer Moin, *Khomeini: Life of the Ayatollah* (London: I. B. Tauris, 1999), 122–127.

83. Tehran 499 to State, November 3, 1964, *FRUS 1964–1968*, XXII, 55.

84. Milani, *Shah*, 311.

85. Memcon, April 12, 1962, *FRUS 1961–1963*, XVII, 243.

86. Carroll to Humphrey, July 27, 1966, *FRUS 1964–1968*, XXII, 163. See also, Johns, "The Johnson Administration, the Shah of Iran," 82–83.

87. After the overthrow of the Iraqi monarchy in 1958 and the subsequent withdrawal of Iraq from the Baghdad Pact, the alliance was renamed the Central Treaty Organization (CENTO) and its headquarters were moved to Ankara.

88. CIA Intelligence Memorandum, "Iran, the Shah, and the Soviets," July 27, 1966, NSF, CFME, Box 138, LBJL. See also Ramazani, *Iran's Foreign Policy*, 329–352.

89. CIA Intelligence Memorandum, "Iran: The Impact of Soviet Arms," February 15, 1967, NSF, CFME, Box 138, LBJL.

90. Homa Katouzian, "Mosaddeq's Government in Iranian History: Arbitrary Rule, Democracy, and the 1953 Coup," in *Mohammad Mosaddeq and the 1953 Coup*, 23.

2   "PROTECT ME": THE NIXON DOCTRINE IN THE PERSIAN GULF

1. United Nations, *Statistical Yearbook 1973* (New York: United Nations, 1974), 582, Table 179; Gasiorowski, *U.S. Foreign Policy*, 143, Table 12; Stockholm International Peace Research Institute, *SIPRI Yearbook 1973: World Armaments and Disarmament* (Stockholm: Almquist & Wiksell, 1973), 238–239, Table 7A.8.

2. Memcon, May 31, 1972, *FRUS 1969–1976*, E-4, 201.

3. The term "twin pillars" does not appear in the documentary record. Following the fall of the shah, it was commonly used by journalists as a shorthand for pre-1979 US policy toward the Persian Gulf and soon gained currency with historians.

4. See W. Taylor Fain, *American Ascendance and British Retreat in the Persian Gulf Region* (New York: Palgrave Macmillan, 2008), 169–200; F. Gregory Gause III, "British and American Policies in the Persian Gulf, 1968–1973," *Review of International Studies* 11, no. 4 (1985): 247–273; Tore T. Petersen, *Richard Nixon, Great Britain and the Anglo-American Alignment in the Persian Gulf and Arabian*

Peninsula: Making Allies out of Clients (Brighton, UK: Sussex Academic Press, 2009), 79–97.

5. In 1968 these British-protected states consisted of the emirates of Abu Dhabi, Ajman, Bahrain, Dubai, Fujaira, Qatar, Ras al-Khaimah, Sharjah, and Umm al-Quwain.

6. See Glen Balfour-Paul, *The End of Empire in the Middle East: Britain's Relinquishment of Power in Her Last Three Arab Dependencies* (Cambridge: Cambridge University Press, 1991).

7. William Roger Louis, "British Withdrawal from the Gulf, 1967–1971," *Journal of Imperial and Commonwealth History* 31, no. 1 (2003): 83–86.

8. "Defence Expenditure Study 6: Long-Term Policy in the Persian Gulf: Report by the Defence Review Working Party," June 7, 1967, FCO 49/10.

9. Stewart to Wilson, February 23, 1965, PREM 13/409.

10. Crawford (Bahrain) to FCO, January 31, 1968, FCO 8/33.

11. Wright (Tehran) to FCO, March 20, 1968, FCO 8/33.

12. "Minutes of Discussions on the Persian Gulf held at the Foreign Office by the Minister of State on 25 and 26 March 1968," FCO 8/33.

13. Denis Wright, *The Memoirs of Sir Denis Wright 1911–1971*, 2 vols., unpublished manuscript, Bodleian Library, University of Oxford, 385–388.

14. Allen (London) to Wright (Tehran), June 14, 1968, FO 1016/755.

15. "Relations Between Saudi Arabia and Iran: The State visit by the Shah to Saudi Arabia (9–14 November 1968) and Its Background," December 3, 1968, FO 1016/870.

16. Mohammad Reza Pahlavi, *The Shah's Story*, trans. Teresa Waugh (London: M. Joseph, 1980), 140. See also Sébastien Fath, *L'Iran et de Gaulle: Chronique d'un Rêve Inachevé* (Neuilly-sur-Seine: EurOrient, 1999).

17. See Kevin Boyle, "The Price of Peace: Vietnam, the Pound, and the Crisis of the American Empire," *Diplomatic History* 27, no. 1 (2003): 37–72; Jeremy Fielding, "Coping with Decline: US Policy toward the British Defense Reviews of 1966," *Diplomatic History* 23, no. 4 (1999): 633–656.

18. Brown (New York) to FCO, January 11, 1968, PREM 13/1999.

19. Johnson to Wilson, January 11, 1968, PREM 13/1999.

20. Urwick (Washington) to Stirling (London), January 18, 1968, FCO 8/36.

21. Lyndon B. Johnson, *The Vantage Point: Perspectives of the Presidency, 1963–1969* (London: Weidenfeld & Nicolson, 1972), 385, 425–437.

22. "Interview with Under Secretary of State Eugene Rostow, 19 January 1968, as Broadcast on Voice of America at 6.00 p.m.," FCO 8/36.

23. Balfour-Paul (Bahrain) to Stirling (London), January 26, 1968, FCO 8/36.

24. Killick (Washington) to Sykes (London), January 25, 1968, FCO 8/36; State to Jeddah, January 24, 1968, *FRUS 1964–1968*, XXI, 124.

25. "Minutes of Discussions with United States Officials at the Foreign Office on 27 March 1968," FCO 8/37.

26. State 108214 to Tehran, February 1, 1968, *FRUS 1964–1968*, XXI, 129.

27. Shah of Iran to Johnson, February 1, 1968, *FRUS 1964–1968*, XXI, 130.

28. Tehran 3869 to State, March 23, 1968, *FRUS 1964–1968*, XXII, 273.

29. Rostow to Johnson, February 6, 1968, *FRUS 1964–1968*, XXI, 135.

30. "Record of Conversation Between the Minister of State for Foreign Affairs and Members of the State Department in Washington at 4.30 p.m. on Wednesday, 15 May 1968," FCO 8/37.

31. "Anglo-American Talks on the Middle East in the State Department, 13 September 1968," FCO 8/37; Memcon, September 13, 1968, *FRUS 1964–1968*, XXI, 156.

32. Theodore Eliot in an interview with William Burr, San Francisco, July 29, 1968, Tape 2A, FISOHC.

33. Foster to Rostow, May 21, 1968, *FRUS 1964–1968*, XXII, 285.

34. State 121476 to Tehran, February 28, 1968, *FRUS 1964–1968*, XXII, 259; Ardeshir Zahedi in an interview with the author, Montreux, June 11, 2009.

35. State 131326 to Tehran, March 16, 1968, *FRUS 1964–1968*, XXII, 269.

36. Dean Rusk in an interview with William Burr, Athens, Georgia, May 23, 1986, Tape 1A, FISOHC.

37. Shah of Iran to Johnson, August 15, 1966, *FRUS 1964–1968*, XXII, 173.

38. See Jesse Ferris, *Nasser's Gamble: How Intervention in Yemen Caused the Six-Day War and the Decline of Egyptian Power* (Princeton, NJ: Princeton University Press, 2013); Abdel Razzaq Takriti, *Monsoon Revolution: Republicans, Sultans, and Empires in Oman, 1965–1976* (Oxford: Oxford University Press, 2013).

39. CIA Intelligence Memorandum 1355/66, May 21, 1966, *FRUS 1964–1968*, XXII, 139.

40. Record of Meeting, February 1, 1968, *FRUS 1964–1968*, XXI, 131.

41. Rostow to Johnson, June 11, 1968, *FRUS 1964–1968*, XXII, 292.

42. McClelland to Handley, August 28, 1968, *FRUS 1964–1968*, XXI, 155.

43. Editorial Note, *FRUS 1969–1976*, I, 29. These ideas had been foreshadowed in Richard Nixon, "Asia after Vietnam," *Foreign Affairs* 46, no. 1 (1967): 113–125.

44. Robert S. Litwak, *Détente and the Nixon Doctrine: American Foreign Policy and the Pursuit of Stability, 1969–1976* (Cambridge: Cambridge University Press, 1984), 135–150; David F. Schmitz, *The United States and Right-Wing Dictatorships: 1965–1989* (Cambridge: Cambridge University Press, 2004), 72–111. For example, on the Nixon Doctrine in Latin America, see Tanya Harmer, "Brazil's Cold War in the Southern Cone, 1970–1975," *Cold War History* 12, no. 4 (2012): 659–681; Tanya Harmer, "Fractious Allies: Chile, the United States, and the Cold War, 1973–76," *Diplomatic History* 37, no. 1 (2013): 109–143.

45. Westad, *Global Cold War*, 197.

46. Raymond L. Garthoff, *Détente and Confrontation: American-Soviet Relations from Nixon to Reagan*, Revised Edition (Washington, DC: Brookings Institution, 1994), 25–39; Litwak, *Détente and the Nixon Doctrine*, 54.

47. See Jussi Hanhimäki, "An Elusive Grand Design," in *Nixon in the World: American Foreign Relations, 1969–1977*, eds. Fredrik Logevall and Andrew Preston (Oxford: Oxford University Press, 2008), 40–41.

48. Nixon to Haldeman, Ehrlichmann, and Kissinger, March 2, 1970, *FRUS 1969–1976*, I, 61.

49. Henry Kissinger in an interview with Faisal bin Salman al-Saud, New York, June 3, 1997, in Faisal bin Salman al-Saud, *Iran, Saudi Arabia and the Gulf: Power Politics in Transition 1968–1971* (London: I. B. Tauris, 2003), 65.

50. Richard M. Nixon, *The Memoirs of Richard Nixon* (New York: Grosset & Dunlap, 1978), 133.

51. See David Greenberg, *Nixon's Shadow: The History of an Image* (New York: W.W. Norton & Company, 2003), 36–72.

52. Milani, *Shah*, 248. Nixon later recalled that he made four trips to Tehran to see the shah during his time out of office in the 1960s. See Nixon, *Real War*, 296.

53. Steven P. Ambrose, *Nixon: The Triumph of a Politician, 1962–1972* (New York: Simon & Schuster, 1989), 106; Armin Meyer, *Quiet Diplomacy: From Cairo to Tokyo in the Twilight of Imperialism* (New York: iUniverse, 2003), 140.

54. Gholam Reza Afkhami, *The Life and Times of the Shah* (Berkeley: University of California Press, 2009), 302–303.

55. Marvin Zonis, *The Political Elite of Iran* (Princeton, NJ: Princeton University Press, 1971), 39–79.

56. Paper prepared by William G. Miller of the Policy Planning Staff of the Department of State, "The 'New Men' and Their Challenge to American Policy in Iran," August 7, 1964, NSF, Files of Robert W. Komer, Box 27, LBJL. See also, Milani, *Persian Sphinx*, 163.

57. Hughes to Rusk, March 27, 1968, *FRUS 1964–1968*, XXII, 274. See also Ali Ansari, *The Politics of Nationalism in Modern Iran* (Cambridge: Cambridge University Press, 2012), 165–179.

58. CIA Special Memorandum 9–68, "The Shah's Increasing Assurance," May 7, 1968, NSF, Files of Harold H. Saunders, Box 4, LBJL.

59. Tehran 789 to State, November 28, 1965, *FRUS 1964–1968*, XXII, 110.

60. On the shah's decision-making style, see Zonis, *Political Elite*, 95.

61. "Program for the Informal Visit to Iran of The Honorable Richard M. Nixon," undated, Wilderness Years, Series 2, Trip File, Iran, RMNL.

62. Handwritten notes by Richard M. Nixon, Wilderness Years, Series 2, Far East and Middle East Trips 1967, RMNL.

63. Address by Richard M. Nixon to the Bohemian Club, San Francisco, July 29, 1967, *FRUS 1969–1976*, I, 2.

64. Pahlavi, *Shah's Story*, 143.

65. Saunders to Kissinger, April 1, 1969, *FRUS 1969–1976*, E-4, 7.

66. NIE 34-69, January 10, 1969, *FRUS 1969–1976*, E-4, 1.

67. Memcon, April 1, 1969, *FRUS 1969–1976*, E-4, 8.

68. Oles M. Smolansky and Bettie M. Smolansky, *The USSR and Iraq: The Soviet Quest for Influence* (Durham, NC: Duke University Press, 1991), 143–187.

69. Memcon, April 1, 1969, *FRUS 1969–1976*, E-4, 6.

70. Asadollah Alam, *Yad'dashtha-yi 'Alam: Virayish va muqaddamah az Ali Naqi Alikhani* [The Alam Diaries: Edited by Alinaghi Alikhani], Vol. I: 1969–1970 (Bethesda, MD: Iranbooks, 1993), 165. The English-language translation of this passage is taken from Alam, *Shah and I*, 50.

71. See Richard M. Schofield, *Evolution of the Shatt Al-'Arab Boundary Dispute* (Wisbech, UK: Middle East & North African Studies Press, 1986), 42–66.

72. Chubin and Zabih, *Foreign Relations of Iran*, 185–187; Ramazani, *Iran's Foreign Policy*, 417–418; Hussein Sirriyeh, "Development of the Iraqi-Iranian Dispute, 1847–1975," *Journal of Contemporary History* 20, no. 3 (1985): 485–487.

73. Alam, *Yad'dashtha-ye 'Alam*, Vol. I, 173–174; Tehran 1399 to State, April 20, 1969, RG59, CFPF 1967–69, Box 2218.

74. Tehran 1340 to State, April 16, 1969, and Tehran 1390 to State, April 19, 1969, RG59, CFPF 1967–69, Box 2218.

75. Gen. Fereydoun Djam in an interview with Habib Ladjevardi, March 10, 1983, London, Tape 4, HIOHP.

76. Tehran 1367 to State, April 18, 1969, RG59, CFPF 1967–69, Box 2218.

77. Gen. Mohammad Fazeli in an interview with Seyed Vali Reza Nasr, Bethesda, May 14, 1991, Tape 1B, FISOHC.

78. Alam, *Yad'dashtha-ye 'Alam*, Vol. I, 175.

79. Tehran 1371 to State, April 18, 1969, *FRUS 1969–1976*, E-4, 11.

80. State 60660 to Tehran, April 19, 1969, RG59, CFPF 1967–-69, Box 2218.

81. Tehran 1401 to State, April 20, 1969, NPM, NSCF, CFME, Box 601.

82. Tehran 1396 to State, April 19, 1969, and Tehran 1398 to State, April 20 1969, RG59, CFPF 1967–69, Box 2218.

83. Alam, *Yad'dashtha-ye 'Alam*, Vol. I, 176.

84. Tehran 1416 to State, April 21, 1969, RG59, CFPF 1967–69, Box 2218.

85. Tehran 1444 to State, April 22, 1969, RG59, CFPF 1967–69, Box 2218.

86. Intelligence Note 295 from Hughes to Rogers, April 22, 1969, *FRUS 1969–76*, E-4, 12. See also Archie Bolster in an interview with William Burr, Washington, March 24, 1988, Tape 3BB, FISOHC.

87. NSSM 66, July 12, 1969, Virtual Library, RMNL.

88. Tehran 4183 to State, October 13, 1969, *FRUS 1969–1976*, E-4, 23.

89. Rogers to Nixon, October 17, 1969, *FRUS 1969–1976*, E-4, 26.

90. Kissinger to Nixon, October 21, 1969, *FRUS 1969–1976*, E-4, 29.

91. Mosbacher to Woods, September 18, 1969, NPM, President's Personal File, White House Social Events 1969–1974, Box 123.

92. Woods to Haldeman, October 6, 1969, NPM, President's Personal File, White House Social Events 1969–1974, Box 123.

93. Memorandum for the Record, October 22, 1969, *FRUS 1969–1976*, E-4, 31.

94. Memcon, October 22, 1969, *FRUS 1969–1976*, E-4, 33–35.

95. Nixon to the Shah of Iran, February 23, 1970, *FRUS 1969–1976*, E-4, 48.

96. Kissinger to Nixon, June 25, 1970, *FRUS 1969–1976*, E-4, 75.

97. Tehran 1247 to State, April 1, 1970, *FRUS 1969–1976*, E-4, 57.

98. Packard to Richardson, April 14, 1970, *FRUS 1969–1976*, E-4, 60.

99. Jack Miklos in an interview with William Burr, Oakland, July 28, 1986, Tape 1D, FISOHC.

100. Memcon, April 14, 1970, *FRUS 1969–1976*, E-4, 61.

101. Saunders to Kissinger, April 16, 1970, *FRUS 1969–1976*, E-4, 63. Helms himself had secured the shah's permission to place these installations in Iran in 1957, when he was chief of operations in the CIA's Directorate of Plans. See Richard Helms with William Hood, *A Look over My Shoulder: A Life in the Central Intelligence Agency* (New York: Random House, 2003), 417. See also Jeffrey T. Richelson, *The Wizards of Langley: Inside the CIA's Directorate of Science and Technology* (Boulder, CO: Westview Press, 2001), 33, 88.

102. Tehran 1019 to State, March 19, 1970, *FRUS 1969–1976*, E-4, 55.

103. Kissinger to Nixon, April 16, 1970, *FRUS 1969–1976*, E-4, 62.

104. Tehran 1626 to State, April 21, 1970, *FRUS 1969–1976*, E-4, 64.

105. Paper prepared by the NSC Staff, June 4, 1970, NPM, NSCIF, Meeting Files, Box H-046. See also, *FRUS 1969–1976*, XXIV, 82, f. 1.

106. Saunders and Kennedy to Kissinger, June 3, 1970, *FRUS 1969–1976*, E-4, 70.

107. Harold Saunders in an interview with the author, Washington, June 27, 2011.

108. Jack Miklos in an interview with William Burr, Oakland, July 31, 1986, Tape 2A, FISOHC.

109. Minutes of a Review Group Meeting, June 5, 1970, *FRUS 1969–1976*, XXIV, 83.

110. Kissinger to Nixon, June 25, 1970, *FRUS 1969–1976*, E-4, 75.

111. See Craig Daigle, *The Limits of Détente: The United States, the Soviet Union and the Arab-Israeli Conflict, 1969–1973* (New Haven, CT: Yale University Press, 2012), 113–154.

112. Roham Alvandi, "Muhammad Reza Pahlavi and the Bahrain Question, 1968–1970," *British Journal of Middle Eastern Studies* 37, no. 2 (2010): 159–177.

113. Kissinger to Nixon, October 22, 1970, *FRUS 1969–1976*, E-4, 91.

114. Douglas MacArthur II in an interview with William Burr, Washington, May 29, 1985, Tape 2A, FISOHC.

115. Tehran 862 to State, NPM, NSCF, CFME, Box 602.

116. Tehran 34 to State, January 5, 1970, and Tehran 2436 to State, June 9, 1970, NPM, NSCF, CFME, Box 601; Research Study RNAS-6 prepared by the Department of State, April 12, 1973, RG59, SNF 1970–73, Box 2380.

117. Tehran 7 to State, January 3, 1970, NPM, NSCF, CFME, Box 601.

118. Memcon, July 24, 1974, *FRUS 1969–1976*, XXVII, 27.

119. Harold Saunders in an interview with William Burr, Washington, February 24, 1987, Tape 2B, FISOHC.

120. See Nathan J. Citino, *From Arab Nationalism to OPEC: Eisenhower, King Saud, and the Making of U.S.-Saudi Relations* (Bloomington: Indiana University Press, 2002).

121. Sisco to Kissinger, November 21, 1969, *FRUS 1969–1976*, XXIV, 133.

122. Morris (Jeddah) to McCarthy (London), December 23, 1968, FO 248/1652.

123. Memcon, March 11, 1969, *FRUS 1969–1976*, XXIV, 72.

124. "Persian Gulf: Annual Review for 1970," January 1, 1971, FCO 8/1570.

125. State 42979 to Jidda, March 24, 1970, *FRUS 1969–1976*, XXIV, 139.

126. Dhahran 112 to State, February 5, 1969, *FRUS 1969–1976*, XXIV, 127.

127. Memcon, May 27, 1971, *FRUS 1969–1976*, XXIV, 151.

128. Henry Kissinger, *Years of Upheaval* (Boston, MA: Little, Brown, 1982), 662.

129. Gen. Mansur Qadar in an interview with Gholam Reza Afkhami, Washington, May 4, 1986, Tapes 6A and 6B, FISOHC.

130. Tehran 2674 to State, May 20, 1971, RG59, SNF 1970–73, Box 2380.

131. Conversation among Nixon, MacArthur, and Haig, April 8, 1971, *FRUS 1969–1976*, E-4, 122.

132. See Noam Kochavi, *Nixon and Israel: Forging a Conservative Partnership* (Albany: State University of New York Press, 2009).

133. See Popp, "An Application of Modernization."

134. Richard Arndt in an interview with William Burr, Washington, May 9, 1988, Tape 1B, FISOHC.

135. NIE 36-6-70, April 7, 1970, *FRUS 1969–1976*, XXIV, 140.

136. Tehran 2648 to State, May 20, 1971, RG59, SNF 1970–73, Box 2380.

137. Memcon, May 31, 1972, *FRUS 1969–1976*, E-4, 201.

138. Tehran 3312 to State, August 2, 1970, NPM, NSCF, CFME, Box 601.

139. Gary S. Samore, "Royal Family Politics in Saudi Arabia (1953–1982)," PhD diss., Harvard University, 1983, 259–264; Alexei Vassiliev, *The History of Saudi Arabia* (London: Saqi Books, 2000), 371–372.

140. Sisco to Kissinger, November 21, 1969, *FRUS 1969–1976*, XXIV, 133.

141. Samore, "Royal Family Politics," 268.

142. NIE 36-6-70, April 7, 1970, *FRUS 1969–1976*, XXIV, 140.

143. Saunders to Kissinger, April 24, 1970, NPM, NSCF, CFME, Box 601.

144. Alexander M. Haig, Jr., with Charles McCarry, *Inner Circles: How America Changed the World, a Memoir* (New York: Warner Books, 1992), 536.

145. Memcon, October 22, 1969, *FRUS 1969–1976*, E-4, 33.

146. Laird to Rogers, October 27, 1970, *FRUS 1969–1976*, E-4, 93; NSDM 92, November 7, 1970, *FRUS 1969–1976*, E-4, 97.

147. Kissinger, *Years of Upheaval*, 667.

148. See Christopher R. W. Dietrich, "'Arab Oil Belongs to the Arabs': Raw Material Sovereignty, Cold War Boundaries, and the Nationalisation of the Iraq Petroleum Company, 1967–1973," *Diplomacy and Statecraft* 22, no. 3 (2011): 450–479.

149. Henry Kissinger, *Years of Renewal* (London: Weidenfeld & Nicolson, 1999), 581.

150. Henry Kissinger, *The White House Years* (London: Weidenfeld & Nicolson, 1979), 1264.

151. Memcon, October 22, 1969, *FRUS 1969–1976*, E-4, 33.

152. Research Memorandum RNA-6 from Hughes to Rogers, February 14, 1969, *FRUS 1969–1976*, E-4, 251.

153. CIA Information Cable, March 9, 1970, *FRUS 1969–1976*, E-4, 267.

154. Tehran A-322 to State, July 8, 1969, RG59, CFPF 1967–69, Box 2218. Iraq did provide some modest material support for Arab and Baluchi separatists in Iran as well as safe-haven for General Teymour Bakhtiar, the first chief of SAVAK who had fallen out with the shah in the early 1960s. See Editorial Note, *FRUS 1969–1976*, XXVII, 204; Abbas Milani, "Teymour Bakhtiar," *Eminent Persians*, Vol. I, 430–437.

155. Alam, *Yad'dashtha-ye 'Alam*, Vol. I, 233.

156. Memcon, October 15, 1969, *FRUS 1969–1976*, E-4, 262; London 598 to State, January 23, 1970, *FRUS 1969–1976*, E-4, 265; McKearney (Baghdad) to Acland (London), January 24, 1970, FCO 17/1240; Symons (Baghdad) to Hinchcliffe (London), January 31, 1970, FCO 17/1240; Balfour Paul (Baghdad) to Tripp (London), January 31, 1970, FCO 17/1240; Alam, *Yad'dashtha-ye 'Alam*, Vol. I, 355–356; Majeed Mehran, *Dar koridorha-ye vezarat-e omur-e kharejeh cheh khabar: Khaterat-e yek diplomat-e qadimi* [In the Corridors of the Ministry of Foreign Affairs: The Memoirs of a Retired Diplomat] (Tehran: Nashr-e Tarikh-e Iran, 2004), 415–418.

157. Eliot to Kissinger, April 13, 1972, *FRUS 1969–1976*, E-4, 305; State 67657 to Tehran, April 19, 1972, RG59, SNF 1970–73, Box 2380.

158. On Soviet-Iranian relations, see Mirfendereski with Ahrar, *Dar hamsayegi-ye khers*; Tahmoures Adamiyat, *Gashti bar guzashtah: Khatirati az safir-e kabir-e Iran dar Shoravi* [A Journey Through the Past: Memoirs of an Imperial Iranian Ambassador to the Soviet Union] (Tehran: Ketab Sera, 1989).

159. Smolansky and Smolansky, *USSR and Iraq*, 164.

160. Moscow 4546 to State, August 13, 1970, *FRUS 1969–1976*, E-4, 274; State to Tehran, London, and Moscow, January 22, 1972, *FRUS 1969–1976*, E-4, 295; CIA Intelligence Memorandum 0865/72, May 12, 1972, *FRUS 1969–1976*, E-4, 307.

161. State Department Briefing Paper, "Iran's Role in Regional Security," May 12, 1972, NPM, NSCF, President's Trip Files, Box 479.

162. Briefing Paper prepared for Nixon, May 18, 1972, *FRUS 1969–1976*, E-4, 308.

163. Memcon, Janaury 13, 1971, *FRUS 1969–1976*, XXIV, 93.

164. Memcon, May 30, 1972, *FRUS 1969–1976*, E-4, 200; Memcon, May 31, 1972, *FRUS 1969–1976*, E-4, 201; Kissinger, *White House Years*, 1264–1265; Kissinger, *Years of Renewal*, 583–584.

165. Kissinger, *Years of Upheaval*, p. 676.

166. Conversation among Nixon, MacArthur, and Haig, April 8, 1971, *FRUS 1969–1976*, E-4, 122.

167. Kissinger, *White House Years*, 1260–1261.

168. Jeremi Suri, *Henry Kissinger and the American Century* (Cambridge, MA: Harvard University Press, 2007), 270.

169. Harold Saunders in an interview with the author, Washington, June 27, 2011.

170. Pahlavi, *Shah's Story*, 144.

171. Ardeshir Zahedi in an interview with the author, Montreux, June 11, 2009.

172. Kissinger, *White House Years*, 1262.

173. Ian Skeet, *OPEC: Twenty-Five Years of Prices and Politics* (Cambridge: Cambridge University Press, 1988), 66–68.

174. See Richard A. Mobley, "The Tunbs and Abu Musa Islands: Britain's Perspective," *Middle East Journal* 57, no. 4 (2003): 627–645.

175. See Richard Sisson and Leo E. Rose, *War and Secession: Pakistan, India, and the Creation of Bangladesh* (Berkeley: University of California Press, 1990).

176. See Jussi Hanhimäki, *The Flawed Architect: Henry Kissinger and American Foreign Policy* (Oxford: Oxford University Press, 2004), 154–184; Robert J. McMahon, "The Danger of Geopolitical Fantasies: Nixon, Kissinger, and the South Asia Crisis of 1971," in *Nixon in the World*, 249–268; Christopher Van Hollen, "The Tilt Policy Revisited: Nixon-Kissinger Geopolitics and South Asia," *Asian Survey* 20, no. 4 (1980): 339–361.

177. Tehran 3328 to State, June 22, 1971, RG59, SNF 1970–73, Box 2378.

178. See Shirin Tahir-Kheli, "Iran and Pakistan: Cooperation in an Area of Conflict," *Asian Survey* 17, no. 5 (1977): 474–490.

179. Tehran 1946 to State, April 15, 1971, RG59, SNF 1970–73, Box 2531.

180. Tehran 4292 to State, August 4, 1971, and Tehran 4462 to State, August 14, 1971, RG59, SNF 1970–73, Box 2533.

181. Tehran 5209 to State, September 17, 1971, and Intelligence Note RNAN-27 prepared by the Department of State, September 27, 1971, RG59, SNF 1970–73, Box 2523.

182. Milani, *Shah*, 322–326.

183. Tehran 6210 to State, November 1, 1971, NPM, NSCF, CFME, Box 602.

184. Haig to Kissinger, January 19, 1972, NPM, NSCF, CFME, Box 643. See also, *FRUS 1969–1976*, XI, 222, f.3.

185. Note prepared by the Department of Defence, December 7, 1971, NPM, NSCIF, Meeting Files (1969–75), WSAGM, Box H-083.

186. Saunders to Kissinger, December 9, 1971, NPM, NSCIF, Meeting Files (1969–75), WSAGM, Box H-083.

187. *FRUS 1969–1976*, XI, 222, f. 4.

188. Conversation between Nixon and Kissinger, December 6, 1971, NPM, White House Tapes, Oval Office, Conversation 630–2.

189. Memcon, December 10, 1971, *FRUS 1969–1976*, XI, 274.

190. President Eisenhower had visited Iran in 1959 and Vice President Johnson had also visited in 1962.

191. The only records of these meetings were kept by Kissinger, who was nearly excluded from attending. General Ellis W. Williamson, then the chief of US military mission in Iran, later recalled that the shah had wanted to meet alone with Nixon and had only consented to Kissinger attending after Nixon insisted. See Gen. Ellis W. Williamson in an interview with William Burr, Arlington, March 11, 1988, Tape 2, FISOHC.

192. Memcon, May 30, 1972, *FRUS 1969–1976*, E-4, 200.

193. Memcon, May 31, 1972, *FRUS 1969–1976*, E-4, 201.

194. Kissinger, *White House Years*, 1264–1265; Kissinger, *Years of Renewal*, 583–584.

195. Asadollah Alam, *Yad'dashtha-ye 'Alam: Virayish va muqaddamah az Ali Naqi Alikhani* [The Alam Diaries: Edited by Alinaghi Alikhani], Volume II: 1970, 1972 (Bethesda, MD: Iranbooks, 1993), 260.

196. Harold Saunders in an interview with William Burr, Washington, February 24, 1987, Tape 2A, FISOHC.

197. Kissinger to Laird and Rogers, July 25, 1972, *FRUS 1969–1976*, E-4, 214.

198. SIPRI, *SIPRI Yearbook 1973*, 238–239, Table 7A.8.

199. Gasiorowski, *U.S. Foreign Policy*, 112, Table 6.

200. See Muhammad Ja'far Chamankar, *Buhran-e Zufar va rezhim-e Pahlavi* [The Dhofar Crisis and the Pahlavi Regime] (Tehran: Institute for Iranian Contemporary Historical Studies, 2004); James F. Goode, "Assisting Our Brothers, Defending Ourselves: The Iranian Intervention in Oman, 1972–1975," *Iranian Studies* (forthcoming 2014).

201. Petersen, *Richard Nixon, Great Britain*, 60.

3 IRAN'S SECRET WAR WITH IRAQ: THE CIA AND THE SHAH-FORSAKEN KURDS

1. Tehran 4639 to State, July 2, 1973, NPM, NSCF, CFME, Box 603.

2. Eliot to Kissinger, December 14, 1972, NPM, NSCF, CFME, Box 602. On the shah's Indian Ocean strategy, see Robert J. Bookmiller, *Engaging Iran: Australian and Canadian Relations with the Islamic Republic* (Dubai: Gulf Research Center, 2009), 27–33; Rouhollah K. Ramazani, "Iran's Search for Regional Coöperation," *Middle East Journal* 30, no. 2 (1976): 173–186.

3. Skeet, *OPEC*, 240.

4. Gasiorowski, *U.S. Foreign Policy*, 112–113.

5. See Ervand Abrahamian, *Radical Islam: The Iranian Mojahedin* (London: I. B. Tauris, 1989); Payman Vahabzadeh, *A Guerrilla Odyssey: Modernization, Secularism, Democracy, and the Fadai Period of National Liberation in Iran* (Syracuse, NY: Syracuse University Press, 2010). On the Third World revolutionary movements in the Middle East and North Africa, see Jeffrey J. Byrne,

"Our Own Special Brand of Socialism: Algeria and the Contest for Modernities in the 1960s," *Diplomatic History* 33, no. 3 (2009): 427–447; Paul Thomas Chamberlin, *The Global Offensive: The United States, the Palestine Liberation Organization, and the Making of the Post-Cold War Order* (New York: Oxford University Press, 2012); Matthew Connelly, *A Diplomatic Revolution: Algeria's Fight for Independence and the Origins of the Post-Cold War Era* (New York: Oxford University Press, 2002); Takriti, *Monsoon Revolution*.

6. Tehran 5142 to State, December 1, 1970, *FRUS 1969–1976*, E-4, 102; Tehran 3878 to State, June 5, 1973, *FRUS 1969–1976*, XXVII, 18.

7. Tehran A-4 to State, January 9, 1973, *FRUS 1969–1976*, XXVII, 1.

8. On Britain's attitude toward the 1937 Treaty, see Schofield, *Evolution of the Shatt Al-'Arab*, 54–55.

9. Military Attaché Report 196-45 from Captain Archibald B. Roosevelt, Jr. (Baghdad), "Tribal Revolt in Kurdistan," August 16, 1945, Papers of Archibald B. Roosevelt, Jr., Manuscript Division, Library of Congress, Washington, DC. "Mulla" is a religious title that refers to Barzani's descent from the Barzinji shai-khly family that was associated with the Qadiri *tariqa* (Sufi order). See Martin Van Bruinessen, *Agha, Sheikh and State: The Social and Political Structures of Kurdistan* (London: Zed Books, 1992), 205–264.

10. See Archie Roosevelt, Jr., "The Kurdish Republic of Mahabad," *Middle East Journal* 1, no. 3 (1947): 247–297. Archibald "Archie" Roosevelt, Jr., was a US military intelligence officer who came to greatly admire Barzani after serving in Iraq during World War II. Like his cousin Kim Roosevelt (the CIA officer responsible for the 1953 coup in Iran), Archie was a grandson of President Theodore Roosevelt and went on to enjoy a long career in the CIA.

11. Research Study RNAS-10 prepared by the Department of State, May 31, 1972, *FRUS 1969–1976*, E-4, 310; Memcon, April 12, 1962, *FRUS 1961–1963*, XVII, 243; Yevgeny Primakov, *Russia and the Arabs: Behind the Scenes in the Middle East from the Cold War to the Present*, trans. Paul Gould (New York: Basic Books, 2009), 326. Massoud Barzani, *Mustafa Barzani and the Kurdish Liberation Movement (1931–1961)*, ed. Ahmed Ferhadi (New York: Palgrave Macmillan, 2003), 135–150.

12. Memcon, April 13, 1962, *FRUS 1961–1963*, XVII, 247; Tehran 1044 to State, January 20, 1966, *FRUS 1964–1968*, XXI, 179.

13. Edgar O'Ballance, *The Kurdish Struggle, 1920–94* (London: Macmillan, 1996), 61; Col. Isa Pejman in an interview with Akbar Etemad, Paris, March 4, 1983 and April 8, 1983, Tape 1B, HIOHP; Abbas William Samii, "The Role of SAVAK in the 1978–1979 Iranian Revolution," PhD diss., University of Cambridge, 1994, 133–135.

14. Watson to Willison, June 12, 1963, FO 371/170421; Shah of Iran to Johnson, January 7, 1964, *FRUS 1964–1968*, XXII, 2.

15. O'Ballance, *Kurdish Struggle*, 84.

16. Jonathan C. Randal, *After Such Knowledge, What Forgiveness? My Encounters with Kurdistan* (New York: Farrar, Strauss and Giroux, 1997), 131–132; Saad Jawad, *Iraq and the Kurdish Question, 1958–1970* (London: Ithaca Press, 1981), 297.

17. Michael Bar-Zahor, "David Ben-Gurion and the Policy of the Periphery," in *Israel in the Middle East*, eds. Itamar Rabinovich and Jehuda Reinharz, Second Edition (Lebanon, NH: University Press of New England, 2008), 191–197; Avi Shlaim, "Israel, the Great Powers, and the Middle East Crisis of 1958," *Journal of Imperial and Commonwealth History* 27, no. 2 (1999): 177–192; Noa Schonmann, "The Phantom Pact: Israel's Periphery Policy in the Middle East," DPhil diss., University of Oxford, 2009.

18. See Uri Bialer, "Fuel Bridge across the Middle East: Israel, Iran, and the Eilat-Ashkelon Oil Pipeline," *Israel Studies* 12, no. 3 (2007): 29–67.

19. Samii, "Role of SAVAK," 149–152; London A-2294 to State, March 8, 1967, RG59, CFPF 1967–69, Box 2218.

20. Samii, "Role of SAVAK," 136.

21. Schonmann, "Phantom Pact," 259.

22. Schonmann, "Phantom Pact," 259.

23. David Kimche, *The Last Option: After Nasser, Arafat and Saddam Hussein, the Quest for Peace in the Middle East* (New York: Charles Scribner's Sons, 1991), 189; Col. Isa Pejman in an interview with Akbar Etemad, Paris, April 8, 1983, Tape 1B, FISOHC; Samii, "Role of SAVAK," 137.

24. Edmund Ghareeb, *The Kurdish Question in Iraq* (Syracuse, NY: Syracuse University Press, 1981), 133; Samii, "Role of SAVAK," 137; Schonmann, "Phantom Pact," 260, f. 179.

25. Baghdad 1312 to State, October 14, 1958, *FRUS 1958–1960*, XII, 138.

26. Baghdad to State, September 20, 1962, *FRUS 1961–1963*, XVIII, 49; State 383 to Baghdad, June 22, 1962, *FRUS 1961–1963*, XVII, 305.

27. See Eric Jacobsen, "A Coincidence of Interests: Kennedy, U.S. Assistance, and the 1963 Iraqi Ba'th Regime," *Diplomatic History* 37, no. 5 (2013): 1029–1059; Weldon C. Matthews, "The Kennedy Administration, Counterinsurgency, and Iraq's First Ba'thist Regime," *International Journal of Middle East Studies* 43, no. 4 (2011): 635–653.

28. Komer to Bundy, March 1, 1963, *FRUS 1961–1963*, XVIII, 305.

29. State CA-9411 to Certain Posts, March 2, 1963, *FRUS 1961–1963*, XVIII, 174; McKesson to Bundy, August 6, 1963, *FRUS 1961–1963*, XVIII, 307; State 331 to Baghdad, April 5, 1963, *FRUS 1961–1963*, XVIII, 208.

30. Baghdad 486 to State, December 16, 1964, *FRUS 1964–1968*, XXI, 171

31. Tehran 1128 to State, April 12, 1965, *FRUS 1964–1968*, XXI, 172. Saunders to Watson, April 29, 1965, NSF, CFME, Box 136, LBJL; Saunders to Joyce, April 30, 1965, Files of Robert W. Komer, Box 28, LBJL.

32. Douglas Little, "The United States and the Kurds: A Cold War Story," *Journal of Cold War Studies* 12, no. 4 (2010): 73.

33. Atherton to Hare, November 1, 1966, *FRUS 1964–1968*, XXI, 185.

34. Baghdad A-424 to State, October 30, 1965, *FRUS 1964–68*, XXI, 177.

35. Baghdad A-625 to State, March 12, 1966; Saunders to Komer, March 23, 1966, NSF, Files of Robert W. Komer, Box 28, LBJL. Rostow to Johnson, February 20, 1967, and Memorandum from the Department of State to Rostow, February 16, 1967, WHCF, Confidential File, CO 124 Iraq, Box 9 [1 of 2], LBJL. Memorandum prepared by Saunders, July 30, 1968, WHCF, Subject File, CO 124 Iraq, Box 41, LBJL.

36. Tehran 7641 to State, December 10, 1968, and Tehran 367 to State, January 29, 1969, RG59, CFPF 1967–69, Box 2218.

37. Memcon, October 15, 1969, *FRUS 1969–1976*, E-4, 262.

38. Tehran 928 to State, March 12, 1970, *FRUS 1969–1976*, E-4, 53.

39. State 37806 to Tehran, March 14, 1970, *FRUS 1969–1976*, E-4, 268.

40. Smolansky and Smolansky, *USSR and Iraq*, 70–76. See also Haim Shemesh, *Soviet-Iraqi Relations, 1968–1988: In the Shadow of the Iraq-Iran Conflict* (Boulder, CO: Lynne Rienner, 1992), 34–35.

41. David McDowall, *A Modern History of the Kurds*, Third Edition (London: I. B. Tauris, 2007), 328.

42. CIA Information Cable, March 9, 1970, *FRUS 1969–1976*, E-4, 267.

43. Beirut A-38 to State, February 2, 1972, *FRUS 1969–1976*, E-4, 297.

44. CIA Informational Cable, August 10, 1970, *FRUS 1969–1976*, E-4, 273.

45. State 67409 to Certain Posts, April 21, 1971, *FRUS 1969–1976*, E-4, 286.

46. State 213299 to Tehran, November 24, 1971, *FRUS 1969–1976*, E-4, 294.

47. Beirut 222 to State, July 16, 1971, *FRUS 1969–1976*, E-4, 292.

48. For a vivid description of the assassination attempt, see John Bulloch and Harvey Morris, *No Friends but the Mountains: The Tragic History of the Kurds* (New York: Oxford University Press, 1992), 133.

49. Beirut 9689 to State, November 3, 1971, *FRUS 1969–1976*, E-4, 293.

50. Marion Farouk-Sluglett and Peter Sluglett, *Iraq since 1958: From Revolution to Dictatorship* (London: I. B. Tauris, 2001), 126–127; Johan Franzén, *Red Star over Iraq: Iraqi Communism before Saddam* (London: Hurst, 2011), 195–206.

51. Smolansky and Smolansky, *USSR and Iraq*, 16–25; Shemesh, *Soviet-Iraqi Relations*, 67–68; Charles Tripp, "Iraq," in *The Cold War in the Middle East*, eds. Yezid Sayigh and Avi Shlaim (Oxford: Clarendon Press, 1997), 203.

52. Moscow 1501 to State, February 18, 1972, *FRUS 1969–1976*, E-4, 298.

53. CIA Information Cable, March 10, 1972, *FRUS 1969–1976*, E-4, 300.

54. Tripp, *History of Iraq*, 189.

55. Farouk-Sluglett and Sluglett, *Iraq since 1958*, 152.

56. Tripp, "Iraq," 190–193; Franzén, *Red Star over Iraq*, 206–243.

57. Saunders to Haig, March 27, 1972, *FRUS 1969–1976*, E-4, 301; Helms to Kissinger, Rogers and Laird, March 31, 1972, *FRUS 1969–1976*, E-4, 303; Memorandum from Killgore to Sisco, April 3, 1972, *FRUS 1969–1976*, E-4, 304.

58. Saunders to Haig, March 27, 1972, *FRUS 1969–1976*, E-4, 301

59. Waller to Sisco, March 9, 1972, *FRUS 1969–1976*, E-4, 299.

60. Saunders to Haig, March 27, 1972, *FRUS 1969–1976*, E-4, 301.

61. Harold Saunders in an interview with William Burr, Washington, February 24, 1987, Tape 2B, FISOHC.

62. State 12737 to Certain Posts, January 22, 1972, *FRUS 1969–1976*, E-4, 295.

63. Beirut A-38 to State, February 2, 1972, *FRUS 1969–1976*, E-4, 297.

64. Saunders to Haig, March 27, 1972, *FRUS 1969–1976*, E-4, 301.

65. Kissinger, *Years of Renewal*, 581.

66. Clive Borrell, "Iraq Politician's Wife Shot in Assassination Attempt," *Times* (London), February 19, 1972. The Ba'thi regime would succeed in assassinating Nayif in London on July 9, 1978.

67. Helms to Kissinger, Rogers, and Laird, March 29, 1972, *FRUS 1969–1976*, E-4, 302; Helms to Kissinger, June 6, 1972, *FRUS 1969–1976*, E-4, 313.

68. Killgore to Sisco, April 3, 1972, *FRUS 1969–1976*, E-4, 304.

69. Killgore to Sisco, April 3, 1972, *FRUS 1969–1976*, E-4, 304.

70. Eliot to Kissinger, April 13, 1972, *FRUS 1969–1976*, E-4, 305. See also Tripp, "Iraq," 202.

71. Kissinger, *Years of Renewal*, 581.

72. Saunders to Haig, March 27, 1972, *FRUS 1969–1976*, E-4, 301.

73. Memorandum prepared by Simcha Dinitz, "The Prime Minister's Conversation with the Shah on Thursday, 18.5.72," On-Line Collection: Prime Minister Golda Meir and the Shah of Iran in 1972 (posted May 15, 2012), Israel State Archives.

74. Helms to Kissinger, June 6, 1972, *FRUS 1969–1976*, E-4, 313.

75. Research Study RNAS-10 prepared by the Department of State, May 31, 1972, *FRUS 1969–1976*, E-4, 310.

76. Memcon, May 30, 1972, *FRUS 1969–1976*, E-4, 200.

77. Memcon, May 31, 1972, *FRUS 1969–1976*, E-4, 201.

78. Alam, *Yad'dashtha-ye 'Alam*, Vol. II, 260.

79. Kissinger, *Years of Renewal*, 583–584.

80. Kissinger, *White House Years*, 1264–1265.

81. Helms to Kissinger, June 6, 1972, *FRUS 1969–1976*, E-4, 313; Harold Saunders in an interview with the author, Washington, June 27, 2011. The Nixon Library has released a copy of Saunders's memorandum, with the names of Idriss Barzani and Mahmoud Uthman not redacted. It is available at NPM, NSCF, CFME, Box 603.

82. Randal, *After Such Knowledge*, 149.

83. Harold Saunders in an interview with William Burr, Washington, February 24, 1987, Tape 2B, FISOHC.

84. Initially, it seems that Kissinger's deputy, Gen. Alexander Haig, was to meet with the Kurdish emissaries. But even this may have been too close for comfort for Kissinger, as the task ultimately fell to Col. Kennedy.

85. Waller to Helms, June 12, 1972, *FRUS 1969–1976*, E-4, 315.

86. Saunders to Haig, June 23, 1972, *FRUS 1969–1976*, E-4, 318.

87. Kissinger to Connally, June 29, 1972, *FRUS 1969–1976*, E-4, 209, f.1. As the State Department was unaware of Nixon's decision to support Barzani, the briefing paper they prepared for Connally's visit advised him to "inform the Shah that the Kurdish situation is a complicated problem in which you strongly doubt that the USG would wish to be involved." See Briefing Paper prepared by the Department of State, "Iranian Interest in Iraqi Kurdistan," undated, RG59, Executive Secretariat, Briefing Books, 1958–1976, LOT 72D373, Box 135.

88. Saunders to Nixon, July 12, 1972, *FRUS 1969–1976*, E-4, 211.

89. Randal, *After Such Knowledge*, p. 153.

90. Memcon, July 5, 1972, *FRUS 1969–1976*, E-4, 319.

91. Kissinger mentions British financial support for the Kurdish operation in his memoirs. See Kissinger, *Years of Renewal*, 584, 589. However, any reference to Britain has been redacted from all US documents, except for a single reference in a memorandum of a conversation between Nixon, Kissinger, and the shah on July 24, 1973, in Washington, obtained by the National Security Archive. See Memorandum prepared by Kissinger for the President's Files, undated, EBB 265, NSA-GWU. Even this reference is redacted in the version of this document that was subsequently published in *FRUS 1969–1976*, XXVII, 25. Furthermore, there is no trace of Britain's role in the Kurdish operation in the records of the Foreign and Commonwealth Office at the UK National Archives.

92. CIA Memorandum, "Prospects and Problems of Assistance to the Kurds," July 18, 1972, *FRUS 1969–1976*, E-4, 321, Attachment B.

93. *CIA: The Pike Report, With an Introduction by Philip Agee* (Nottingham, UK: Spokesman Books, 1977), 212.

94. CIA Memorandum, "Prospects and Problems of Assistance to the Kurds," July 18, 1972, *FRUS 1969–1976*, E-4, 321, Attachment B.

95. Kissinger, *Years of Renewal*, 585.

96. Kissinger to the 40 Committee, undated, *FRUS 1969–1976*, E-4, 322.

97. NSDM 40, February 17, 1970, *FRUS 1969–1976*, II, 203. See also "Note on U.S. Covert Actions," *FRUS 1969–1976*, XXVII.

98. Haig to Kissinger, July 28, 1972, *FRUS 1969–1976*, E-4, 321.

99. For a firsthand account of the culture of secrecy in the Nixon White House, see David R. Young, "The Presidential Conduct of American Foreign Policy, 1969–1973," DPhil diss., University of Oxford, 1981.

100. See Seymour Hersh, *The Price of Power: Kissinger in the Nixon White House* (London: Faber, 1983), 542,f.

101. See Stanley I. Kutler, ed., *Watergate: A Brief History with Documents* (Chichester, UK: Wiley-Blackwell, 2010).

102. Helms to Kissinger, November 13, 1972, NPM, NSCF, CFME, Box 603.

103. Kissinger to Nixon, October 5, 1972, *FRUS 1969–1976*, E-4, 325.

104. Arthur Lowrie in an interview with Patricia Lessard and Theodore Lowrie, December 23, 1989, The Foreign Affairs Oral History Collection of the Association for Diplomatic Studies and Training.

105. Baghdad A-6 to State, December 1, 1972, *FRUS 1969–1976*, E-4, 328.

106. Baghdad 92 to State, December 19, 1972, *FRUS 1969–1976*, E-4, 329.

107. NIE 36-2-72, December 21, 1972, *FRUS 1969–1976*, E-4, 330.

108. NIE 36-2-72, December 21, 1972, *FRUS 1969–1976*, E-4, 330.

109. Helms with Hood, *Look over My Shoulder*, 409–412.

110. CIA Station in Tehran to Helms, December 11, 1972, CIA-Helms.

111. CIA Station in Tehran to Helms, January 11, 1973, CIA-Helms.

112. Thomas Powers, *The Man Who Kept the Secrets: Richard Helms and the CIA* (New York: Alfred A. Knopf, 1979), 277–312.

113. James Schlesinger in an interview with William Burr, Washington, May 15, 1986, Tape 1A, FISOHC.

114. See Manouchehr Hashemi, *Davari: Sukhan-i dar karnameh-ye Savak* [Judgement: Some Remarks about SAVAK] (London: Aras, 1994), 494–507.

115. Kissinger to Nixon, March 29, 1973, *FRUS 1969–1976*, XXVII, 207.

116. Retired CIA officer who served as the liaison with Barzani, in an interview with the author, December 13, 2011.

117. Kissinger to Nixon, March 29, 1973, *FRUS 1969–1976*, XXVII, 207.

118. Helms to Kissinger, April 6, 1973, CIA-Helms.

119. State 118336 to Tehran, June 18, 1973, NPM, NSCF, CFME, Box 603; Memorandum prepared by Kissinger for the President's File, undated, EBB 265, NSA-GWU.

120. Iraq had severed diplomatic relations with Iran after the shah's seizure of the Persian Gulf islands of Abu Musa and the Tunbs in November 1971. On the talks between Iran and Iraq, see Tehran 2915 to State, April 28, 1973, and Ankara 5217 to State, June 29, 1973, RG59, SNF 1970–73, Box 2380; Ramsbotham (Tehran) to FCO, April 30, 1973, FCO 8/2094; Tehran 2990 to State, May 1, 1973, and Tehran 3383 to State, May 16, 1973, NPM, NSCF, CFME, Box 603; Baghdad 266 to State, May 17, 1973, *FRUS 1969–1976*, XXVII, 215.

121. Tehran 3548 to State, May 22, 1973, RG59, SNF 1970–73, Box 2380.

122. Baghdad 266 to State, May 17, 1973, NPM, NSCF, CFME, Box 603.

123. Tehran 3974 to State, June 9, 1973, RG59, SNF 1970–73, Box 2380.

124. Ramsbotham (Tehran 333) to FCO, April 19, 1973, and Ramsbotham (Tehran 334) to FCO, April 19, 1973, FCO 8/2094.

125. Renwick (Paris) to Wright (London), May 28, 1973, and Ramsbotham (Tehran) to FCO, May 31, 1973, FCO 8/2094.

126. Walters to Kissinger, Rogers and Schlesinger, July 23, 1973, NPM, NSCF, VIP Visits, Box 920.

127. Helms to CIA Official, June 9, 1973, and CIA Official to Helms, June 11, 1973, CIA-Helms.

128. Baghdad to State, June 24, 1973, *FRUS 1969–1976*, XXVII, 217.

129. Jim Hoagland, "The Kurds Gird for Another War," *Washington Post*, June 24, 1973.

130. Helms to Kissinger, July 9, 1973, *FRUS 1969–1976*, XXVII, 222.

131. Walters to Kissinger, July 26, 1973, *FRUS 1969–1976*, XXVII, 225. This message was delivered to the shah at Saadabad Palace on July 17, though he was "unaware" that the CIA had obtained a copy, most likely from the two Kurdish envoys who met with Helms and Callahan on July 6.

132. Tehran 4475 to State, June 25, 1973, *FRUS 1969–1976*, XXVII, 218.

133. Memorandum from Kissinger for the President's File, undated, EBB 265, NSA-GWU.

134. Memorandum from Kissinger for the President's File, undated, *FRUS 1969–1976*, XXVII, 28.

135. Zahedi had resigned from his post as foreign minister earlier that year, after repeated clashes with Prime Minister Amir-Abbas Hoveyda. The shah then sent him as ambassador to Washington, where he stayed until the 1978–1979 Iranian Revolution. See Milani, *Persian Sphinx*, 244–250.

136. Memcon, August 3, 1973, *FRUS 1969–1976*, XXVII, 31.

137. Memcon, July 23, 1973, *FRUS 1969–1976*, XXVII, 24. Helms also mentioned that the Kurds had been asking both the Kuwaitis and Saudis for financial support, but they had been "reluctant to contribute so far."

138. Memcon, July 24, 1973, *FRUS 1969–1976*, XXVII, 27.

139. Memcon, July 27, 1973, *FRUS 1969–1976*, XXVII, 30.

140. *FRUS 1969–1976*, XXVII, 225, f.3.

141. Colby to Kissinger, August 7, 1973, *FRUS 1969–1976*, XXVII, 227.

142. Kissinger to Helms, Augsut 16, 1973, *FRUS 1969–1976*, XXVII, 229; Helms to Kissinger, August 17, 1973, CIA-Helms. The precise figure for US cash payments to the Kurds has been redacted from these documents. However, a 50 percent increase in the 1972 figure of $3 million would take the annual cash payments up to $4.5 million.

143. Kissinger, *Years of Renewal*, 585. In 1972, the total Iranian annual subsidy for the Kurds, including cash and arms, had been $9 million.

144. Editorial Note, *FRUS 1969–1976*, XXXVIII, 16. Kissinger's decision on the Kurds' subvention was relayed to the shah on August 24, even though it was not approved by Nixon until September 6 and ratified by the 40 Committee until September 7. See Kissinger to Nixon, September 6, 1973, *FRUS 1969–1976*, XXVII, 233.

145. Helms to Kissinger, Augsut 25, 1973, CIA-Helms. See also *FRUS 1969–1976*, XXVII, 229, f.3.

146. Memcon, July 23, 1973, *FRUS 1969–1976*, XXVII, 24.

147. Minutes of Senior Review Group Meeting, July 20, 1973, *FRUS 1969–1976*, XXVII, 23.

148. Baghdad 202 to State, April 10, 1973, *FRUS 1969–1976*, XXVII, 212.

149. Eliot to Kissinger, March 3, 1973, *FRUS 1969–1976*, XXVII, 205; Memcon, April 6, 1973, *FRUS 1969–1976*, XXVII, 209.

150. Baghdad 379 to State, July 1, 1973, *FRUS 1969–1976*, XXVII, 219.

151. Baghdad 373 to State, July 1, 1973, *FRUS 1969–1976*, XXVII, 220. Lowrie had made similar arguments at the regional chiefs of mission conference in Tehran on April 23–24. See Lowrie to Korn, April 30, 1973, *FRUS 1969–1976*, XXVII, 214.

152. Research Study prepared in the Bureau of Intelligence and Research, August 23, 1973, *FRUS 1969–1976*, XXVII, 230.

153. CIA Weekly Summary 0387/73, September 14, 1973, CREST.

154. McDowall, *Modern History*, 332–335.

155. *FRUS 1969–1976*, XXVII, 237, f. 2.

156. Asadollah Alam, *Yad'dashtha-ye 'Alam: Virayish va muqaddamah az Alinaqi Alikhani* [The Alam Diaries: Edited by Alinaghi Alikhani], Vol. III: 1973–1974 (Bethesda, MD: Iranbooks, 1995), 222.

157. Helms to Kissinger, October 16, 1973, NSA, KSWWOF, Box 19, GRFL.

158. Kissinger, *Years of Renewal*, 587.

159. Kissinger to Colby, October 16, 1973, NSA, KSWWOF, Box 19, GRFL; Kissinger to Helms, October 16, 1973, CIA-Helms.

160. Scowcroft to Nixon, November 9, 1973, NPM, NSCF, CFME, Box 603.

161. Kissinger, *Years of Renewal*, 585.

162. Kissinger, *Years of Upheaval*, 675–676.

163. Farouk-Sluglett and Sluglett, *Iraq since 1958*, 149–170; Franzén, *Red Star over Iraq*, 206–215; Smolansky and Smolansky, *USSR and Iraq*, 111–117.

164. Memorandum from the Department of State for Kissinger, March 3, 1973, NPM, NSCF, CFME, Box 603.

165. Skeet, *OPEC*, 240.

166. Prohaska to Waldheim, March 8, 1974, S-0904-022-04, UNARMS; CIA Weekly Summary 0011/74, March 15, 1974, CREST.

167. "Meeting Held at the Iraqi Foreign Ministry in Baghdad on Monday, 8 April 1974, at 5.30pm," S-0904-0022-08, UNARMS.

168. Diplomatic Report 167/75, "Iraq and the Kurds," February 23, 1975, FCO 8/2535.

169. Helms to Scowcroft, March 18, 1974, CIA-Helms. See also another copy of this document in *FRUS 1969–1976*, XXVII, 242.

170. Helms to Scowcroft, March 20, 1974, CIA-Helms; Colby to Kissinger, March 21, 1974, *FRUS 1969–1976*, XXVII, 243.

171. Kissinger, *Years of Renewal*, 588–589.

172. Scowcroft to Helms, March 26, 1974, *FRUS 1969–1976*, XXVII, 244.

173. CIA Memorandum for Kissinger, March 21, 1974, NPM, NSCF, CFME, Box 603. See also another copy of this document in *FRUS 1969–1976*, XXVII, 243.

174. Helms to Scowcroft, March 18, 1974, *FRUS 1969–1976*, XXVII, 242.

175. Memcon, March 21, 1974, 01078, DNSA.

176. Kissinger to Nixon, April 11, 1974, NSA, KSWWOF, Box 19, GRFL. See also another copy of this document in *FRUS 1969–1976*, XXVII, 246.

177. Kissinger to Helms, undated, NSA, KSWWOF, Box 19, GRFL. This is most likely the April 19 message that is referred to in *FRUS 1969–1976*, XXVII, 246, f.4.

178. Helms to Kissinger, April 17, 1974, *FRUS 1969–1976*, XXVII, 247.

179. Helms to Kissinger, April 22, 1974, *FRUS 1969–1976*, XXVII, 248.

180. Helms to Kissinger, May 21, 1974, CIA-Helms.

181. Baghdad 221 to State, April 11, 1974, *FRUS 1969–1976*, XXVII, 245.

182. Baghdad 280 to State, May 1, 1974, *FRUS 1969–1976*, XXVII, 249.

183. Minutes of the Secretary's Principals and Regionals Staff Meeting, April 23, 1974, 01111, DNSA.

184. Walter LaFeber, *America, Russia and the Cold War, 1945–2006*, Tenth Edition (Boston: McGraw-Hill, 2008), 275.

185. Tehran 3088 to State, April 20, 1974, NPM, NSCF, CFME, Box 603.

186. United Nations, Security Council, "Letter Dated 12 February 1974 from the Deputy Permanent Representative of Iraq to the United Nations Addressed to the President of the Security Council," February 12, 1974, S/11216, ODS; United Nations, Security Council, "Note by the President of the Security Council," February 28, 1974, S/11229, ODS.

187. "Meeting Held at the National Assembly in Baghdad on Thursday, 18 April 1974, at 6.30 p.m.," S-0904-0022-08, UNARMS.

188. Weckmann-Munoz to Waldheim, April 30, 1974, S-0904-0022-11, UNARMS.

189. Weckmann-Munoz to Waldheim, April 25, 1974, S-0303-0003-01, UNARMS.

190. Weckmann-Munoz to Waldheim, April 30, 1974, S-0904-0022-11, UNARMS.

191. United Nations, Security Council, "Report by the Secretary-General on the Implementation of the Consensus adopted by the Security Council on 28 February 1974 Regarding the Complaint by Iraq Concerning Incidents on Its Frontier with Iran," May 20, 1974, S/11921, ODS.

192. United Nations, Security Council, Resolution 348, May 28, 1974, S/RES/348, ODS.

193. Arbuthnott (Tehran) to Clark (London), June 13, 1974, FCO 8/2307.

194. Colby to Kissinger, May 23, 1974, *FRUS 1969–1976*, XXVII, 250.

195. Kissinger to Nixon, June 24, 1974, NSA, KSWWOF, Box 19, GRFL.

196. Helms to Scowcroft, July 8, 1974, CIA-Helms.

197. Tehran 6159 to State, July 25, 1974, NPM, NSCF, CFME, Box 603.

198. Asadollah Alam, *Yad'dashtha-ye 'Alam: Virayish va muqaddamah az Alinaqi Alikhani* [The Alam Diaries: Edited by Alinaghi Alikhani], Vol. IV: 1974–1975 (Bethesda, MD: IBEX, 2000), 145.

199. United Nations—New York 2065 to State, June 5, 1974, *FRUS 1969–1976*, XXVII, 252; State 121821 to United Nations—New York, June 8, 1974, *FRUS 1969–1976*, XXVII, 253.

200. Tehran 6206 to State, July 28, 1974, NPM, NSCF, CFME, Box 603. Alam, *Yad'dashtha-ye 'Alam*, Vol. IV, 154–155.

201. Baghdad 1109 to State, August 2, 1974, NPM, NSCF, CFME, Box 603; State 170249 to Tehran, August 5, 1974, *FRUS 1969–1976*, XXVII, 256.

202. Tabriz 20 to State, September 4, 1974, *FRUS 1969–1976*, XXVII, 261.

203. Baghdad 564 to State, August 29, 1974, *FRUS 1969–1976*, XXVII, 260.

204. Tehran 6788 to State, August 14, 1974, and Baghdad 583 to State, September 7, 1974, RG59, CFPF 1973–76, AAD. Browne (Tehran) to Williams (London), August 22, 1974, and Parsons (Tehran) to FCO, September 4, 1974, FCO 8/2315.

205. Note prepared by the Government of Israel, August 24, 1974, NSA, KSWWOF, Box 19, GRFL.

206. "Cable from Jerusalem Translated by Shalev and Dictated to General Scowcroft," August 24, 1975, NSA, KSWWOF, Box 19, GRFL.

207. Note prepared by the Government of Israel, "Assistance to Kurds," August 22, 1974, NSA, KSWWOF, Box 19, GRFL; Scowcroft to Helms, August 24, 1974, CIA-Helms.

208. Scowcroft to Helms, August 22, 1974, *FRUS 1969–1976*, XXVII, 258.

209. Intelligence Note prepared in the Bureau of Intelligence and Research, November 18, 1974, *FRUS 1969–1976*, XXVII, 267, Tab B.

210. Helms to Scowcroft, August 25, 1974, CIA-Helms.

211. Memcon, August 26, 1974, NSA, Memcons, Box 5, GRFL. Helms to Scowcroft, August 24, 1974, Scowcroft to Helms, August 24, 1974, and Kissinger to Helms, August 26, 1974, CIA-Helms.

212. CIA Memorandum for Ford, August 30, 1974, NSA, PCFMESA, Box 14, GRFL.

213. Memcon, September 17, 1974, NSA, KSWWOF, Box 19, GRFL; Memcon, December 23, 1974, 01463, DNSA.

214. Tehran 10954 to State, December 30, 1974, NSA, PCFMESA, Box 14, GRFL.

215. Baghdad 564 to State, August 29, 1974, NSA, PCFMESA, Box 14, GRFL. Taqa was referring to the 1971 Indo-Pakistan War, which led to East Pakistan's independence as Bangladesh.

216. State 262660 to Tehran, November 28, 1974, NSA, PCFMESA, Box 13, GRFL.

217. Kissinger to Ford, September 6, 1974, NSA, PCFMESA, Box 12, GRFL.

218. Helms to Kissinger, August 25, 1974, CIA-Helms.

219. Parsons (Tehran) to FCO, September 11, 1974, FCO 8/2307.

220. Graham (Baghdad) to FCO, November 27, 1974, FCO 8/2309.

221. Parsons (Tehran) to Wright (London), October 24, 1974, FCO 8/2308.

222. Barzani to Kissinger, October 22, 1974, NSA, KSWWOF, Box 19, GRFL.

223. Parsons (Tehran) to the Ministry of Defense, September 10, 1974, FCO 8/2307; CIA Memorandum, "Defense and Humanitarian Support for General Barzani," October 31, 1974, NSA, KSWWOF, Box 19, GRFL; Intelligence Note prepared in the Bureau of Intelligence and Research, November 18, 1974, *FRUS 1969–1976*, XXVII, 267, Tab B.

224. Parsons (Tehran) to FCO, December 18, 1974, FCO 8/2309. The Iraqis mistakenly claimed that American-made "Hawk" missiles had brought down the Iraqi jets in December. See Hyland to Sisco, December 16, 1974, *FRUS 1969–1976*, XXVII, 267.

225. Parsons (Tehran) to FCO, November 28, 1974, FCO 8/2309. On the Iraqi Kurdish refugees in Iran, see Prohaska to Waldheim, October 9, 1974, S-0904-0022-11, UNARMS.

226. Intelligence Note prepared in the Bureau of Intelligence and Research, November 18, 1974, *FRUS 1969–1976*, XXVII, 267, Tab B.

227. Memcon, October 13, 1974, 01366, DNSA.

228. Memcon, October 19, 1974, 01377, and Memcon, October 22, 1974, 01379, DNSA.

229. Scowcroft to Ford, November 3, 1974, NSA, Trip Briefing Books and Cables for HAK, Box 3, GRFL.

230. Memcon, November 7, 1974, 01405, DNSA.

231. Kissinger, *Years of Renewal*, 591–592.

232. Memcon, November 16, 1974, 01417, DNSA.

233. Tehran 8821 to State, October 21, 1974, RG59, CFPF 1973–76, AAD.

234. Tehran 10592 to State, December 16, 1974, NSA, PCFMESA, Box 14, GRFL.

235. Amman 7404 to State, December 11, 1974, NSA, PCFMESA, Box 22, GRFL.

236. Intelligence Note prepared in the Bureau of Intelligence and Research, November 18, 1974, *FRUS 1969–1976*, XXVII, 267, Tab B.

237. Lait (Baghdad) to Richardson (London), November 23, 1974, and Balfour Paul (Amman) to FCO, January 13, 1975, FCO 8/2546.

238. Amman 166 to State, January 10, 1975, NSA, PCFMESA, Box 22, GRFL.

239. Cowgill (Tehran) to Norburry (London), January 8, 1975, FCO 8/2546.

240. Campbell to Bolster, December 26, 1974, RG59, Records Relating to Iran, 1965–1975, LOT 77D400, Box 11; Neumann to Bolster, December 26, 1974, *FRUS 1969–1976*, XXVII, 269.

241. Alam, *Yad'dashtha-ye 'Alam*, Vol. IV, 267.

242. Tehran 10954 to State, December 30, 1974, NSA, PCFMESA, Box 14, GRFL.

243. Parsons (Tehran) to Weir (London), January 2, 1975, FCO 8/2546.

244. Memcon, January 16, 1975, 01477, DNSA.

245. Ankara 904 to State, Janaury 31, 1975, RG59, CFPF 1973–76, AAD. Graham (Baghdad) to Weir (London), February 6, 1975, FCO 8/2534.

246. Graham (Baghdad) to Lucas (London), February 13, 1975, FCO 8/2535; Graham (Baghdad) to Lucas (London), February 6, 1975, FCO 8/2546.

247. Parsons (Tehran) to Weir (London), February 13, 1975, FCO 8/2535.

248. Kissinger, *Years of Renewal*, 591.

249. Barzani to Kissinger, January 22, 1975, NSA, KSWWOF, Box 19, GRFL.

250. Rodman to Kissinger, February 6, 1975, NSA, KSWWOF, Box 19, GRFL.

251. Scowcroft to Ford, February 19, 1975, NSA, KSWWOF, Box 19, GRFL.

252. Kissinger, *Years of Renewal*, p. 593. Kissinger to Barzani, February 20, 1975, NSA, KSWWOF, Box 19, GRFL.

253. Defense Intelligence Agency Notice, March 7, 1975, *FRUS 1969–1976*, XXVII, 273.

254. Col. Isa Pejman in an interview with Habib Ladjevardi, Paris, March 4, 1983, Tape 1, HIOHP.

255. Alam, *Yad'dashtha-ye 'Alam*, Vol. IV, 340–345.

256. Helms to Scowcroft, March 8, 1975, *FRUS 1969–1976*, XXVII, 275; *CIA: The Pike Report*, 213; Jim Hoagland, "The Kurds Betrayed: Web of Deceit," *Washington Post*, March 25, 1975.

257. Kimche, *Last Option*, 195.

258. Trita Parsi, *Treacherous Alliance: The Secret Dealings of Israel, Iran, and the United States* (New Haven, CT: Yale University Press, 2007), 56.

259. Parsons (Tehran) to FCO, March 10, 1975, FCO 8/2535.

260. TOHAK38 from Helms to Kissinger, March 9, 1975, DDRAC, Box 9, GRFL.

261. Tehran 2254 to State, March 10, 1975, NSA, PCFMESA, Box 14, GRFL.

262. Memcon, February 7, 1975, NSA, Memcons, Box 9, GRFL.

263. Briefing paper for Nixon prepared by the Department of State, July 1973; and Kissinger to Nixon, July 23, 1973, NPM, NSCF, VIP Visits, Box 920.

264. Kissinger, *Years of Renewal*, 590, 593–594.

265. HAKTO16 from Kissinger to Scowcroft, March 9, 1975, DDRAC, Box 9, GRFL.

266. Gen. Brent Scowcroft in an interview with the author, Washington, December 16, 2011.

267. Memcon, March 9, 1975, 01522, DNSA.

268. The Israeli envoy in Tehran, Uri Lubrani, expressed similar sentiments. See Tehran 2351 to State, March 13, 1975, *FRUS 1969–1976*, XXVII, 279.

269. CIA Intelligence Memorandum, "Iran's Arab World Initiatives and their Implications," January 14, 1975, CREST; CIA Intelligence Memorandum, "Iran: The Shah's Lending Binge," December 1974, 00918, DNSA.

270. Memcon, March 9, 1975, NSA, Kissinger Reports on USSR, China and Middle East Discussions, Box 3, GRFL.

271. Tehran 1188 to State, March 10, 1975, NSA, KSWWOF, Box 19, GRFL.

272. CIA Weekly Summary 0013/75, March 28, 1975, CREST.

273. CIA Memorandum for Scowcroft, March 13, 1975, NSA, KSWWOF, Box 19, GRFL.

274. Kissinger, *Years of Renewal*, 594–596.

275. Scowcroft to Helms, March 10, 1975, NSA, KSWWOF, Box 19, GRFL.

276. Alam, *Yad'dashtha-ye 'Alam*, Vol. IV, 326–327, 359.

277. Randal, *After Such Knowledge*, 166.

278. Helms to Scowcroft, March 10, 1975, CIA-Helms.

279. HAKTO52 from Kissinger to Scowcroft, March 15, 1975, DDRAC, Box 9, GRFL; Scowcroft to Helms, March 16, 1975, *FRUS 1969–1976*, XXVII, 281.

280. TOHAK141 from Helms to Kissinger, March 19, 1975, DDRAC, Box 9, GRFL.

281. Tehran 2272 to State, March 11, 1975, NSA, PCFMESA, Box 14, GRFL. Jim Hoagland, "The Death of a People," *Washington Post*, April 6, 1975.

282. Defense Intelligence Agency Appraisal, October 6, 1975, *FRUS 1969–1976*, XXVII, 300; McDowall, *Modern History*, 338–340; O'Ballance, *Kurdish Struggle*, 98–99.

283. Temple (Baghdad) to McCluney (London), April 5, 1975, and Westmacott (Tehran) to Williams (London), May 7, 1975, FCO 8/2546.

284. C. L. Sulzberger, "To Be Obscurely Hanged," *New York Times*, March 12, 1975.

285. "The Kurds Have No Friends," *Washington Post*, March 25, 1975.

286. Joseph Kraft, "What Restrains the Shah?" *Washington Post*, April 27, 1975.

287. Kissinger to Ford, May 7, 1975, NSA, Presidential Briefing Material for VIP Visits, Box 9, GRFL.

288. Memcon, May 15, 1975, NSA, Memcons, Box 11, GRFL.

289. Minutes of the Secretary's Principals' and Regionals' Staff Meeting, May 16, 1975, 01624, DNSA.

290. Kissinger to Ford, May 19, 1975, Presidential Handwriting File, Box 6, GRFL. On Meany's support for Barzani, see David A. Korn, "The Last Years of Mustafa Barzani," *Middle East Quarterly*, 1/2 (1994), available at: <http://www.meforum.org/220/the-last-years-of-mustafa-barzani>.

291. See Cynthia M. Nolan, "Seymour Hersh's Impact on The CIA," *International Journal of Intelligence and Counterintelligence* 12, no. 1 (1999): 18–34.

292. Colby to Kissinger, June 4, 1975, *FRUS 1969–1976*, XXVII, 289.

293. See US House of Representatives, Ninety-Fourth Congress, First Session, Select Committee on Intelligence, "U.S. Intelligence Agencies and Activities: The Performance of the Intelligence Community," September 11, 12, 18, 25, 30, 1975; and October 7, 30, 31, Part 2 (Washington, DC: US Government Printing Office, 1975), 913–919; Gerald K. Haines, "The Pike Committee Investigations and the CIA," *Studies in Intelligence* 42, no. 5 (1999): 84.

294. Memcon, October 31, 1975, NSA, Memcons, Box 16, GRFL.

295. John Crewdson, "U.S. Said to Arm Iraqi Kurds in 72," *New York Times*, November 2, 1975.

296. Tehran 10655 to State, November 3, 1975, *FRUS 1969–1976*, XXVII, 301.

297. Joseph Fitchett, "Kurds Say CIA Betrayed Them," *Washington Post*, November 13, 1975; Korn, "Last Years."

298. "Kurdish Rebels in Iraq Gave Three Rugs to Kissinger," *New York Times*, January 26, 1976; Maxine Cheshire, "Now You See Them. . .," *Washington*

Post, January 29, 1976. See also Rodman to Covey, November 10, 1975, and Catto to Scowcroft, February 12, 1976, NSA, KSWWOF, Box 19, GRFL; Koplowitz to Helms, March 26, 1976, and Blee to Helms, March 30, 1976, CIA-Helms.

299. William Safire, "Mr. Ford's Secret Sellout," *New York Times*, February 5, 1976.

300. Memorandum prepared for Ron Nessen, "Safire Column on U.S. Policy Toward the Kurds," February 5, 1976, Ron Nessen Papers, Box 123, GRFL. "Column by Safire on Kurds Assailed," *New York Times*, February 6, 1976.

301. Telcon between Kissinger and Osborn, 2.50 p.m, February 12, 1976, DNSA.

302. Telcon between Kissinger and Dinitz, 3.00 p.m, February 12, 1976, State-Kissinger.

303. Aaron Latham, "The Kissinger-Safire Feud," *New York* (Magazine), March 29, 1976, 34–36.

304. William Safire, "Son of 'Secret Sellout,'" *New York Times*, February 12, 1976.

305. Bernard Gwertzman, "Kissinger Assails Report by Pike as 'Malicious Lie,'" *New York Times*, February 13, 1976; Murrey Marder, "Kissinger Hits Leaks of Pike Report," *Washington Post*, February 13, 1976.

306. Haines, "Pike Committee," 89.

307. "The Report on the CIA That President Ford Doesn't Want You to Read," *Village Voice*, February 16, 1976.

308. William Safire, "Mr. Ford's Cover-Up," *New York Times*, April 12, 1976; Memcon, April 12, 1976, NSA, Memcons, Box 19, GRFL.

309. See, for example, Aaron Latham, "What Kissinger Was Afraid of in the Pike Papers," *New York* (Magazine), October 4, 1976, 50–68.

310. Memcon, July 8, 1976, NSA, Memcons, Box 20, GRFL. Telcon between Kissinger and Koppel, 12.30 p.m., July 9, 1976, State-Kissinger.

311. See Louise Fawcett, "Down But Not Out? The Kurds in International Politics," *Review of International Studies* 27, no. 1 (2001): 109–118.

312. Korn, "Last Years"; Ratliff to Kissinger, July 24, 1975, *FRUS 1969–1976*, XXVII, 293; Atherton to Kissinger, August 5, 1976, *FRUS 1969–1976*, XXVII, 315.

313. Minutes of the Secretary's Staff Meeting, July 30, 1976, 02000, DNSA.

314. Kissinger, *Years of Renewal*, 578, 596.

315. *CIA: The Pike Report*, 198.

316. Henry Kissinger, "Hard Choices to Make in the Gulf," *Washington Post*, May 5, 1991.

317. Jim Hoagland, "The Kurds Gird for Another War," *Washington Post*, June 24, 1973.

318. Randal, *After Such Knowledge*, 157.

319. Alam, *Yad'dashtha-ye 'Alam*, Vol. IV, 211.

4   A FORD, NOT A NIXON: THE UNITED STATES AND THE
SHAH'S NUCLEAR DREAMS

1. See James Cannon, *Time and Change: Gerald Ford's Appointment with History* (Ann Arbor: The University of Michigan Press, 1998).

2. Alam, *Yad'dashtha-ye 'Alam*, Vol. IV, 205.

3. See Mario Del Pero, *The Eccentric Realist: Henry Kissinger and the Shaping of American Foreign Policy* (Ithaca, NY: Cornell University Press), 110–144; Robert D. Schulzinger, "Détente in the Nixon-Ford Years," in *The Cambridge History of the Cold War, Volume II: Crises and Détente*, eds. Melvyn P. Leffler and Odd Arne Westad (Cambridge: Cambridge University Press, 2010), 388–392.

4. "The Master Builder of Iran," *Newsweek*, October 14, 1974. See also Editorial Note, *FRUS 1969–1976*, XXVII, 84.

5. Maw to Kissinger, September 8, 1975, *FRUS 1969–1976*, E-3, 254. See also Mark Philip Bradley, "American Vernaculars: The United States and the Global Human Rights Imagination," *Diplomatic History* 38, no. 1 (2014): 1–21; Barbara Keys, "Congress, Kissinger, and the Origins of Human Rights Diplomacy," *Diplomatic History* 34, no. 5 (2010): 823–851; Sarah B. Snyder, " 'A Call for U.S. Leadership': Congressional Activism on Human Rights," *Diplomatic History* 37, no. 2 (2013): 372–397.

6. C. L. Sulzberger, "The Shah (II): Authority," *New York Times*, March 22, 1975.

7. Tehran 2069 to State, March 4, 1975, *FRUS 1969–1976*, XXVII, 111. See also Milani, *Persian Sphinx*, 275–280.

8. Intelligence Information Cable, May 8, 1975, *FRUS 1969–1976*, XXVII, 120.

9. See Afshin Matin-Asgari, *Iranian Student Opposition to the Shah* (Costa Mesa, CA: Mazda, 2002).

10. Mojahedin-e Khalq militants were reportedly responsible for killing two members of the U.S. military mission in Tehran in May 1975 and three American defense contractors in August 1976. See Tehran 4788 to State, May 21, 1975, *FRUS 1969–1976*, XXVII, 128; Report Prepared in the Bureau of Intelligence and Research, October 7, 1975, *FRUS 1969–1976*, XXVII, 146; Tehran 8696 to State, August 28, 1976, *FRUS 1969–1976*, XXVII, 186.

11. U.S. House of Representatives, Ninety-Fourth Congress, Second Session, Committee on International Relations, Subcommittee on International Organisations, "Human Rights in Iran," August 8, 1976, and September 8, 1976 (Washington, DC: US Government Printing Office, 1976). See also Tehran 8376 to State, August 18, 1976, *FRUS 1969–1976*, XXVII, 184; Huddle to Naas, August 20, 1976, *FRUS 1969–1976*, XXVII, 185.

12. Bill, *Eagle and the Lion*, 319–378.

13. Kissinger to Rogers and Laird, July 25, 1972, *FRUS 1969–1976*, E-4, 214.

14. Ingersoll to Kissinger, December 12, 1974, and Kennedy and Oakley to Kissinger, December 13, 1974, NSA, PCFMESA, Box 12, GRFL.

15. This is Kissinger's handwritten instruction on the December 13 memorandum from Kennedy and Oakley, cited above. See also Davis to Springsteen, February 10, 1975, NSA, PCFMESA, Box 12, GRFL.

16. Sullivan to Clements, January 23, 1975, *FRUS 1969–1976*, XXVII, 99.

17. Schlesinger to Ford, undated [September 2, 1975], NSA, PCFMESA, Box 13, GRFL. See also Schlesinger to Ford, September 2, 1975, *FRUS 1969–1976*, XXVII, 142.

18. On the Kissinger-Schlesinger rivalry, see Hanhimäki, *Flawed Architect*, 363–364; Kissinger, *Years of Renewal*, 177–182.

19. Cooper, *Oil Kings*, 172–173.

20. Memcon, August 17, 1974, NSA, Memcons, Box 5, GRFL.

21. James Schlesinger in an interview with William Burr, Washington, May 15, 1986, Tape 1A, FISOHC.

22. This chapter builds on the work of William Burr, who is responsible for locating and making available many of the US government documents cited here. See Burr, "A Brief History."

23. Richard G. Hewlett and Jack M. Holt, *Atoms for Peace and War, 1953–1961: Eisenhower and the Atomic Energy Commission* (Berkley: University of California Press, 1989), 305–325.

24. "Address before the General Assembly of the United Nations on Peaceful Uses of Atomic Energy," New York, December 8, 1953, *Public Papers of the Presidents: Dwight D. Eisenhower, 1953* (Washington, DC: US Government Printing Office, 1960), 256.

25. "Agreement for Cooperation between the Government of the United States of America and the Government of Iran Concerning Civil Uses of Atomic Energy," *United States Treaties and Other International Agreements*, Vol. 10, Part 1, 1959 (Washington, DC: US Government Printing Office, 1960), 733–738.

26. "Atomic Energy: Application of Safeguards by the IAEA to the United States-Iran Cooperation Agreement," *Treaties and Other International Acts Series*, 6390 (Washington, DC: US Government Printing Office, 1968).

27. Tehran 66 to State, January 5, 1972, NPM, NSCF, CFME, Box 602.

28. On the Johnson administration and the non-proliferation regime, see Hal Brands, "Rethinking Nonproliferation: LBJ, the Gilpatric Committee, and U.S. National Security Policy," *Journal of Cold War Studies* 8, no. 2 (2006): 83–113.

29. On the Nixon administration's proliferation pessimism, see Francis J. Gavin, "Nuclear Nixon: Ironies, Puzzles, and the Triumph of Realpolitik," in *Nixon in the World*, ed. Fredrick Lovegall and Andrew Preston, 139–140; Michael J. Brenner, *Nuclear Power and Non-Proliferation: The Remaking of U.S. Policy* (Cambridge: Cambridge University Press, 1981), 63.

30. Skeet, *OPEC*, 99–104, 240.

31. Hossein Razavi and Firouz Vakil, *The Political Environment of Economic Planning in Iran, 1971–1983: From Monarchy to Islamic Republic* (Boulder, CO: Westview, 1984), 71, Table 4.1.

32. Afkhami, *Life and Times*, 346–347.

33. See Abbas Milani, "Akbar Etemad," in *Eminent Persians*, Vol. I, 134–138.

34. Akbar Etemad in an interview with Farrokh Ghaffari, Paris, October 27, 1982, Tape A-4B, FISOHC.

35. Gholam Reza Afkhami, ed., *San'at-e petroshimi-e Iran: Az aghaz ta astane-ye enqelab* [The Evolution of Iran's Petrochemical Industry], Interview with Baqer Mostowfi, Managing Director of the National Iranian Petrochemical Company, 1964–1978 (Bethesda, MD: Foundation for Iranian Studies, 2001).

36. Khodadad Farmanfarmaian in an interview with Habib Ladjevardi, Cambridge, MA, January 19, 1983, Tape 15, HIOHP. See also Abbas Milani, "Aziz, Khodadad, Maryam, & Sattareh Farmanfarma'ian," in *Eminent Persians*, Vol. I, 143–151.

37. Akbar Etemad in an interview with Gholam Reza Afkhami, London, Septemer 5, 1995, Tape C1-1A, FISOHC.

38. Razavi and Vakil, *Political Environment*, 66–67.

39. Akbar Etemad in an interview with Gholam Reza Afkhami, Bethesda, MD, April 11, 1996, Tape C2-2B, FISOHC.

40. Clyde H. Farnsworth, "France Gives Iran Stake in Uranium," *New York Times*, Janaury 4, 1975; CIA Memorandum, "Israel and Iran in Sub-Saharan Africa," June 19, 1975, CREST; Thomas O'Toole, "S. Africa Set To Sell Iran Uranium Ore," *Washington Post*, October 12, 1975; Tehran A-76 to State, April 15, 1976, Tehran A-69 to State, May 11, 1977, EBB 268, NSA-GWU. See also David Patrikarakos, *Nuclear Iran: The Birth of an Atomic State* (London: I. B. Tauris, 2012), 35–47.

41. J. Samuel Walker, "Nuclear Power and Nonproliferation: The Controversy over Nuclear Exports," *Diplomatic History* 25, no. 2 (2001): 218.

42. The nuclear-armed People's Republic of China took the Chinese seat at the United Nations from Taiwan in October 1971.

43. Asadollah Alam, *Yad'dashtha-ye 'Alam: Virayish va muqaddamah az Alinaqi Alikhani* [The Alam Diaries: Edited by Alinaghi Alikhani], Vol. V: 1975–1976 (Bethesda, MD: Ibex, 2003), 361.

44. Akbar Etemad in an interview with Gholam Reza Afkhami, London, September 5, 1995, Tape C1-3A, FISOHC.

45. Tehran 1477 to State, February 23, 1974, NPM, NSCF, CFME, Box 603.

46. Tehran 1783 to State, March 6, 1974, RG59, CFPF 1973–76, AAD.

47. State 48689 to Tehran, March 12, 1974, RG59, CFPF 1973–76, AAD.

48. CIA Memorandum, "Briefing of State in Preparation for Commission on Cooperation with Iran," September 13, 1974, CREST. See also Hamblin, "The Nuclearization of Iran."

49. Tehran 2091 to State, March 15, 1974, RG59, CFPF 1973-76, AAD.

50. NSSM 202, May 23, 1974, Virtual Library, RMNL. See also Brenner, *Nuclear Power*, 62–75; Walker, "Nuclear Power," 220–225.

51. NSDM 255, June 3, 1974, Virtual Library, RMNL. See also Brenner, *Nuclear Power*, 93–97.

52. State 98119 to Jerusalem, May 11, 1974, RG59, CFPF 1973-76, AAD; US House of Representatives, Ninety-Third Congress, Second Session, Committee on Foreign Relations, Subcommittee on International Organizations and Movements and on the Near East and South Asia, "U.S. Foreign Policy and the Export of Nuclear Technology to the Middle East," June 25, 1974; July 9 and 18, 1974; September 16, 1974 (Washington, DC: US Government Printing Office, 1974), 28–30.

53. Brenner, *Nuclear Power*, 49–51.

54. Akbar Etemad in interview with Farrokh Ghaffari, Paris, October 27, 1982, Tape A-6A, FISOHC.

55. Tehran 4169 to State, RG59, CFPF 1973–76, AAD; Friedman to Sober, June 17, 1974, EBB 268, NSA-GWU.

56. Drew Middleton, "Who's Next in Atom Club?" *New York Times*, May 26, 1974. James. F. Clarity, "Iran Negotiates for Nuclear Energy Aid," *New York Times*, May 27, 1974.

57. Tehran 4059 to State, May 21, 1974, RG59, CFPF 1973–76, AAD.

58. Brenner, *Nuclear Power*, 72; Walker, "Nuclear Power," 222.

59. "Atom Energy Pact with Israel Seen," *New York Times*, June 15, 1974; John W. Finney, "U.S. Will Rely on Controls on Military Nuclear Uses," *New York Times*, June 15, 1974.

60. Atherton to Kissinger, June 20, 1974, EBB 268, NSA-GWU.

61. Ronald Koven, "Iran Eyes Nuclear Weapons," *Washington Post*, June 24, 1974.

62. Paris 15305 to State, June 24, 1974, EBB 268, NSA-GWU.

63. Paris 15445 to State, June 24, 1974, EBB 268, NSA-GWU.

64. Tehran 5192 to State, June 24, 1974, EBB 268, NSA-GWU; Takashi Oka, "France and Iran Sign Aid Pacts," *Christian Science Monitor*, June 24, 1974; "France and Iran Sign $4-Billion Accord; Shah Will Receive 5 Nuclear Reactors," *New York Times*, June 24, 1974.

65. Noyes to Schlesinger, June 1974, EBB 268, NSA-GWU.

66. Tehran 5564 to State, July 8, 1974, RG59, CFPF 1973–76, AAD.

67. "France Gets $4 Billion in Iran Trade," *Washington Post*, June 28, 1974.

68. Marshall to Cotter, January 7, 1975, FOIA Request by William Burr, NSA-GWU.

69. James Schlesinger in an interview with William Burr, Washington, May 15, 1986, Tape 1A, FISOHC.

70. Tehran 5465 to State, July 3, 1974, RG59, CFPF 1973–76, AAD.

71. Tehran 5510 to State, July 5, 1974, RG59, CFPF 1973–76, AAD.

72. Tehran 5652 to State, July 10, 1974, RG59, CFPF 1973–76, AAD.

73. Zahedi to Korologos, September 17, 1974, WHCF, Subject File ND 20, Box 71, GRFL; Senator Hartke (D-IN), "Iran's Proposal for a Nuclear Free Zone in the Middle East Region," *Congressional Record*, 120:23, September 11, 1974, S30768.

74. Daryoush Bayandor in correspondence with the author, July 11, 2010.

75. State 236975 to Moscow, October 27, 1974, NSA, Presidential Country Files for Europe and Canada, Box 20, GRFL; United Nations—New York 4684 to State, November 2, 1974, RG59, CFPF 1973–76, AAD.

76. United Nations, General Assembly, Resolution 3263, "Establishment of Nuclear-Weapon-Free Zone in the Middle East," December 9, 1974, A/RES/3263(XXIX), ODS.

77. SNIE 4-1-74, August 23, 1974, EBB 268, NSA-GWU.

78. US Congress, Ninety-Third Congress, Second Session, Joint Committee on Atomic Energy, Subcommittee on Military Applications, "Proliferation of Nuclear Weapons," September 10, 1974 (Washington, DC: US Government Printing Office, 1974), 30–31.

79. See Brenner, *Nuclear Power*, 14–16.

80. Tehran 5389 to State, July 1, 1974, EBB 268, NSA-GWU; Tehran 5458 to State, July 3, 1974, NPM, NSCF, CFME, Box 603; Tehran 8057 to State, September 24, 1974, RG59, CFPF 1973–76, AAD.

81. Tehran 8883 to State, October 22, 1974, NSA, PCFMESA, Box 14, GRFL.

82. Akbar Etemad in an interview with Gholam Reza Afkhami, London, September 5, 1995, Tape C1-2A, FISOHC.

83. Memcon, November 2, 1974, *FRUS 1969–1976*, XXVII, 88.

84. On the genesis of the multinational plant concept, see Brenner, *Nuclear Power*, 98–100.

85. Ingersoll to Ford, December 4, 1974, EBB 268, NSA-GWU.

86. Tehran 9039 to State, October 25, 1974, RG59, CFPF 1973–76, AAD.

87. Tehran 8541 to State, October 9, 1974, RG59, CFPF 1973–76, AAD.

88. Atherton to Kissinger, December 6, 1974, and Gammon to Sober and Clingan, December 11, 1974, EBB 268, NSA-GWU.

89. Ray had stepped down as chairman of the AEC when the Commission was abolished under the Energy Reorganization Act of 1974. The AEC's functions were split between two new agencies: the Energy Research and Development Administration, which took charge of US civilian and military nuclear policy, and the Nuclear Regulatory Commission, which took over the regulation of the nuclear industry, including the authority to veto nuclear exports.

90. Paris 1949 to State, January 23, 1975, and Tehran 813 to State, January 28, 1975, RG59, CFPF 1973–76, AAD.

91. Tehran 1393 to State, February 12, 1975, RG59, CFPF 1973–76, AAD.

92. Akbar Etemad in an interview with Gholam Reza Afkhami, London, September 5, 1995, Tape C1-3A, FISOHC.

93. State 35095 to Tehran, February 15, 1975, RG59, CFPF 1973–76, AAD.

94. State 73577 to Tokyo, April 1, 1975, RG59, CFPF 1973–76, AAD.

95. Elliott to Scowcroft, March 12, 1975, and Ingersoll to Scowcroft, March 10, 1975, NSC, IR, Box 34, GRFL; NSSM 219, March 14, 1975, Digital Library, GRFL.

96. "A Nuclear Iran?" *Washington Post*, March 10, 1975.

97. Joseph Kraft, "What Restrains the Shah," *Washington Post*, April 27, 1975.

98. Report prepared by the NSSM 219 Working Group, "Nuclear Cooperation Agreement with Iran," April 1975, and Davis to the various members of the NSC, April 15, 1975, NSC, IR, Box 34, GRFL.

99. Tehran 3437 to State, April 15, 1975, EBB 268, NSA-GWU.

100. Ingersoll to Kissinger, April 18, 1975, NSC, IR, Box 34, GRFL.

101. Iklé to Davis, April 16, 1975, NSC, IR, Box 34, GRFL; Sievering to Elliott, April 18, 1975, NSC, IR, Box 59, GRFL.

102. Schlesinger to Kissinger, April 25, 1975, EBB 268, NSA-GWU.

103. Elliott to Kissinger, April 19, 1975, NSC, IR, Box 59, GRFL.

104. NSDM 292, April 22, 1975, Digital Library, GRFL.

105. State 105820 to Tehran, May 6, 1975, RG59, CFPF 1973–76, AAD.

106. Briefing paper prepared by the Department of State, "Peaceful Nuclear Cooperation," May 1975, EBB 268, NSA-GWU.

107. Walker, "Nuclear Power," 227. See also Brenner, *Nuclear Power*, 92–93.

108. Abraham A. Ribicoff, "A Market-Sharing Approach to the World Nuclear Sales Problem," *Foreign Affairs* 54, no. 4 (1976): 770.

109. "Iran: Oil, Grandeur and a Challenge to the West," *Time*, November 4, 1974.

110. John Carvel, "Shah Gives Britain Word of Warning," *Guardian*, January 29, 1974.

111. Tehran 83 to State, January 6, 1975, RG59, CFPF 1973-76, AAD; Henry Tanner, "Shah Gives Sadat Strong Backing For Arab Cause," *New York Times*, January 13, 1975.

112. Tehran 1733 to State, February 23, 1975, RG59, CFPF 1973–76, AAD. See also, Trita Parsi, "Israel and the Origins of Iran's Arab Option: Dissection of a Strategy Misunderstood," *Middle East Journal* 60, no. 3 (2006): 493–512; Rouhallah K. Ramazani, "Iran and the Arab-Israeli Conflict," *Middle East Journal* 32, no. 4 (1978): 413–428.

113. John W. Finney, "Arms Sale to Iran Scored As Drain on U.S. Military," *New York Times*, January 2, 1975.

114. Jackson to Kissinger, March 22, 1975, RG59, Records Relating to Iran, 1965–1975, LOT77D400, Box 11.

115. John Kifner, "Iranian Program Debated at M.I.T," *New York Times*, April 27, 1975.

116. Buratti to the Members of the Corporation Joint Advisory Committee on Institute-Wide Affairs and the Ad Hoc Advisory Committee to Consider MIT's International Commitments, June 3, 1975, Council of Economic Advisers, Box 92, GRFL.

117. Cooper, *Oil Kings*, 176.

118. Tehran 6939 to State, July 17, 1975, EBB 268, NSA-GWU.

119. Kissinger to Ford, May 15, 1975, NSA, Presidential Briefing Material for VIP Visits, Box 9, GRFL.

120. Memcon, May 15, 1975, NSA, Memcons, Box 11, GRFL.

121. Tehran 6441 to State, July 5, 1975, NSA, PCFMESA, Box 14, GRFL.

122. Jack Anderson, "Whatever the Shah Wants?" *Washington Post*, June 22, 1975; Jack Anderson, "U.S. Aides Demolish Shah Arguments," *Washington Post*, June 27, 1975; Jack Anderson and Les Whitten, "Iran May be Spending Beyond Means," *Washington Post*, July 31, 1975. See also Cooper, *Oil Kings*, 268–273.

123. Jack Anderson and Les Whitten, "CIA Study Finds Shah Insecure," *Washington Post*, July 11, 1975.

124. According to Earnest Oney, then the chief of the Greece, Turkey, and Iran Section of the CIA's Office of Current Intelligence, the profiles of the shah contained no such conclusions. See Earnest R. Oney in an interview with Seyed Vali Reza Nasr, Washington, May 29, 1991, Tape 2B, FISOHC. One such profile, dated October 23, 1978, is cited in Milani, *Shah*, 377, f.27.

125. United Nations—Vienna 8210 to State, September 25, 1975, RG59, CFPF 1973–76, AAD.

126. "Summary of a discussion between Dwight J. Porter and Mr. Akbar Etemad, President, Iran Atomic Energy Organization, Vienna, September 22 and 23," undated, NSC, IR, Box 59, GRFL.

127. Tehran 10396 to State, October 23, 1975, RG59, CFPF 1973–76, AAD.

128. The Verification Panel was an NSC committee that dealt with issues relating to arms control and disarmament. Ingersoll to Kissinger, October 26, 1975, and Elliott to Davis, November 20, 1975, NSC, IR, Box 59, GRFL.

129. Davis to various members of the NSC, November 20, 1975, with attached study prepared by the NSC Verification Panel's Non-Proliferation Working Group, "Nuclear Agreement with Iran," NSC, IR, Box 59, GRFL.

130. State 254826 to Tehran, November 25, 1975, EBB 268, NSA-GWU.

131. "Recession's Impact on Iran," *Business Week*, November 17, 1975; Tehran 11089 to State, November 13, 1975, NSC, IR, Box 59, GRFL.

132. See Shane J. Maddock, *Nuclear Apartheid: The Quest for American Atomic Supremacy from World War II to the Present* (Chapel Hill: University of North Carolina Press, 2010).

133. Tehran 11089 to State, November 13, 1975, EBB 268, NSA-GWU.

134. All of the relevant agencies weighed into the debate, except for the CIA. Curiously, the CIA representative on the VPWG sent a brief note to the NSC staff secretary saying that the Agency had "no comments or recommendations to make" on the VPWG study. See CIA Memorandum for Davis, November 26, 1975, NSC, IR, Box 59, GRFL.

135. Tehran 11539 to State, November 26, 1975, EBB 268, NSA-GWU.

136. Rumsfeld to Scowcroft, December 4, 1975, NSC, IR, Box 59, GRFL.

137. New Dehli 17228 to State, December 29, 1975, RG59, CFPF 1973–76, AAD.

138. State 304414 to Tehran, December 30, 1975, RG59, CFPF 1973–76, AAD.

139. Akbar Etemad in an interview with Gholam Reza Afkhami, London, September 5, 1995, Tape C1-3A, FISOHC.

140. Tehran 73 to State, January 5, 1976, EBB 268, NSA-GWU.

141. Seamans to Scowcroft, December 17, 1975, NSC, IR, Box 59, GRFL.

142. Springsteen to Scowcroft, January 31, 1976, NSC, IR, Box 59, GRFL.

143. William Branigin, "Iran, U.S. Near Nuclear Deal," *Washington Post*, June 14, 1976; Akbar Etemad in interview with Farrokh Ghaffari, Paris, October 27, 1982, Paris, Tape A-6B, FISOHC.

144. Springsteen to Scowcroft, January 13, 1976, NSC, IR, Box 59, GRFL.

145. Brenner, *Nuclear Power*, 74.

146. Iklé to Scowcroft, January 19, 1976, NSC, IR, Box 59, GRFL.

147. Harry B. Ellis, "U.S., Iran Nuclear Talks Stalled," *Christian Science Monitor*, February 26, 1976.

148. See Cannon, *Time and Change*; Yanek Mieczkowski, *Gerald Ford and the Challenges of the 1970s* (Lexington: The University Press of Kentucky, 2005).

149. Scowcroft to Ford, January 26, 1976, and Elliott, Marcum, and Oakley to Scowcroft, January 23, 1976, NSC, IR, Box 59, GRFL.

150. Scowcroft to various members of the NSC, February 4, 1976, NSC, IR, Box 59, GRFL.

151. Ford to the Shah of Iran, February 21, 1976, NSA, PCWFL, Box 2, GRFL.

152. Scowcroft to Ford, undated [February 1976], (Action 992), and Elliot to Scowcroft, February 19, 1976, NSA, PCWFL, Box 2, GRFL.

153. David Burnham, "U.S. Export Ban on Nuclear Equipment Urged by Former Atomic Energy Chief," *New York Times*, Janaury 20, 1976.

154. Seamans to Ford, March 15, 1976, CREST.

155. Shah of Iran to Ford, March 4, 1976, NSA, PCWFL, Box 2, GRFL.

156. Seamans to Ford, March 15, 1976, CREST; Scowcroft to Ford, March 22, 1976, NSA, PCWFL, Box 2, GRFL.

157. Kratzer and Atherton to Kissinger, March 26, 1976, EBB 268, NSA-GWU.

158. Robison to Kissinger, April 14, 1976, EBB 268, NSA-GWU; Springsteen to Scowcroft, April 16, 1976, NSC, IR, Box 64, GRFL.

159. Ikle to Scowcroft, March 29, 1976; Elliott and Oakley to Scowcroft, April 16, 1976, NSC, IR, Box 64, GRFL.

160. Rumsfeld to Scowcroft, April 7, 1976, NSC, IR, Box 64, GRFL.

161. Scowcroft to Ford, April 19, 1976, NSC, IR, Box 64, GRFL.

162. NSDM 324, April 20, 1976, Digital Library, GRFL.

163. Memcon, May 12, 1976, EBB 268, NSA-GWU.

164. State 116392 to Tehran, May 12, 1976; Tehran 4920 to State, May 16, 1976, NSA, PCFMESA, Box 14, GRFL; Tehran 5765 to State, June 7, 1976, EBB 268, NSA-GWU.

165. State TOSEC110175 to Tehran, April 27, 1976, NSA, Trip Briefing Books and Cables of HAK, Box 34, GRFL.

166. Paul L. Joskow, "The International Nuclear Industry Today: The End of the American Monopoly," *Foreign Affairs* 54, no. 4 (1976): 788–803.

167. Craig R. Whitney, "Bonn's Atom Offer to Iran Stirs a Debate on Sharing," *New York Times*, April 18, 1976.

168. Memcon, May 12, 1976, EBB 268, NSA-GWU.

169. James Reston, "The Nuclear Power Race," *New York Times*, June 4, 1975; "Nuclear Madness," *New York Times*, June 13, 1975.

170. Brenner, *Nuclear Power*, 91, 117–118; Walker, "Nuclear Power," 234–235.

171. Memcon, May 12, 1976, EBB 268, NSA-GWU. Elliott and Oakley to Scowcroft, July 12, 1976, NSA, PCFMESA, Box 27, GRFL.

172. Memcon, July 2, 1976, EBB 268, NSA-GWU.

173. State 132760 to Tehran, May 28, 1976; State 135520 to Tehran, June 2, 1976; Tehran 5735 to State, June 7, 1976, EBB 268, NSA-GWU.

174. Tehran 7485 to State, July 23, 1976, EBB 268, NSA-GWU.

175. "Kissinger Arrives in Iran for Economic Discussions," *Los Angeles Times*, August 6, 1976.

176. Oakley to Scowcroft, July 26, 1976, NSA, International Economic Affairs Staff Files, Box 1, GRFL.

177. U.S. Senate, Committee on Foreign Relations, Subcommittee on Foreign Assistance, *U.S. Military Sales to Iran* (Washington, DC: US Government Printing Office, 1976), iii, xiii.

178. "Iran and the Arms Trade," *Washington Post*, August 5, 1976; Tom Wicker, "President and Shah," *New York Times*, July 6, 1976.

179. "Iran Accused at Meeting Here of Torture and Repression; Speakers Urge 'Tyranny' End," *New York Times*, February 29, 1976; Reza Baraheni, "Torture in Iran; 'It is a Hell Made by One Man for Another Man,'" *New York Times*, April 21, 1976; Victor A. Lusinchi, "Torture and Denials of Rights Laid to Iran by Jurists' Group," *New York Times*, May 29, 1976.

180. Memcon, August 3, 1976, NSA, Memcons, Box 20, GRFL.

181. Tehran 7886 to State, August 3, 1976, EBB 268, NSA-GWU.

182. Lahore SECTO20089 to State, August 8, 1976, NSA, Trip Briefing Books and Cables for HAK, Box 40, GRFL.

183. Scowcroft to Ford, August 9, 1976, NSA, Trip Briefing Books and Cables for HAK, Box 40, GRFL.

184. Tehran SECTO20064 to State, August 7, 1976, NSA, Trip Briefing Books and Cables for HAK, Box 40, GRFL.

185. Brenner, *Nuclear Power*, 100–115. Walker, "Nuclear Power," 234–236.

186. "France Agrees to Provide Iran Nuclear Plants," *Washington Post*, October 7, 1976; "French Sign Iran A-Deal, Assail U.S." *New York Times*, October 8, 1976.

187. State 264470 to Tehran, October 27, 1976, NSA, PCFMESA, Box 14, GRFL.

188. "Statement on Nuclear Policy," October 28, 1976, *Public Papers of the Presidents: Gerald R. Ford, 1976–77, Book III* (Washington, DC: US Government Printing Office, 1979), 2763–2778.

189. Ford to the Shah of Iran, October 29, 1976, NSA, Presidential Correspondence with Foreign Leaders, Box 2, GRFL.

190. See, for example, Patrick Tyler, *A World of Trouble: The White House and the Middle East—from the Cold War to the War on Terror* (New York: Farrar, Straus and Giroux, 2009), 210–248.

191. Burr, "Brief History," 28–32.

192. Gasiorowski, *U.S. Foreign Policy*, 112, Table 6.

CONCLUSION

1. "Notes on People," *New York Times*, April 29, 1980.

2. Letter from Hewitt to Kissinger, April 30, 1980, James A. Bill Papers, Box 35, Swem Library, College of William and Mary.

3. CBS News, "The Kissinger-Shah Connection?" May 4, 1980, *60 Minutes Verbatim* (New York: Arno Press, 1980), 507–512. See also William Bundy, *A Tangled Web: The Making of Foreign Policy in the Nixon Presidency* (London: I. B. Tauris, 1998), 217–219, 327–331, 507–509; and Walter Isaacson, *Kissinger: A Biography* (London: Faber & Faber, 1992), 562–565.

4. Marlise Simons, "Shah, Entourage In Mexico with Aid of Kissinger," *Washington Post*, June 11, 1979.

5. "Kissinger Interceded for Shah in Mexico, As Did the State Dept.," *New York Times*, June 12, 1979.

6. Nixon, *Real War*, 297. See also, Anson, *Exile*, 210–211; Pahlavi, *Enduring Love*, 322; Shawcross, *Shah's Last Ride*, 240.

7. "Nixon Pays Shah Visit in Mexico," *New York Times*, July 14, 1979.

8. "Carter Emissary Dissuaded Shah from U.S. Exile," *New York Times*, April 20, 1979.

9. Zbigniew Brzezinski, *Power and Principle: Memoirs of the National Security Adviser, 1977–1981* (New York: Farrar, Straus, Giroux, 1983), 474.

10. Hamilton Jordan, *Crisis: The Last Years of the Carter Presidency* (New York: G. P. Putnam and Sons, 1982), 31.

11. On Carter's decision to admit the shah, see Emery, *US Foreign Policy*, 136–138; Sick, *All Fall Down*, 176–186.

12. Anthony Lewis, "Mr. Kissinger's Role," *New York Times*, November 26, 1979.

13. Henry Kissinger, *For the Record: Selected Statements, 1977–1980* (London: Weidenfeld and Nicolson and Michael Joseph, 1981), 254–255.

14. "Shah Said to Welcome Invitation from Sadat When Treatment Ends," *New York Times*, November 11, 1979; Shawcross, *Shah's Last Ride*, 288.

15. John Lewis Gaddis, *Strategies of Containment: A Critical Appraisal of American National Security Policy during the Cold War*, Revised and Expanded Edition (New York: Oxford University Press, 2005), 302.

16. Kissinger to Nixon, undated, *FRUS 1969–1976*, I, 39. See also Paul Chamberlin, "A World Restored: Religion, Counterrevoluion, and the Search for Order in the Middle East," *Diplomatic History* 32, no. 3 (2008): 443.

17. "The State of the Union, Address Delivered before a Joint Session of the Congress," January 23, 1980, *Public Papers of the Presidents: Jimmy Carter 1980–1981, Book I* (Washington, DC: US Government Printing Office, 1981), 197.

18. Olav Njolstad, "Shifting Priorities: The Persian Gulf in U.S. Strategic Planning in the Carter Years," *Cold War History* 4, no. 3 (2004): 21–55; William E. Odom, "The Cold War Origins of the U.S. Central Command," *Journal of Cold War Studies* 8, no. 2 (2006): 52–82.

19. Bill, *Eagle and the Lion*, 210.

20. Jeremi Suri, *Power and Protest: Global Revolution and the Rise of Détente* (Cambridge, MA: Harvard University Press, 2003), 88–130, 176–178.

21. Jeremi Suri, *Henry Kissinger and the American Century* (Cambridge, MA: The Belknap Press of Harvard University Press, 2007), 270.

22. Amin Saikal, *The Rise and Fall of the Shah* (Princeton, NJ: Princeton University Press, 1980), 202–203.

23. See Matthew Jones, "A 'Segregated' Asia?: Race, the Bandung Conference, and Pan-Asianist Fears in American Thought and Policy, 1954–1955," *Diplomatic History* 29, no. 5 (2005): 841–868; Michael E. Latham, "The Cold War in the Third World, 1963–1975," in *Cambridge History of the Cold War*, Vol. II, 259–280; Mark Atwood Lawrence, "The Rise and Fall of Nonalignment," in *The Cold War in the Third World*, ed. Robert J. McMahon (New York: Oxford University Press, 2013), pp. 139–155; Jason Parker, "Cold War II: The Eisenhower Administration, the Bandung Conference, and the Reperiodization of the Postwar Era," *Diplomatic History* 30, no. 5 (2006): 867–892.

24. See Parsi, *Treacherous Alliance*, 223–237.

25. "Address before a Joint Session of the Congress on the State of the Union," January 29, 2002, *Public Papers of the Presidents: George W. Bush, 2002, Book I* (Washington, DC: US Government Printing Office, 2004), 131.

26. Bill, *Eagle and the Lion*, 192; Marvin Zonis, *Majestic Failure: The Fall of the Shah* (Chicago: The University of Chicago Press, 1991).

Bibliography

ARCHIVAL COLLECTIONS

United States

US National Archives and Records Administration (NARAII), College Park, Maryland
    Central Intelligence Agency Records Search Tool (CREST)
    General Records of the Department of State, Record Group 59 (RG59)
        Central Foreign Policy Files (CFPF), 1967–69
        Central Foreign Policy Files (CFPF), 1973–76, Access to Archival Databases
            (AAD), available at: <http://aad.archives.gov/aad/>
        Executive Secretariat, Briefing Books, 1958–1976, LOT 72D373
        Records Relating to Iran, 1965–1975, LOT 77D400
        Subject Numeric Files (SNF), 1970–73
John F. Kennedy Presidential Library (JFKL), Boston, Massachusetts
    Presidential Papers
        National Security Files, Series: Robert W. Komer
        President's Office Files
Lyndon B. Johnson Presidential Library (LBJL), Austin, Texas
    National Security Files (NSF)
        Country File Middle East (CFME)
        Files of Harold H. Saunders
        Files of Robert W. Komer
    White House Central File (WHCF)
        Confidential File
        Subject File
Richard M. Nixon Presidential Library (RMNL), Yorba Linda, California
    Pre-Presidential Papers
    Wilderness Years, Series 2
        Trip File, Iran

Far East and Middle East Trips 1967
Virtual Library, available at: http://www.nixonlibrary.gov/virtuallibrary/
Richard M. Nixon Presidential Materials Project (NPM), College Park, Maryland
(Relocated to the RMNL in 2010)
National Security Council Files (NSCF)
Country Files—Middle East (CFME)
President's Trip Files
VIP Visits
National Security Council Institutional Files (NSCIF)
Meeting Files
Washington Special Actions Group Meetings (WSAGM)
President's Personal File
White House Social Events 1969–1974
White House Tapes
Gerald R. Ford Presidential Library (GRFL), Ann Arbor, Michigan
Council of Economic Advisers
Declassified Documents Remote Archive Capture (DDRAC)
Digital Library, available at: <http://www.fordlibrarymuseum.gov/library/docs.asp>
National Security Advisor (NSA)
International Economic Affairs Staff Files
Kissinger Reports on USSR, China and Middle East Discussions
Kissinger-Scowcroft West Wing Office Files (KSWWOF)
Memoranda of Conversations (Memcons)
Presidential Briefing Material for VIP Visits
Presidential Correspondence with Foreign Leaders (PCWFL)
Presidential Country Files for Europe and Canada
Presidential Country Files for the Middle East and South Asia (PCFMESA)
Trip Briefing Books and Cables for HAK
National Security Council (NSC)
Institutional Records (IR)
Presidential Handwriting File
Ron Nessen Papers
White House Central Files (WHCF)
Subject File
Georgetown University Library, Washington, DC
Papers of Richard M. Helms
Library of Congress, Washington, DC
Papers of Archibald B. Roosevelt, Jr.
Swem Library, College of William and Mary, Williamsburg, Virginia
Papers of James A. Bill

United Kingdom

The National Archives, Kew, Richmond, Surrey

    FO 248: Foreign Office and Foreign and Commonwealth Office: Embassy and Consulates, Iran (formerly Persia): General Correspondence

    FO 371: Foreign Office: Political Departments: General Correspondence from 1906–1966

    FO 1016: India Office and Successors: Political Residencies and Agencies, Persian Gulf: Correspondence and Papers

    FCO 8: Foreign Office and Foreign and Commonwealth Office: Arabian Department and Middle East Department: Registered Files (B and NB Series)

    FCO 17: Foreign Office, Eastern Department and Successors: Registered Files (E and NE Series)

    FCO 49: Foreign and Commonwealth Office and Predecessors: Planning Staff and Commonwealth Policy and Planning Department: Registered Files (PP, ZP and RS Series)

    PREM 13: Prime Minister's Office: Correspondence and Papers, 1964–1970

United Nations

United Nations Archives and Records Management Section (UNARMS), New York

United Nations Office Documents System (ODS), available at: <http://documents.un.org/>

PUBLISHED GOVERNMENT DOCUMENTS

CIA: The Pike Report, With an Introduction by Philip Agee. Nottingham, UK: Spokesman Books, 1977.

Congressional Record

Foreign Relations of the United States (FRUS) (Washington, DC: US Government Printing Office)

    1946

        VII: The Near East and Africa (1969)

    1949

        VI: The Near East, South Asia, and Africa (1977)

    1952–1954

        X: Iran, 1952–1954 (1989)

    1958–1960

        XII: Near East Region; Iraq; Iran; Arabian Peninsula (1992)

    1961–1963

XVII: Near East, 1961–1962 (1994)

XVIII: Near East, 1962–1963 (1995)

1964–1968

XXI: Near East Region; Arabian Peninsula (2000)

XXII: Iran (1999)

1969–1976

I: Foundations of Foreign Policy, 1969–1972 (2003)

XI: South Asia Crisis, 1971 (2005)

XXIV: Middle East Region and Arabian Peninsula, 1969–1972; Jordan, September 1970 (2008)

XXVII: Iran; Iraq, 1973–1976 (2012)

XXXVIII: Foundations of Foreign Policy, 1973–1976 (2012)

E-3: Documents on Global Issues, 1973–1976 (2009)

E-4: Documents on Iran and Iraq, 1969–1972 (2006)

Public Papers of the Presidents: Dwight D. Eisenhower, 1953. Washington, DC: US Government Printing Office, 1960.

Public Papers of the Presidents: Gerald R. Ford, 1976–77, Book III. Washington, DC: US Government Printing Office, 1979.

Public Papers of the Presidents: Jimmy Carter 1980–1981, Book I. Washington, DC: US Government Printing Office, 1981.

Public Papers of the Presidents: George W. Bush, 2002, Book I. Washington, DC: US Government Printing Office, 2004.

Treaties and Other International Acts Series, 6390. Washington, DC: US Government Printing Office, 1968.

US Congress, Ninety-Third Congress, Second Session, Joint Committee on Atomic Energy, Subcommittee on Military Applications, "Proliferation of Nuclear Weapons," September 10, 1974. Washington, DC: US Government Printing Office, 1974.

US House of Representatives, Ninety-Third Congress, Second Session, Committee on Foreign Relations, Subcommittee on International Organizations and Movements and on the Near East and South Asia, "U.S. Foreign Policy and the Export of Nuclear Technology to the Middle East," June 25, 1974; July 9 & 18, 1974; September 16, 1974. Washington, DC: US Government Printing Office, 1974.

US House of Representatives, Ninety-Fourth Congress, First Session, Select Committee on Intelligence, "U.S. Intelligence Agencies and Activities: The Performance of the Intelligence Community," September 11, 12, 18, 25, 30, 1975; and October 7, 30, 31, 1975, Part 2. Washington, DC: US Government Printing Office, 1975.

US House of Representatives, Ninety-Fourth Congress, Second Session, Committee on International Relations, Subcommittee on International Organizations, "Human Rights in Iran," August 8, 1976, and September 8, 1976. Washington, DC: US Government Printing Office, 1976.

US Senate, Committee on Foreign Relations, Subcommittee on Foreign Assistance, *U.S. Military Sales to Iran*. Washington, DC: US Government Printing Office, 1976.

United States Treaties and Other International Agreements, Vol. 10, Part 1, 1959. Washington, DC: US Government Printing Office, 1960.

ONLINE DOCUMENT COLLECTIONS

Cold War International History Project (CWIHP), Woodrow Wilson International Center for Scholars, Washington, DC

"New Evidence on the Iran Crisis 1945–46: From the Baku Archives," *Cold War International History Project Bulletin* 12/13 (2001): 309–314. Available at: <http://www.wilsoncenter.org/publication/bulletin-no-1213-fallwinter-2001>

Yegorova, Natalia I., *The "Iran Crisis" of 1945–46: A View from the Russian Archives*, Working Paper 15. Washington, DC: CWIHP, 1996. Available at: <http://www.wilsoncenter.org/publication/the-iran-crisis-1945-46-view-the-russian-archives>

National Security Archive, George Washington University (NSA-GWU), Washington, DC

Digital National Security Archive (DNSA), available at: <http://nsarchive.chadwyck.com/>

Electronic Briefing Book (EBB) 265, available at: <http://www2.gwu.edu/~nsarchiv/NSAEBB/NSAEBB265/>

Electronic Briefing Book (EBB) 268, available at:

<http://www2.gwu.edu/~nsarchiv/nukevault/ebb268/index.htm>

Henry Kissinger Telephone Transcripts (State-Kissinger), U.S. Department of State Electronic Reading Room, available at: <http://foia.state.gov/Search/Collections.aspx>

Israel State Archives, On-Line Collection: Prime Minister Golda Meir and the Shah of Iran in 1972, available at: <http://www.archives.gov.il/ArchiveGov/pirsumyginzach/TeudaBareshet/GoldaShah/>

Special Collection: A Life in Intelligence—The Richard Helms Collections (CIA-Helms), US Central Intelligence Agency Electronic Reading Room, available at: <http://www.foia.cia.gov/collection/life-intelligence-richard-helms-collection>

MEMOIRS, DIARIES, AND CONTEMPORANEOUS PUBLICATIONS

Adamiyat, Tahmoures, *Gashti bar guzashtah: Khatirati az safir-e kabir-e Iran dar Shoravi* [A Journey Through the Past: Memoirs of an Imperial Iranian Ambassador to the Soviet Union]. Tehran: Ketab Sera, 1989.

Afkhami, Gholam Reza, ed., *San'at-e petroshimi-e Iran: Az aghaz ta astane-ye enqelab* [The Evolution of Iran's Petrochemical Industry], Interview with Baqer Mostowfi, Managing Director of the National Iranian Petrochemical Company, 1964–1978. Bethesda, MD: Foundation for Iranian Studies, 2001.

Alam, Asadollah, *The Shah and I: The Confidential Diary of Iran's Royal Court, 1969–1977*, trans. ed. Alinaghi Alikhani. London: I. B. Tauris, 1991.

Alam, Asadollah, *Yad'dashtha-ye 'Alam: Virayish va muqaddamah az Ali Naqi Alikhani* [The Alam Diaries: Edited by Alinaghi Alikhani], Vol. I: 1969–1970. Bethesda: Iranbooks, 1993.

Alam, Asadollah, *Yad'dashtha-ye 'Alam: Virayish va muqaddamah az Ali naqi Alikhani* [The Alam Diaries: Edited by Alinaghi Alikhani], Vol. II: 1970, 1972. Bethesda, MD: Iranbooks, 1993.

Alam, Asadollah, *Yad'dashtha-ye 'Alam: Virayish va muqaddamah az Alinaqi Alikhani* [The Alam Diaries: Edited by Alinaghi Alikhani], Vol. III: 1973–1974. Bethesda, MD: Iranbooks, 1995.

Alam, Asadollah, *Yad'dashtha-ye 'Alam: Virayish va muqaddamah az Alinaqi Alikhani* [The Alam Diaries: Edited by Alinaghi Alikhani], Vol. IV: 1974–1975. Bethesda, MD: Ibex, 2000.

Alam, Asadollah, *Yad'dashtha-ye 'Alam: Virayish va muqaddamah az Alinaqi Alikhani* [The Alam Diaries: Edited by Alinaghi Alikhani], Vol. V: 1975–1976. Bethesda, MD: Ibex, 2003.

Alam, Asadollah, *Yad'dashtha-ye 'Alam: Virayish va muqaddamah az Alinaqi Alikhani* [The Alam Diaries: Edited by Alinaghi Alikhani], Vol. VI: 1976–1977. Bethesda, MD: Ibex, 2007.

Brzezinski, Zbigniew, *Power and Principle: Memoirs of the National Security Adviser, 1977–1981*. New York: Farrar, Straus, Giroux, 1983.

Haig, Alexander M., Jr., with Charles McCarry, *Inner Circles: How America Changed the World, a Memoir*. New York: Warner Books, 1992.

Hashemi, Manouchehr, *Davari: Sukhan-i dar karnameh-ye Savak* [Judgment: Some Remarks about SAVAK]. London: Aras, 1994.

Helms, Richard, with William Hood, *A Look over My Shoulder: A Life in the Central Intelligence Agency*. New York: Random House, 2003.

Jordan, Hamilton, *Crisis: The Last Years of the Carter Presidency*. New York: G. P. Putnam and Sons, 1982.

Joskow, Paul L., "The International Nuclear Industry Today: The End of the American Monopoly," *Foreign Affairs* 54, no. 4 (1976): 788–803.

Kennedy, John F., *The Strategy of Peace*, ed. Allan Nevis. New York: Harper & Row, 1960.

Kimche, David, *The Last Option: After Nasser, Arafat and Saddam Hussein, the Quest for Peace in the Middle East*. New York: Charles Scribner's Sons, 1991.

Johnson, Lyndon B., *The Vantage Point: Perspectives of the Presidency, 1963–1969*. London: Weidenfeld & Nicolson, 1972.

Kissinger, Henry, *The White House Years*. London: Weidenfeld & Nicolson, 1979.

Kissinger, Henry, *For the Record: Selected Statements, 1977–1980*. London: Weidenfeld and Nicolson and Michael Joseph, 1981.

Kissinger, Henry, *Years of Upheaval*. Boston: Little, Brown, 1982.

Kissinger, Henry, *Years of Renewal*. London: Weidenfeld & Nicolson, 1999.

Mehran, Majeed, *Dar koridorha-ye vezarat-e omur-e kharejeh cheh khabar: Khaterat-e yek diplomat-e qadimi* [In the Corridors of the Ministry of Foreign Affairs: The Memoirs of a Retired Diplomat]. Tehran: Nashr-e Tarikh-e Iran, 2004.

Meyer, Armin, *Quiet Diplomacy: From Cairo to Tokyo in the Twilight of Imperialism*. New York: iUniverse, 2003.

Mirfendereski, Ahmad, with Ahmad Ahrar, *Dar hamsayegi-ye khers: Diplomasi va siyasat-e khareji-ye Iran, az 3 Shahrivar 1320 ta 22 Bahman 1357* [Neighboring the Bear: Iranian Diplomacy and Foreign Policy, 1941–1980]. Tehran: Elm, 2003.

Nixon, Richard M., "Asia after Vietnam," *Foreign Affairs* 46, no. 1 (1967): 113–125.

Nixon, Richard M., *The Memoirs of Richard Nixon*. New York: Grosset & Dunlap, 1978.

Nixon, Richard M., *The Real War*. London: Sidgwick & Jackson, 1980.

Pahlavi, Farah, *An Enduring Love: My Life with the Shah, A Memoir*. New York: Hyperion, 2004.

Pahlavi, Mohammad Reza, *Mission for My Country*. London: Hutchinson, 1961.

Pahlavi, Mohammad Reza, *The Shah's Story*, trans. Teresa Waugh. London: M. Joseph, 1980.

Ribicoff, Abraham A., "A Market-Sharing Approach to the World Nuclear Sales Problem," *Foreign Affairs* 54, no. 4 (1976): 763–787.

Roosevelt, Kermit, *Countercoup: The Struggle for the Control of Iran* (New York: McGraw-Hill, 1979).

Woodhouse, C. M., *Something Ventured*. London: Granada, 1982.

Wright, Denis, *The Memoirs of Sir Denis Wright 1911–1971 in Two Volumes*, Volume II, unpublished manuscript, Bodleian Library, University of Oxford.

INTERVIEWS

Author's Interviews and Correspondence
    Retired CIA officer
    Daryoush Bayandor
    Harold Saunders
    Gen. Brent Scowcroft
    Ardeshir Zahedi
Foundation for Iranian Studies Oral History Collection (FISOHC)
    Richard Arndt
    Archie Bolster
    Theodore Eliot

Akbar Etemad
Gen. Mohammad Fazeli
Douglas MacArthur II
Jack Miklos
Earnest Oney
Gen. Mansur Qadar
Dean Rusk
Harold Saunders
James Schlesinger
Gen. Ellis Williamson
Harvard Iranian Oral History Project (HIOHP)
Ali Amini
Gen. Fereydoun Djam
Khodadad Farmanfarmaian
Col. Isa Pejman
The Foreign Affairs Oral History Collection of the Association for Diplomatic
  Studies and Training
Theodore Eliot
Arthur Lowrie

PERIODICALS AND BROADCASTS

60 Minutes Verbatim. New York: Arno Press, 1980.
Business Week
Christian Science Monitor
Economist (London)
Guardian
Los Angeles Times
New York (Magazine)
New York Times
Newsweek
Time (Magazine)
Times (London)
Village Voice
Washington Post

SECONDARY SOURCES

Abrahamian, Ervand, *Radical Islam: The Iranian Mojahedin.* London: I.
  B. Tauris, 1989.
Abrahamian, Ervand, *Tortured Confessions: Prisons and Public Recantations in Modern
  Iran.* Berkeley: University of California Press, 1999.

Afkhami, Gholam Reza, *The Life and Times of the Shah*. Berkeley: University of California Press, 2009.

Alvandi, Roham, "Muhammad Reza Pahlavi and the Bahrain Question, 1968–1970," *British Journal of Middle Eastern Studies* 37, no. 2 (2010): 159–177.

Alvandi, Roham, "Nixon, Kissinger, and the Shah: The Origins of Iranian Primacy in the Persian Gulf," *Diplomatic History* 36, no. 2 (2012): 337–372.

Alvandi, Roham, "Flirting with Neutrality: the Shah, Khrushchev, and the 1959 Soviet-Iranian Negotiations," *Iranian Studies* (forthcoming 2014).

Alvandi, Roham, "The Shah's Détente with Khrushchev: Iran's 1962 Missile Base Pledge to the Soviet Union," *Cold War History* (forthcoming 2014).

Ambrose, Steven P., *Nixon: The Triumph of a Politician, 1962–1972*. New York: Simon & Schuster, 1989.

Amini, Iraj, *Bar bal-e bohran: Zendegi-ye siyasi-ye Ali Amini* [On the Wings of Crisis: The Political Life of Ali Amini]. Tehran: Nashr-e Mahi, 2009.

Ansari, Ali M., "The Myth of the White Revolution: Mohammad Reza Shah, 'Modernization' and the Consolidation of Power," *Middle Eastern Studies* 37, no. 3 (2001): 1–24.

Ansari, Ali M., *The Politics of Nationalism in Modern Iran*. Cambridge: Cambridge University Press, 2012.

Anson, Robert Sam, *Exile: The Unquiet Oblivion of Richard M. Nixon*. New York: Simon & Schuster, 1984.

Ashton, Nigel J., *Eisenhower, Macmillan and the Problem of Nasser: Anglo-American Relations and Arab Nationalism, 1955–59*. London: Macmillan, 1996.

Ashton, Nigel J., ed., *The Cold War in the Middle East*. London: Routledge, 2007.

Ashton, Nigel J., *King Hussein of Jordan: A Political Life*. New Haven, CT: Yale University Press, 2008.

Azimi, Fakhreddin, *Iran: The Crisis of Democracy*. New York: St. Martin's Press, 1989.

Balfour-Paul, Glen, *The End of Empire in the Middle East: Britain's Relinquishment of Power in Her Last Three Arab Dependencies*. Cambridge: Cambridge University Press, 1991.

Bar-Zahor, Michael, "David Ben-Gurion and the Policy of the Periphery," in *Israel in the Middle East*, eds. Itamar Rabinovich and Jehuda Reinharz, Second Edition (Lebanon, NH: University Press of New England, 2008), 191–197.

Barzani, Massoud, *Mustafa Barzani and the Kurdish Liberation Movement (1931–1961)*, ed. Ahmed Ferhadi. New York: Palgrave Macmillan, 2003.

Bayne, E. A., *Persian Kingship in Transition*. New York: American Universities Field Staff, 1968.

Behrooz, Maziar, *Rebels with a Cause: The Failure of the Left in Iran*. London: I. B. Tauris, 1999.

de Bellaigue, Christopher, *Patriot of Persia: Muhammad Mossadegh and a Very British Coup*. London: Bodley Head, 2012.

Bialer, Uri, "Fuel Bridge across the Middle East: Israel, Iran, and the Eilat-Ashkelon Oil Pipeline," *Israel Studies* 12, no. 3 (2007): 29–67.

Bill, James A., *The Eagle and the Lion: The Tragedy of American-Iranian Relations*. New Haven, CT: Yale University Press, 1988.

Bill, James A., and Wm. Roger Louis, eds., *Musaddiq, Iranian Nationalism and Oil*. London: I. B. Tauris, 1988.

Bookmiller, Robert J., *Engaging Iran: Australian and Canadian Relations with the Islamic Republic*. Dubai: Gulf Research Center, 2009.

Bostock, Frances, and Jeffrey Jones, *Planning and Power in Iran: Ebtehaj and Economic Development under the Shah*. London: Frank Cass, 1989.

Boyle, Kevin, "The Price of Peace: Vietnam, the Pound, and the Crisis of the American Empire," *Diplomatic History* 27, no. 1 (2003): 37–72.

Bradley, Mark Philip, "American Vernaculars: The United States and the Global Human Rights Imagination," *Diplomatic History* 38, no. 1 (2014): 1-21.

Brands, Hal, "Rethinking Nonproliferation: LBJ, the Gilpatric Committee, and U.S. National Security Policy," *Journal of Cold War Studies* 8, no. 2 (2006): 83–113.

Brenner, Michael J., *Nuclear Power and Non-Proliferation: The Remaking of U.S. Policy*. Cambridge: Cambridge University Press, 1981.

Bull, Hedley, *The Anarchical Society: A Study of Order in World Politics*. New York: Columbia University Press, 1977.

Bulloch, John, and Harvey Morris, *No Friends but the Mountains: The Tragic History of the Kurds*. New York: Oxford University Press, 1992.

Bundy, William, *A Tangled Web: The Making of Foreign Policy in the Nixon Presidency*. London: I. B. Tauris, 1998.

Burr, William, "A Brief History of U.S.-Iranian Nuclear Negotiations," *Bulletin of Atomic Scientists* 65, no. 1 (2009): 21–34.

Byrne, Jeffrey J., "Our Own Special Brand of Socialism: Algeria and the Contest for Modernities in the 1960s," *Diplomatic History* 33, no. 3 (2009): 427–447.

Cannon, James, *Time and Change: Gerald Ford's Appointment with History*. Ann Arbor: The University of Michigan Press, 1998.

Castiglioni, Claudia, "'I Can Start a Revolution but You Won't Like the Result': The United States and Iran in the Decade of Development," in *The Middle East and the Cold War: Between Security and Development*, eds. Massimiliano Trentin and Matteo Gerlini (Newcastle, UK: Cambridge Scholars Publishing, 2012), 105–127.

Chamankar, Muhammad Ja'far, *Buhran-e Zufar va rezhim-e Pahlavi* [The Dhofar Crisis and the Pahlavi Regime]. Tehran: Institute for Iranian Contemporary Historical Studies, 2004.

Chamberlin, Paul, "A World Restored: Religion, Counterrevoluion, and the Search for Order in the Middle East," *Diplomatic History* 32, no. 3 (2008): 441–469.

Chamberlin, Paul, *The Global Offensive: The United States, the Palestine Liberation Organization, and the Making of the Post-Cold War Order*. New York: Oxford University Press, 2012.

Chubin, Shahram, and Sepehr Zabih, *The Foreign Relations of Iran: A Developing State in a Zone of Great-Power Conflict*. Berkeley: University of California Press, 1974.

Citino, Nathan J., *From Arab Nationalism to OPEC: Eisenhower, King Saud, and the Making of U.S.-Saudi Relations*. Bloomington: Indiana University Press, 2002.

Collier, David R., "To Prevent a Revolution: John F. Kennedy and the Promotion of Democracy in Iran," *Diplomacy & Statecraft* 24, no. 3 (2013): 456–475.

Connelly, Matthew, *A Diplomatic Revolution: Algeria's Fight for Independence and the Origins of the Post-Cold War Era*. New York: Oxford University Press, 2002.

Cooper, Andrew Scott, *The Oil Kings: How the U.S., Iran, and Saudi Arabia Changed the Balance of Power in the Middle East*. New York: Simon & Schuster, 2011.

Cottam, Richard W., *Iran and the United States: A Cold War Case Study* (Pittsburgh, PA: University of Pittsburgh Press, 1988).

Daigle, Craig, *The Limits of Détente: The United States, the Soviet Union and the Arab-Israeli Conflict, 1969–1973*. New Haven, CT: Yale University Press, 2012.

Del Pero, Mario, *The Eccentric Realist: Henry Kissinger and the Shaping of American Foreign Policy*. Ithaca, NY: Cornell University Press.

Dietrich, Christopher R. W., "'Arab Oil Belongs to the Arabs': Raw Material Sovereignty, Cold War Boundaries, and the Nationalization of the Iraq Petroleum Company, 1967–1973," *Diplomacy and Statecraft* 22, no. 3 (2011): 450–479.

Doenecke, Justus D., "Revisionists, Oil and Cold War Diplomacy," *Iranian Studies* 3, no. 1 (1970): 23–33.

Elm, Mostafa, *Oil, Power, and Principle: Iran's Nationalization and Its Aftermath*. Syracuse, NY: Syracuse University Press, 1992.

Emery, Christian, *US Foreign Policy and the Iranian Revolution: The Cold War Dynamics of Engagement and Strategic Alliance*. Basingstoke, UK: Palgrave Macmillan, 2013.

Fain, W. Taylor, *American Ascendance and British Retreat in the Persian Gulf Region*. New York: Palgrave Macmillan, 2008.

Farouk-Sluglett, Marion, and Peter Sluglett, *Iraq since 1958: From Revolution to Dictatorship*. London: I. B. Tauris, 2001.

Fath, Sébastien, *L'Iran et de Gaulle: Chronique d'un Rêve Inachevé*. Neuilly-sur-Seine : EurOrient, 1999.

Fawcett, Louise L., *Iran and the Cold War: The Azerbaijan Crisis of 1946*. Cambridge: Cambridge University Press, 1992.

Fawcett, Louise L., "Down But Not Out? The Kurds in International Politics," *Review of International Studies* 27, no. 1 (2001): 109–118.

Ferris, Jesse, *Nasser's Gamble: How Intervention in Yemen Caused the Six-Day War and the Decline of Egyptian Power*. Princeton, NJ: Princeton University Press, 2013.

Fielding, Jeremy, "Coping with Decline: US Policy toward the British Defense Reviews of 1966," *Diplomatic History* 23, no. 4 (1999): 633–656.

Franzén, Johan, *Red Star over Iraq: Iraqi Communism before Saddam*. London: Hurst, 2011.

Gaddis, John Lewis, *Strategies of Containment: A Critical Appraisal of American National Security Policy during the Cold War*, Revised and Expanded Edition. New York: Oxford University Press, 2005.

Garthoff, Raymond L., *Détente and Confrontation: American-Soviet Relations from Nixon to Reagan*, Revised Edition. Washington, DC: Brookings Institution, 1994.

Gasiorowski, Mark J., *U.S. Foreign Policy and the Shah: Building a Client State in Iran*. Ithaca, NY: Cornell University Press, 1991.

Gasiorowski, Mark J., "The Qarani Affairs and Iranian Politics," *International Journal of Middle East Studies* 25, no. 4 (1993): 625–644.

Gasiorowski, Mark J., "The CIA Looks Back at the 1953 Coup in Iran," *Middle East Report* 216 (2000), 4–5.

Gasiorowski, Mark J., "US Intelligence Assistance to Iran, May-October 1979," *Middle East Journal* 66, no. 4 (2012): 613–627.

Gasiorowski, Mark J., and Malcolm Byrne, eds., *Mohammad Mosaddeq and the 1953 Coup in Iran*. Syracuse, NY: Syracuse University Press, 2004.

Gause, F. Gregory, III, "British and American Policies in the Persian Gulf, 1968–1973," *Review of International Studies* 11, no. 4 (1985): 247–273.

Gerges, Fawaz A., *The Superpowers and the Middle East: Regional and International Politics, 1955–1967*. Boulder, CO: Westview Press, 1994.

Ghareeb, Edmund, *The Kurdish Question in Iraq*. Syracuse, NY: Syracuse University Press, 1981.

Goode, James F., *The United States and Iran, 1946–51: The Diplomacy of Neglect*. London: Macmillan, 1989.

Goode, James F., "Reforming Iran during the Kennedy Years," *Diplomatic History* 15, no. 1 (1991): 13–29.

Goode, James F., *The United States and Iran: In the Shadow of Musaddiq*. Basingtoke, UK: Macmillan, 1997.

Goode, James F., "Assisting Our Brothers, Defending Ourselves: The Iranian Intervention in Oman, 1972–1975," *Iranian Studies* (forthcoming 2014).

Greenberg, David, *Nixon's Shadow: The History of an Image*. New York: W. W. Norton, 2003.

Haines, Gerald K., "The Pike Committee Investigations and the CIA," *Studies in Intelligence* 42, no. 5 (1999): 81–92.

Halliday, Fred, *Revolution and Foreign Policy: The Case of South Yemen, 1967–1987*. Cambridge: Cambridge University Press, 1989.

Hamblin, Jacob Darwin, "The Nuclearization of Iran in the Seventies," *Diplomatic History* (forthcoming 2014).

Hamzavi, A. H., "Iran and the Tehran Conference," *International Affairs* 20, no. 2 (1944): 192–203.

Hanhimäki, Jussi, *The Flawed Architect: Henry Kissinger and American Foreign Policy*. Oxford: Oxford University Press, 2004.

Harmer, Tanya, "Brazil's Cold War in the Southern Cone, 1970–1975," *Cold War History* 12, no. 4 (2012): 659–681.

Harmer, Tanya, "Fractious Allies: Chile, the United States, and the Cold War, 1973–76," *Diplomatic History* 37, no. 1 (2013): 109–143.

Hasanli, Jamil, *At the Dawn of the Cold War: The Soviet-American Crisis over Iranian Azerbaijan, 1941–1946*. Lanham: Rowman & Littlefield, 2006.

Heiss, Mary Ann, *Empire and Nationhood: the United States, Great Britain, and Iranian Oil, 1950–1954*. New York: Columbia University Press, 1997.

Hersh, Seymour, *The Price of Power: Kissinger in the Nixon White House*. London: Faber, 1983.

Hewlett, Richard G., and Jack M. Holt, *Atoms for Peace and War, 1953–1961: Eisenhower and the Atomic Energy Commission*. Berkley: University of California Press, 1989.

Isaacson, Walter, *Kissinger: A Biography*. London: Faber & Faber, 1992.

Jacobsen, Eric, "A Coincidence of Interests: Kennedy, U.S. Assistance, and the 1963 Iraqi Ba'th Regime," *Diplomatic History* 37, no. 5 (2013): 1029–1059.

Jawad, Saad, *Iraq & the Kurdish Question, 1958–1970*. London: Ithaca Press, 1981.

Johns, Andrew L., "The Johnson Administration, the Shah of Iran, and the Changing Pattern of U.S.-Iranian Relations, 1965–1967: 'Tired of Being Treated like a Schoolboy,' " *Journal of Cold War Studies* 9, no. 2 (2007): 64–94.

Jones, Matthew, "A 'Segregated' Asia?: Race, the Bandung Conference, and Pan-Asianist Fears in American Thought and Policy, 1954–1955," *Diplomatic History* 29, no. 5 (2005): 841–868.

Katouzian, Homa, *Musaddiq and the Struggle for Power in Iran*. London: I. B. Tauris, 1990.

Katouzian, Homa, *The Persians: Ancient, Medieval and Modern Iran*. New Haven, CT: Yale University Press, 2009.

Katz, Mark N., *Russia and Arabia: Soviet Foreign Policy toward the Arabian Peninsula*. Baltimore, MD: The Johns Hopkins University Press, 1986.

Keys, Barbara, "Congress, Kissinger, and the Origins of Human Rights Diplomacy," *Diplomatic History* 34, no. 5 (2010): 823–851.

Kochavi, Noam, *Nixon and Israel: Forging a Conservative Partnership*. Albany: State University of New York Press, 2009.

Korn, David A., "The Last Years of Mustafa Barzani," *Middle East Quarterly*, 1/2 (1994), available at: <http://www.meforum.org/220/the-last-years-of-mustafa-barzani>.

Kuniholm, Bruce R., *The Origins of the Cold War in the Near East: Great Power Conflict and Diplomacy in Iran, Turkey, and Greece*. Princeton, NJ: Princeton University Press, 1980.

Kutler, Stanley I., ed., *Watergate: A Brief History with Documents*. Chichester, UK: Wiley-Blackwell, 2010.

LaFeber, Walter, *America, Russia and the Cold War, 1945–2006*, Tenth Edition. Boston: McGraw-Hill, 2008.

Leffler, Melvyn P., and Odd Arne Westad, eds., *The Cambridge History of the Cold War, Volume II: Crises and Détente*. Cambridge: Cambridge University Press, 2010.

Little, Douglas, *American Orientalism: the United States and the Middle East since 1945* (Chapel Hill: University of North Carolina Press, 2004).

Little, Douglas, "The United States and the Kurds: A Cold War Story," *Journal of Cold War Studies* 12, no. 4 (2010): 63–98.

Litwak, Robert S., *Détente and the Nixon Doctrine: American Foreign Policy and the Pursuit of Stability, 1969–1976*. Cambridge: Cambridge University Press, 1984.

Logevall, Fredrik, and Andrew Preston, eds., *Nixon in the World: American Foreign Relations, 1969–1977*. Oxford: Oxford University Press, 2008.

Louis, William Roger, "British Withdrawal from the Gulf, 1967–1971," *Journal of Imperial and Commonwealth History* 31, no. 1 (2003): 83–108.

Louis, William Roger, *Ends of British Imperialism: The Scramble for Empire, Suez and Decolonisation*. London: I. B. Tauris, 2006.

Lundestad, Geir, "Empire by Invitation? The United States and Western Europe, 1945–1952," *Journal of Peace Research* 23, no. 3 (1986): 263–277.

Lytle, Mark H., *The Origins of the Iranian-American Alliance, 1941–1953*. London: Holmes & Meier, 1987.

Maddock, Shane J., *Nuclear Apartheid: The Quest for American Atomic Supremacy from World War II to the Present*. Chapel Hill: University of North Carolina Press, 2010.

Matin-Asgari, Afshin, *Iranian Student Opposition to the Shah*. Costa Mesa, CA: Mazda, 2002.

Matthews, Weldon C., "The Kennedy Administration, Counterinsurgency, and Iraq's First Ba'thist Regime," *International Journal of Middle East Studies* 43, no. 4 (2011): 635–653.

McDowall, David, *A Modern History of the Kurds*, Third Edition. London: I. B. Tauris, 2007.

McFarland, Stephen L., "A Peripheral View of the Origins of the Cold War: The Crises in Iran, 1941–47," *Diplomatic History* 4, no. 4 (1980): 333–352.

McGlinchey, Stephen, "Lyndon B. Johnson and Arms Credit Sales to Iran 1964–1968," *Middle East Journal* 67, no. 4 (2013): 229–247.

McGlinchey, Stephen, "Richard Nixon's Road to Tehran: The Making of the U.S.-Iran Arms Agreement of May 1972," *Diplomatic History* 37, no. 4 (2013): 841–860.

McMahon, Robert J., ed. *The Cold War in the Third World*. New York: Oxford University Press, 2013.

Mieczkowski, Yanek, *Gerald Ford and the Challenges of the 1970s*. Lexington: The University Press of Kentucky, 2005.

Milani, Abbas, *The Persian Sphinx: Amir Abbas Hoveyda and the Riddle of the Iranian Revolution*. London: I. B. Tauris, 2000.

Milani, Abbas, *Eminent Persians: The Men and Women Who Made Modern Iran, 1941–1979*, Volumes I–II (Syracuse, NY: Syracuse University Press; and New York: Persian World Press, 2008).

Milani, Abbas, *The Shah*. New York: Palgrave Macmillan, 2011.

Mobley, Richard A., "The Tunbs and Abu Musa Islands: Britain's Perspective," *Middle East Journal* 57, no. 4 (2003): 627–645.

Moin, Baqer, *Khomeini: Life of the Ayatollah*. London: I. B. Tauris, 1999.

Motter, T. H. Vail, *The Persian Corridor and Aid to Russia*. Washington, DC: Office of the Chief of Military History, Department of the Army, 1952.

Nemchenok, Victor V., " 'That So Fair a Thing Should Be So Frail:' The Ford Foundation and the Failure of Rural Development in Iran, 1953–1964," *Middle East Journal* 63, no. 2 (2009): 261–284.

Nemchenok, Victor V., "In Search of Stability Amid Chaos: US Policy Toward Iran, 1961–63," *Cold War History* 10, no. 3 (2010): 341–369.

Njolstad, Olav, "Shifting Priorities: The Persian Gulf in U.S. Strategic Planning in the Carter Years," *Cold War History* 4, no. 3 (2004): 21–55.

Nolan, Cynthia M., "Seymour Hersh's Impact on The CIA," *International Journal of Intelligence and Counterintelligence* 12, no. 1 (1999): 18–34.

O'Ballance, Edgar, *The Kurdish Struggle, 1920–94*. London: Macmillan, 1996.

Odom, William E., "The Cold War Origins of the U.S. Central Command," *Journal of Cold War Studies* 8, no. 2 (2006): 52–82.

Parker, Jason, "Cold War II: The Eisenhower Administration, the Bandung Conference, and the Reperiodization of the Postwar Era," *Diplomatic History* 30, no. 5 (2006): 867–892.

Parsi, Trita, "Israel and the Origins of Iran's Arab Option: Dissection of a Strategy Misunderstood," *Middle East Journal* 60, no. 3 (2006): 493–512.

Parsi, Trita, *Treacherous Alliance: The Secret Dealings of Israel, Iran, and the United States*. New Haven, CT: Yale University Press, 2007.

Patrikarakos, David, *Nuclear Iran: The Birth of an Atomic State*. London: I. B. Tauris, 2012.

Petersen, Tore T., *Richard Nixon, Great Britain and the Anglo-American Alignment in the Persian Gulf and Arabian Peninsula: Making Allies out of Clients*. Brighton, UK: Sussex Academic Press, 2009.

Pfau, Richard, "The Legal Status of American Forces in Iran," *Middle East Journal* 28, no. 2 (1974): 141–153.

Popp, Roland, "Benign Intervention? The Kennedy Administration's Push for Reform in Iran," in *John F. Kennedy and the 'Thousand Days': New Perspectives on the Foreign and Domestic Policies of the Kennedy Administration*, eds. Manfred Berg and Andreas Etges (Heidelberg: Universitatsverlag Winter, 2007), 197–219.

Popp, Roland, "An Application of Modernization Theory during the Cold War? The Case of Pahlavi Iran," *International History Review* 30, no. 1 (2008): 76–98.

Powers, Thomas, *The Man Who Kept the Secrets: Richard Helms and the CIA*. New York: Alfred A. Knopf, 1979.

Primakov, Yevgeny, *Russia and the Arabs: Behind the Scenes in the Middle East from the Cold War to the Present*, trans. Paul Gould. New York: Basic Books, 2009.

Raine, Fernande S., "Stalin and the Creation of the Azerbaijan Democratic Party in Iran, 1945," *Cold War History* 2, no. 1 (2001): 1–38.

Rakove, Robert B., *Kennedy, Johnson, and the Nonaligned World*. Cambridge: Cambridge University Press, 2013.

Ramazani, Rouhollah K., *Iran's Foreign Policy 1941–1973: A Study of Foreign Policy in Modernizing Nations*. Charlottesville: University Press of Virginia, 1975.

Ramazani, Rouhollah K., "Iran's Search for Regional Coöperation," *Middle East Journal* 30, no. 2 (1976): 173–186.

Ramazani, Rouhollah K., "Iran and the Arab-Israeli Conflict," *Middle East Journal* 32, no. 4 (1978): 413–428.

Randal, Jonathan C., *After Such Knowledge, What Forgiveness? My Encounters with Kurdistan*. New York: Farrar, Strauss and Giroux, 1997.

Razavi, Hossein, and Firouz Vakil, *The Political Environment of Economic Planning in Iran, 1971–1983: From Monarchy to Islamic Republic*. Boulder, CO: Westview, 1984.

Richelson, Jeffrey T., *The Wizards of Langley: Inside the CIA's Directorate of Science and Technology*. Boulder, CO: Westview Press, 2001.

Roosevelt, Archie, Jr., "The Kurdish Republic of Mahabad," *Middle East Journal* 1, no. 3 (1947): 247–297.

Rubin, Barry, *Paved with Good Intentions: The American Experience and Iran*. New York: Oxford University Press, 1980.

Saikal, Amin, *The Rise and Fall of the Shah*. Princeton, NJ: Princeton University Press, 1980.

Samii, Abbas William, "The Role of SAVAK in the 1978–1979 Iranian Revolution," PhD diss., University of Cambridge, 1994.

Samore, Gary S., "Royal Family Politics in Saudi Arabia (1953–1982)," PhD diss., Harvard University, 1983.

al-Saud, Faisal bin Salman, *Iran, Saudi Arabia and the Gulf: Power Politics in Transition 1968–1971*. London: I. B. Tauris, 2003.

Sayigh, Yezid, and Avi Shlaim, eds., *The Cold War and the Middle East*. Oxford: Clarendon Press, 1997.

Schayegh, Cyrus, "Iran's Karaj Dam Affair: Emerging Mass Consumerism, the Politics of Promise, and the Cold War in the Third World," *Comparative Studies in Society and History* 54, no. 3 (2012): 612–643.

Schmitz, David F., *The United States and Right-Wing Dictatorships: 1965–1989*. Cambridge: Cambridge University Press, 2004.

Schofield, Richard M., *Evolution of the Shatt Al-'Arab Boundary Dispute*. Wisbech, UK: Middle East & North African Studies Press, 1986.

Schonmann, Noa, "The Phantom Pact: Israel's Periphery Policy in the Middle East," DPhil diss., University of Oxford, 2009.

Shannon, Matthew K., "Losing Hearts and Minds: American-Iranian Relations and International Education during the Cold War," PhD diss., Temple University, 2013.

Shawcross, William, *The Shah's Last Ride: The Story of the Exile, Misadventures and Death of the Emperor*. London: Chatto & Windus, 1989.

Shemesh, Haim, *Soviet-Iraqi Relations, 1968–1988: In the Shadow of the Iraq-Iran Conflict*. Boulder, CO: Lynne Rienner, 1992.

Shlaim, Avi, "Israel, the Great Powers, and the Middle East Crisis of 1958," *Journal of Imperial and Commonwealth History* 27, no. 2 (1999): 177–192.

Shlaim, Avi, *Lion of Jordan: The Life of King Hussein in War and Peace*. London: Allen Lane, 2007.

Sick, Gary, *All Fall Down: America's Fateful Encounter with Iran*. London: I. B. Tauris, 1985.

Sirriyeh, Hussein, "Development of the Iraqi-Iranian Dispute, 1847–1975," *Journal of Contemporary History* 20, no. 3 (1985): 483–492.

Sisson, Richard, and Leo E. Rose, *War and Secession: Pakistan, India, and the Creation of Bangladesh*. Berkeley: University of California Press, 1990.

Skeet, Ian, *OPEC: Twenty-Five Years of Prices and Politics*. Cambridge: Cambridge University Press, 1988.

Smith, Tony, "New Bottles for New Wine: A Pericentric Framework for the Study of the Cold War," *Diplomatic History* 24, no. 4 (2000): 567–591.

Smolansky, Oles M., and Bettie M. Smolansky, *The USSR and Iraq: The Soviet Quest for Influence*. Durham, NC: Duke University Press, 1991.

Snyder, Sarah B. "'A Call for U.S. Leadership': Congressional Activism on Human Right," *Diplomatic History* 37, no. 2 (2013): 372–397.

Summit, April R., "For a White Revolution: John F. Kennedy and the Shah of Iran," *Middle East Journal* 58, no. 4 (2004): 560–575.

Suri, Jeremi, *Power and Protest: Global Revolution and the Rise of Détente*. Cambridge, MA: Harvard University Press, 2003.

Suri, Jeremi, *Henry Kissinger and the American Century*. Cambridge, MA: Harvard University Press, 2007.

Tahir-Kheli, Shirin, "Iran and Pakistan: Cooperation in an Area of Conflict," *Asian Survey* 17, no. 5 (1977): 474–490.

Takriti, Abdel Razzaq, *Monsoon Revolution: Republicans, Sultans, and Empires in Oman, 1965–1976*. Oxford: Oxford University Press, 2013.

Trenta, Luca, "The Champion of Human Rights Meets the King of Kings: Jimmy Carter, the Shah, and Iranian Illusions and Rage," *Diplomacy & Statecraft* 24, no. 3 (2013): 476–498.

Tyler, Patrick, *A World of Trouble: The White House and the Middle East—from the Cold War to the War on Terror*. New York: Farrar, Straus and Giroux, 2009.

Vahabzadeh, Payman, *A Guerrilla Odyssey: Modernization, Secularism, Democracy, and the Fadai Period of National Liberation in Iran*. Syracuse, NY: Syracuse University Press, 2010.

Van Bruinessen, Martin, *Agha, Sheikh and State: The Social and Political Structures of Kurdistan*. London: Zed Books, 1992.

Van Hollen, Christopher, "The Tilt Policy Revisited: Nixon-Kissinger Geopolitics and South Asia," *Asian Survey* 20, no. 4 (1980): 339–361.

Vassiliev, Alexei, *The History of Saudi Arabia*. London: Saqi Books, 2000.

Walker, Samuel, "Nuclear Power and Nonproliferation: The Controversy over Nuclear Exports," *Diplomatic History* 25, no. 2 (2001): 215–249.

Warne, Andrew, "Psychoanalyzing Iran: Kennedy's Iran Task Force and the Modernization of Orientalism, 1961–3," *International History Review* 35, no. 2 (2013): 396–422.

Westad, Odd Arne, *The Global Cold War: Third World Interventions and the Making of Our Times*. Cambridge: Cambridge University Press, 2007.

Yaqub, Salim, *Containing Arab Nationalism: The Eisenhower Doctrine and the Middle East*. Chapel Hill: The University of North Carolina Press, 2004.

Yeselson, Abraham, *United States-Persian Diplomatic Relations 1883–1921*. New Brunswick, NJ: Rutgers University Press, 1956.

Yeşilbursa, Behçet Kemal, *The Baghdad Pact: Anglo-American Defence Policies in the Middle East, 1950–1959*. London: Frank Cass, 2005.

Young, David R., "The Presidential Conduct of American Foreign Policy, 1969–1973," DPhil diss., University of Oxford, 1981.

Zonis, Marvin, *The Political Elite of Iran*. Princeton, NJ: Princeton University Press, 1971.

Zonis, Marvin, *Majestic Failure: The Fall of the Shah*. Chicago: The University of Chicago Press, 1991.

Index